T0197111

COMPARATIVE **MODELS** OF DEVELOPMENT

COMPARATIVE
MODELS OF
DEVELOPMENT
Challenges to the American-Western System

HOWARD J. WIARDA, PH.D.

With the Assistance of Carolin Maney Purser, Ph.D.,

COMPARATIVE MODELS OF DEVELOPMENT
CHALLENGES TO THE AMERICAN-WESTERN SYSTEM

iUniverse books may be ordered through booksellers or by contacting:

iUniverse
1663 Liberty Drive
Bloomington, IN 47403
www.iuniverse.com
1-800-Authors (1-800-288-4677)

ISBN: 978-1-5320-2858-8 (sc)
ISBN: 978-1-5320-2857-1 (e)

Library of Congress Control Number: 2017912430

Print information available on the last page.

iUniverse rev. date: 09/05/2017

CONTENTS

LIST OF TABLES

FOREWORD

This was the last of my husband's, Howard John Wiarda, books. It was written as a conversation with students. He wanted to get them excited about countries and regions around the world. As a conversation, Howard used almost no jargon and concentrated on conveying his knowledge based in theoretic frameworks as well as his adventurous life experiences. For those who are interested in other works by Howard, there is a list of more than one hundred titles he authored, co-authored, or edited. Many of these titles were published in several languages including Spanish, Portuguese, Chinese, Japanese, French, Italian, and German. Howard passed away September 12, 2016, in Athens, GA, where he was the Dean Rusk Professor of International Relations at the School of Public and International Affairs, after a brief illness.

Iêda Siqueira Wiarda, Ph.D.

Library of Congress Analyst (Ret.)

PREFACE

I have been traveling, studying, and exploring the world by now for over fifty years, since that great wave of "new nations" emerged onto the world scene in the late 1950s, early 1960s, and forever changed the global system of international politics. My first published studies dealt with Latin America but I've also done research, lived, and traveled in Europe, West and East; Russia; East, South, and Southeast Asia; the Middle East; and North and Southern Africa – a total of 106 countries. I now consider myself not just a regional specialist but a global analyst; my areas of specialization include international relations, comparative politics, development studies, and foreign policy.

Much has changed, of course, in the preceding half-century: the newfound prosperity of East Asia, the rise of China, the collapse of the Soviet Union and then the resurgence under Vladimir Putin, democratization and development in Latin America, Africa's emergence, unimagined oil wealth in the Persian Gulf, India's rise out of poverty, and the economic takeoff of other developing countries. It just so happens that the emergence of the developing nations over the last five or six decades corresponds almost exactly with my own academic career and research specializations during the same time period.

I've long been interested in distinct models of development – capitalist, Marxist, corporatist, democratic, autocratic – and have written extensively about them.[1] But now some things new are happening out there: not just a new paradigm shift but a more fundamental reordering of world politics. The world is no longer the same as it once was.

I see two major overarching trends. The first is that the U.S. and the Western-favored model of development, which we can call democratic, free market, free trade – in short, the so-called "Washington Consensus" – is no longer the only or the dominant global model to which all or most nations aspire. It is being challenged or even in some countries replaced by the autocratic model of Putin in Russia, the state-capitalist model of East Asia, China's phenomenally successful accomplishments, an Islamic model or models in the Middle East, and a variety of authoritarian and corporatist regimes throughout the world. Not only is the U.S. or Western model no longer the only or most popular one out there, it is also being replaced or supplanted by these others in terms of delivery of real goods, services, and economic development.

The second trend, closely related, is the decline of the American or, more broadly, Western system of world order or power politics. At the conclusion of the Cold War only one superpower was left, the United States; it was a unipolar world. The U.S. and its Western allies were not only dominant, they were able to impose their system of world order – democracy, a modern-mixed economy, a liberalized trade system, globalization – on the rest of the world. But that is no longer true either: we are now witnessing the resurgence of Russia, the rise of China, Brazil, India, and "the Rest," the challenge of fundamentalist Islam in the Middle East, renewed nationalism and disruptive identity politics in many parts of the world, growing independence from U.S. tutelage, and a corresponding desire in many Third World areas to do it "our way," independent of the West.[2]

These two macro trends – away from the U.S. or Western model of development and away from the American/Western system of world order – are, of course, interrelated. In terms of its ability to deliver economic development, the U.S. model in the wake of the worldwide economic crash that began in 2009 no longer looks very attractive. And in terms of the world power balance in 2015 as compared to 1991 when the Soviet Union collapsed, the U.S. is no longer the world's only superpower or able to impose its will on the rest of the world.

Both these trends receive major attention in this book. Proceeding regionally – the U.S. and Western Europe, Russia, Eastern Europe, East and Southeast Asia, South Asia, the Middle East, Latin America, Africa – we trace the rise of new developmentalist models in the world, challenging or replacing the U.S.-favored one. Secondly, we analyze the rise of new global power relationships – by Russia, China, Iran, Isis, and others – that are simultaneously challenging the Western system of global order – what we have long referred to as the "international community' but which is now often only an "alliance of the willing" – i.e., not much of an "alliance" or "community" at all. Both these major trends point to the relative decline, over time, of the previously dominant U.S. and Western models, and correspondingly of the rise of a world of nations that is much more discordant, out of sync, and going their own way than was the case previously.

In the course of this long, five-decade and ongoing career, I have incurred many debts, to organizations, institutions and to individuals. Among the institutions which not only provided me with an academic or think tank "home" but also assisted my research in tangible ways are the University of Florida, the University of Massachusetts, Harvard University, the American Enterprise Institute for Public Policy Research (AEI), the Foreign Policy Research Institute (FPRI), the National War College, the Center for Strategic and International Studies (CSIS), the Woodrow International Center for Scholars, the University of Georgia, and the National Defense University Center for Hemispheric Defense Studies. I am grateful to all these institutions for their encouragement and support.

Among individuals, fellow political scientist (and spouse!) Iêda Siqueira Wiarda has been my strongest supporter and indispensable helpmate for all of this half-century. Children Kristy Lynn, Howard E., and Jonathan accompanied me on our travels and adventures in these early years and also provided for a wonderful family life. Numerous graduate students and research assistants, most recently Megan Lounsbury and Carolin Maney, provided ideas and worked over the years on the cumulative projects that went into this book. Doris Holden has been my indispensable typist, word processor, computer expert, editor, and friend for some forty years by now; I hope she does not retire before

I do. Of course, none of these institutions or individuals is responsible for this, the final product; that responsibility is mine alone.

Howard J. Wiarda

Tower Villas

Arlington, VA

Spring, 2015

CHAPTER 1

INTRODUCTION: DEVELOPMENT AND BEYOND

It is now exactly fifty years, half a century, since that great wave of new nations – "developing" or "emerging" or "Third World" countries – burst onto the world scene in the late 1950s, early 1960s. In the space of a few short years in those decades, the membership of countries in the United Nations General Assembly doubled – and then doubled again.

Surely those events are so dramatic and important that now, half a hundred years later, we ought to take stock of what happened, how successful (or unsuccessfully) these nations have been, their impact on the Political Science field of Comparative Politics (essentially, Comparative Politics went from the study of Europe to the study of these developing countries), and the implications of these massive changes for foreign policy (again, a shift from Central Europe – Berlin, the Iron Curtain, the East-West struggle – as the focus of the Cold War to a focus on revolutionary change, or the potential thereof, in Asia, Africa, the Middle East and Latin America).

The emergence of all these new nations onto the world's economic, political, and strategic radar screens completely changed the field of Comparative Politics, as well as the fields of international relations and security studies. Comparative Politics went through a massive paradigm shift: a completely new way of thinking about the world and how to study it. Heretofore, Comparative Politics had focused almost exclusively on Europe and, within that narrow geographic area, only four countries: Great Britain, France, Germany, and the Soviet Union. Indeed, when I first started to teach Comparative Politics, those were the only countries included in the catalogue description and which we were *required* to teach – as if all of Comparative Politics could be encompassed in those four countries! Only rarely were there books or courses that covered other European countries, Asia, Latin America, the Middle East, or Africa.

Paradigm Shifts in Comparative Politics

We can date precisely when this paradigm, this focus of Comparative Politics, began to shift. In 1954, Roy Macridis, a Professor of Political Science at Brandeis University, published his tub-thumping, rabble-rousing, and, at the time, controversial little book (seventy-seven pages), *The Study of Comparative Government*,[3] in which he took the profession apart for its narrowness, its parochialism, its ethnocentrism, its institutional analysis to the exclusion of all other factors, and its exclusively European focus. In the next few years, as independence dawned for a host of new nations, the first few books on the new or emerging nations began to appear, culminating in 1960 in Gabriel A.

Almond and James S. Coleman's (eds.) massively influential *The Politics of the Developing Areas*.[4] That book and the subsequent literature on development that followed in the 1960s influenced an entire generation of young political scientists to study the developing areas rather than just Western Europe.

From that point on, corresponding *exactly* with the sudden emergence of all those new nations, the focus of comparative politics would shift away from Europe and toward the developing nations. The number of books and articles on development and the developing nations *far outstripped* the number on Europe. Another measure of this paradigm shift: the membership roles of the regional professional associations for Asia, Africa, the Middle East, and especially Latin America grew (in the latter case) to *ten or twelve* times the membership of the European Studies Association. All the best young minds in the profession turned their attention and specializations to the developing areas, while Europe was largely left to the older generation.

Further paradigm shifts were under way. Macridis had not only critiqued the exclusively European-centered focus of Comparative Politics but also its focus on institutions. That focus was understandable in the European, or American, contexts where institutions mainly work as intended and as the laws and constitutions prescribe. But in the developing countries institutions seldom work as the laws say: for example, in Latin America as well as Africa there are beautiful laws and constitutions proclaiming democracy, the separation of powers, and human rights; but that has not meant these countries were actually, or even very often, governed by democratic precepts. Therefore, the argument was, instead of institutions, in the developing areas we would have to study more informal processes of politics: patronage networks, family and clan politics, tribal, caste, ethnic, religious, and clientelistic networks. This focus on informal politics would, therefore, require, an entirely different way of studying the Third World, including cultural anthropology, political sociology, international dependency relations, and other interdisciplinary approaches.

A similar paradigm shift was about to occur – indeed, was already occurring, with regard to the West's, especially the United States', Cold War foreign policy, with which development studies were often closely intertwined. Through the 1950s Western foreign policy, and with that the study of international relations, had concentrated, of course, on the Soviet Union and, within that focus, on the Soviet threat to Western Europe; hence, the attention given to Berlin, the Iron Curtain dividing Europe in two, and the possibility of a Soviet tank attack across the North European plain. But then with the Chinese revolution culminating in 1948, the Korean civil war (1950-52), the revolution in Cuba (1957-59), and the threat of revolutionary Marxism in such key countries and areas as India, the Philippines, Egypt, Indonesia, Southern Africa, and Latin America, the focus of the Cold War shifted away from Central Europe and *to* the developing areas.

Indeed, it is worth noting here the connection between the academic paradigm shift to the developing nations *and* the West's new Cold War preoccupation with the Third World: quite a number of the early studies of development, and even the university-based academic centers set up to study them, were sponsored with U.S. government funds – often covertly using CIA money.[5]

These are interesting, exciting, and provocative themes. Hence, in this book, which takes a regional approach to development and international relations – first, Europe and America; then, Russia and Eastern Europe; next, East, Southeast, and South Asia; then, the Middle East, Latin America, and Sub-Saharan Africa – the following, overarching issues are emphasized:

- First, how do we understand and interpret the developing areas? What is the intellectual history that runs from developmentalism and political culture studies, to dependency theory and political economy, to corporatism, to state-society relations, to the world systems approach, to the "new" institutionalism, to indigenous theories of social change, and so on to the present? Which of these approaches have stood the test of time, which are most useful in helping us understand the developing areas?

- Why are the gaps increasing rather than shrinking between the rich and the poor, both *within* these countries and as between the developed countries and developing ones? What are the exceptions and why?

- What works in development and what doesn't? Why are some countries prospering and others not? Why do some countries "get it" – how to achieve development – and others do not?

- Why have some countries and regions adapted to the newer pressures of globalization, democratization, and new markets, and others have not? Why does the Middle East, Southeast Asia, Sub-Saharan Africa, and much of Latin America still lag behind while others – East Asia, now China, Eastern Europe, and the countries of the Persian Gulf – are forging ahead?
- What is it that accounts for these differences between the success stories, the also-rans, and the failures? Is it culture (including religion), is it institutions, is it social structure, or how geography and resources affect development?
- What are the implications of the answers we give to the questions above for policy, the United States, the Western Alliance, and others? What are we doing right or wrong in development? What could we do better? Is there a formula for success?
- How are these vast changes affecting world power balances? Is the U.S.-favored system of liberal internationalism, equilibrium, and balance of power breaking down?

In answering these questions, this book takes both a regional and a global approach. That is, the individual chapters each have a regional focus – North America, Europe, East and Southeast Asia, South Asia, the Middle East, Latin America, and Sub-Saharan Africa. In each of these regional chapters we try to be as comprehensive as possible, surveying the history, culture, socioeconomic background, government institutions, and foreign policy orientation. But our real interest is in the global themes listed above – what works in development, is there a model, why some countries succeed and others don't, what is the formula for success, how is the world power balance being affected?

This is an audacious project, both in its scope and the geographic areas covered. No one person can know all countries (193 at present and still counting) and all the world's geographic regions and culture areas. Certainly, the present author would not, in all modesty, make that claim. On the other hand, I have traveled to, lived in, and studied *all* of these world regions and visited and worked in over hundred countries. I know most of these regions and countries pretty well. Hence, if anyone can successfully bring off a large, global study like this, this author can. Or at least I can try.

Our focus in this book, therefore, is on *grand, global, comparative systems*; a *worldwide systems approach*. The whole world, as the saying goes, is our oyster. And in that big world, a world that is increasingly globalized, there are many intriguing issues that we all must wonder about. Why did North America and Western Europe forge ahead in centuries past and become wealthy, global leaders, and world powers? Why did East Asia, which once was on an even level with Europe, first fall behind and then catch up to become the world's most dynamic area? Why did South America lag behind its New World rival, North America? What's wrong with the Middle East, which was once a leader in mathematics, science, arts, philosophy, and astronomy? And what of poor, underdeveloped Africa, always far behind all of the other regions? It is to provide answers to these and other questions that we have written this book.

In my research, travel, and writing, I have come to use three categories to describe most of the world's nations. The first category, consisting mainly of countries in the First World – North America, Western Europe, and East Asia (Japan and the Four Little Tigers, including South Korea, Taiwan, Hong Kong, and Singapore) – are countries that "get it." They are wealthy, literate, democratic, and efficient. Moreover, they "get it" in the sense of adapting to the modern world and to globalization. These are countries where you would want to live. Included in my list are a handful of countries – Chile, Uruguay, Australia, New Zealand, Costa Rica, and maybe South Africa – outside these main geographic areas.

A second category of countries is comprised of those that "get it" intellectually but are still underdeveloped in infrastructure, public administration, and good governance and, therefore, are still unable to reach their potential. Their aspirations and goals outrun their capacities to produce and deliver. In this category, I place much of Eastern Europe, such Latin American countries as Brazil and Mexico, several of the Persian Gulf oil sheikdoms, and in Southeast Asia, Malaysia, the Philippines, and Indonesia. In some of my writings I call these countries and regions "Second World" – not in the old-fashioned sense of being developed communist countries but in the newer sense of being *former* underdeveloped or Third World countries, now on the way to development but only part way there yet, and with such significant blockages (corruption, inefficiency, clientelism, and bureaucratic bumbling) in some cases that they may be permanently confined to this category. You could live in most of these countries but only with considerable despair, frustration, and difficulty.

A third category is those countries which don't yet get it or, even if they do, have rejected what it takes to achieve development and modernization. Most of these countries are poor, backward, unhappy, and not yet integrated into the modern, globalized world. In this category I place the less-developed countries of Central and South America, much of the Arab Middle East and North Africa (MENA), almost all of Sub-Saharan Africa, and those areas of Asia and Southeast Asia not yet embracing or caught up in the successful Asian model of development. These are generally countries of low literacy, high corruption, low life expectancy, and high crime and violence. For the most part, unless you are an assistance or humanitarian worker, you would not want to live in these places.

Of course, there are many mixed cases. Southern Europe (Greece, Italy, Portugal, and Spain) often hovers between First and my Second Worlds – politically democratic but socially and economically a decidedly mixed bag. South Africa is the most developed country in Africa but it could slip back to Third World status. In the Middle East, Morocco, Lebanon, Jordan, the Gulf states, Tunisia, and Turkey have achieved a level of development not present elsewhere, but their status is still precarious. In South Asia, large and important India seems to fit into all three of my categories at once, while Pakistan appears to be falling from Category 2 back into the "not-getting-it" category. Around the world there are other mixed systems like these or others (Argentina, Egypt, and Bangladesh) that seem to go back and forth between hopefulness and despair.

Despite these mixed cases, my three-part division of the world's nations seems to hold up pretty well, at least as a tentative hypothesis. At a minimum, it provides a handy organizing and classifying device. Note especially that my categories are no longer tied to the old, pre-1990 Cold War-era classification (capitalist, communist, and developing) but represent a new, updated system that both reflects newer trends *and* is tied in with globalization/modernization indices. I offer these categories not as a rigid or fixed set of blinders, however, but as a heuristic device useful both for categorizing nations and for showing dynamically how it is possible to go, as in my "mixed" cases, from one category to another.

To facilitate comparative analysis, each chapter employs a common analytical framework and outline. For each country and region of the world, we begin with a statement of that country's/region's unique developmental model. To understand how it got that way, we then proceed to a discussion of the country's or region's geography, resources, history, and political culture. To analyze change within this context, we next look at socioeconomic data and how the country or region has modernized over the years. We then look at institutions to see if the country's political and governmental institutions, including civil society, are up to the task of development. Finally, and in summing up, we offer an assessment of the country's/region's developmental model and its future.

This book covers roughly a fifty-year time span, from the late 1950s, early 1960s, and the emergence of a host of new and developing nations onto the world scene, until today. In the course of that half-century, we have seen some remarkable changes in the world and in the nations that make it up: far more new and interesting countries to study, far more democracies than ever before, new paths to economic and social development, the collapse of the Soviet model of development, and now globalization. This book sets out to chart and analyze these momentous changes over the last half-century.

Interestingly, that half-century of immense change corresponds with my own half-century career as a scholar of developing, emerging nations. I did my first academic studies of developing nations, mainly Latin America, in the late 1950s at the University of Michigan, precisely when all those new nations in Africa, Asia, and the Middle East were becoming independent for the first time. It was an exciting time to be a student of development and of the newest nations. Completing my Ph.D. in1965, I am this year, 2015, completing my fiftieth year of teaching and research at the university level. What an incredible ride and learning experience it has been!

Models of Development and Change

In this book, we are concerned with *models* of national development. Which *models* work and work best, and which do not. Each country or regional chapter begins with a discussion of that country's or region's model of development. But models are not formed in a vacuum; to understand each particular country or regional model, we will also need information on the country's/region's history culture, geography resources, socioeconomic level, and government or political institutions. The model employed in each country or region is closely related to these background factors.

What we find, in general, is that there is no one, single model, no magic formula, no panacea. What works in one area or country may not work in another. There are no pat solutions, nor will a cookie-cutter approach (one size, one shape, one formula for all) do. Instead, any model used must be adapted and shaped to fit the country or region under review. There is no one model for national success, despite what we hear from such countries as China, Brazil, Singapore (all success stories in their own ways), or Washington for that matter. There are many routes to development and a pluralism of models. That said, however, there are patterns and trends that tell us some models work better than others.

These comments have particular relevance for the United States and for U.S. foreign policy. At the heart of the U.S. tradition, of American beliefs and culture, is the belief that America is a "beacon on a hill," an example, a model, an "exceptional country," and an inspiration for other countries. Moreover, as a reflection of these beliefs as well as our historic missionary tradition, America has sought to export our traditions and institutions to other countries. We really believe that, as a country and culture, our institutions are the best ever invented and that we have a moral duty and obligation to export them to other, less-developed countries. This injunction to spread our best features abroad applies to our free-market economic institutions which we believe account for America's phenomenal wealth and prosperity, our political institutions and human rights which we believe are the best ever invented and are universally applicable, and our foreign policy and security umbrella which we believe are benign and in the best interests of all nations.

There are numerous problems with this formulation. First, how do we know that all other countries desire to imitate our institutions, or want them in precisely the same form or to the same degree as in America? Second, there is the problem of resources: what if you are a poor country and have no rich resources (oil, coal, or iron ore) as the United States did in its early stages of development? Third and extremely important: do we know that our culture and institutions will fit or work or "deliver" in countries whose history, religion, overall culture, and sociology are so much different from our own? Think, recently, of the unsuccessful efforts of the U.S. to bring *our* institutions and *our* ways of doing things to such culturally different countries as Afghanistan, Haiti, Iraq, or, going back all the way, Vietnam.

The answer is that, with some few exceptions (Germany and Japan after World War II and under the control of U.S. occupation armies; South Korea and Taiwan, similarly occupied or heavily dependent on the U.S.), the U.S. model fits only incompletely and uncomfortably in countries, especially non-Western ones, where the cultures and societies are so different from our own. Interestingly, most of these countries discovered during the Cold War (Cuba, China, North Korea, and Vietnam were exceptions) that the Soviet Communist model did not fit very well either. Nor is the East Asian (Japan, South Korea, Taiwan, Singapore, Hong Kong, and now China) model entirely appropriate in their circumstances either.

The truth is that there are a variety of models "out there" from which countries can choose. Just as there are many responses to globalization, so there are also many routes to development. Not just one or two or three (as above) but many. And countries need to pick and choose carefully among them. Instead of a straight path, the image we should have is of a lattice or trellis upon which the flowers of development grow, with many of its members pointing upward but also with crisscrossing and sideward patterns that account for mistakes, sideward lurches (as in Egypt recently) or even reversals of growth. We need such a more complex, pluralist, and multifaceted image of development strategies to account for the full range of options available.

Of course, you will want to pick and choose among the best developmental models available. And, let us face it: some requirements may be universal – population control, for example, or education, or social services, or honest government, or foreign investment and balanced budgets. But within these constraints, there are still many options.

You may wish, for instance, as Japan, South Korea, and Taiwan did in their early stages of growth, and now China and other successful modernizers do, to borrow certain factors from the West: technologies, Western industrial models, and models of efficient bureaucratic behavior. And then adapt them, as these countries did, to their own cultures and circumstances. Or you may wish to borrow the best features from several successful countries. And then blend these, as all the successful developers have done, with your own, indigenous, home-grown culture and way of doing things. Such an eclectic strategy will not guarantee success but it certainly offers the best possibilities for it.

This book suggests that there is no one, single, path to development – neither the U.S. model nor any other. Instead, within a context of certain universal norms and best practices, and diverse routes from which to pick and choose, countries and their leaders must decide, within the realities of their own situations and resources, which path is best for them. To do that correctly – for example, Lee Quan Yew in Singapore – requires a high degree of education, intelligence, wide experience of living and traveling abroad, good judgment, pragmatism, and sound economic and political decisions and management. It is not an easy task; only the most skilled can bring it off.

In this book, we assess the distinct routes to development that different countries and regions have taken. How are these decisions a product of their own cultures, histories, and societies? What factors, or what combination of factors, work best? In this survey, we will be treating the "first developers," in the United States and Western Europe, then moving east to Russia and Eastern Europe, next East Asia and around to South Asia (India, Pakistan, Sri Lanka, and Bangladesh), then the Middle East, Latin America, and Sub-Saharan Africa. It is a grand tour of all the major countries and regions, and of what works best in development and what doesn't. We hope you'll come along for the ride and the excitement.

A Divergence: The World's Best Countries

When we talk of models and what works in development and what doesn't, inevitably we arrive at rankings. Despite the more extreme claims of cultured relativism and multiculturalism, some countries work better and are nicer to live in than others. Recently, *Newsweek Magazine* came up with its own measure of the "Best Country in the World." *Newsweek* based its ranking on five criteria of national well-being: economic dynamism, education, health, quality of life, and governance or the political environment. Obviously, these rankings are not perfect and there are numerous flaws in the methodology, but here are the overall rankings *Newsweek* came up with (see Table 1.1). They help illustrate what it's possible to do with a single, global model of development.

Note that Finland (clean, developed, highly educated, efficient, non-corrupt, high-tech, and globalized) tops the list as *Newsweek*'s "Best Country," and that thirteen of the top twenty (and Twenty-eight of the top forty) are in Europe. Broken down by categories (the five criteria used by *Newsweek*), the best countries in each category were: for quality of life, Germany followed by the United States; for economic dynamism, Singapore followed by the United States; for education, Finland, followed by South Korea; health, Japan followed by Switzerland; and political environment, Finland again, plus Switzerland, the other Scandinavian countries, and the Netherlands.

It is striking that the same countries – Finland, Switzerland, Luxembourg, Sweden, Australia, Norway, Canada, Japan, Denmark, the Netherlands, Germany, New Zealand, South Korea, and Singapore (but not always the U.S.!) – tend to show up in the top five or ten on *all* the criteria.

What do these "best" and "successful" nations have in common? Almost all of them are small, energetic, democratic, efficient, clean, low corruption, and well managed. Using these criteria, these are "quality countries," countries that "get it." Note also that with the exception of

Japan, South Korea, and Singapore, all of the top twenty are West European countries or, like the U.S., Australia, or New Zealand, fragments or products of European culture and civilization.

It is apparent that the small size of a country lends itself, other things being equal, to efficiency, transparency, and good government. What these countries have in common, therefore, whether talking of health care, education, quality of life, or other public policy issues is that they are efficient, well-governed, and *manageable*. Beyond a certain point (some say five million people; others, fifteen million) countries tend to become more complex, often unmanageable, and to get out-of-hand. Bigger than that, governments tend to lose touch with their own people, bureaucracies become insufficient and unresponsive, and public services suffer.

TABLE 1.1
WORLD'S BEST COUNTRIES,
ACCORDING TO NEWSWEEK[1]

1	Finland	21	Spain	41	Panama	61	Kazakhstan	81	Vietnam
2	Switzerland	22	Israel	42	Peru	62	Colombia	82	South Africa
3	Sweden	23	Italy	43	United Arab Emirates	63	Philippines	83	Syria
4	Australia	24	Slovenia	44	Uruguay	64	Saudi Arabia	84	Guatemala
5	Luxembourg	25	Czech Republic	45	Mexico	65	Tunisia	85	Algeria
6	Norway	26	Greece	46	Argentina	66	Sri Lanka	86	Ghana
7	Canada	27	Portugal	47	Jamaica	67	Morocco	87	Kenya
8	Netherlands	28	Croatia	48	Brazil	68	Paraguay	88	Bangladesh
9	Japan	29	Poland	49	Ukraine	69	Azerbaijan	89	Pakistan
10	Denmark	30	Chile	50	Cuba	70	Ecuador	90	Madagascar
11	United States	31	Slovakia	51	Russia	71	Venezuela	91	Senegal
12	Germany	32	Estonia	52	Turkey	72	El Salvador	92	Yemen
13	New Zealand	33	Hungary	53	Jordan	73	Indonesia	93	Tanzania
14	United Kingdom	34	Lithuania	54	Qatar	74	Egypt	94	Ethiopia
15	South Korea	35	Costa Rica	55	Dominican Republic	75	Nicaragua	95	Mozambique
16	France	36	Latvia	56	Belarus	76	Honduras	96	Uganda
17	Ireland	37	Malaysia	57	Albania	77	Bolivia	97	Zambia
18	Austria	38	Bulgaria	58	Thailand	78	India	98	Cameroon
19	Belgium	39	Romania	59	China	79	Iran	99	Nigeria
20	Singapore	40	Kuwait	60	Oman	80	Botswana	100	Burkina Faso

That said, look at the list of the ten best *large* and populous countries (Table 1.2). Japan now tops the list,

---

[1] Rana Foroohar, "The Best Countries in the World," *Newsweek* (August, 2010)

followed by the United States, Germany, the United Kingdom, France, Italy, Mexico, Brazil, Russia and Turkey. I would agree with the Japan ranking at Number One: it is a remarkably efficient, disciplined, well-organized, well-managed country. While I'm glad the U.S. made Number Two on the list, I believe Germany – well-managed, well-organized, efficient – should displace the U.S. in that position. After these top three, there is a sharp drop-off to the numbers four, five, and six – United (no longer so united!) Kingdom, France, and Italy – on the list. And then an even sharper drop-off to the next four, all of which could be considered former Third World but still developing and transitional countries: Mexico, Brazil, Russia, and Turkey. It's not easy to be a big, developing country and, at the same time, be efficient, well managed, and deliver public services.

Newsweek's ranking, while far from perfect, illustrates what it's now possible to do with large, global mega-data. We employ some of the same or similar data in this book: data on literacy worldwide, population, urbanization, and especially per capita (per person) income levels. With this kind of quantitative data now available from the United Nations, the World Bank, and other sources, one can go a long way toward ranking countries and measuring their developmental success. At the same time, while this data is extremely useful, we also rely in this book on more qualitative interpretation: issues of culture, geography, history, resources, location, and sociopolitical behavior. Using both quantitative and qualitative information, we are able to systematically and comparatively analyze and assess the current development status and prospects for the world's main regions.

TABLE 1.2
BEST LARGE COUNTRIES

Japan
United States
Germany
United Kingdom
France
Italy
Mexico
Brazil
Russia
Turkey

The Security Dimension

So far, we have focused mainly on issues of national economic, social, and political development. On the *domestic* side of the equation: how and by what methods or models was it possible to achieve development and a high lifestyle ranking. Now it is time to turn to the strategic or security side: the world's changing international power relationships.

During the long, forty-five-year Cold War (1946-1991), the world system was essentially bipolar: the United States and the Western Alliance versus the Soviet Union. The two great superpowers vied for control, at first in Central Europe (Berlin, Germany, the Wall, the Iron Curtain) and then in the Third World as more and more countries in Africa, the Caribbean, the Middle East, and Southeast Asia threw off the yoke of colonialism and moved toward independence. The two major international models available – the American "developmentalist" model and Soviet-style Marxism-Leninism – reflected the world's two-power struggle. In addition, some Third World governments expressed admiration for a "Maoist" model (also Marxist-Leninist but peasant-based) and some opted for a supposed "third way" between capitalism and socialism, but few of these other options worked out very well: it was essentially a bipolar world.

When the Soviet Union imploded and collapsed in 1991, the bipolar world system which had been dominant for the previous near-half-century also collapsed. Instead of the United States and the Soviet Union, it was now the United States alone: what columnist Charles Krauthammer called a "Unipolar Moment."[6] France and Great Britain had been exhausted as major powers over the previous hundred years; Germany would wrestle with issues of national reunification for the next two decades; Japan's economy was about to go into recession; China was still a poor Marxist regime; and "The Rest" (Brazil, India, Mexico, South Africa, and Indonesia) had yet to rise. The U.S. had emerged overwhelmingly victorious in the Cold War; no other country was in a position to challenge it.

Krauthammer urged that the United States take advantage of its "unipolar moment" to impose its will on the rest of the world. And in a sense, it did that, though often reluctantly, sporadically, and not necessarily militarily. For this period of the 1990s was a period of relative global peace and of the triumph of liberal internationalism: in the absence of the Soviet threat, the Clinton Administration turned its attention to human rights, democratization, and the hoped-for resolution of international conflicts through such global bodies as the United Nations, the World Trade Organization (WTO), the World Bank, and so on.

Recall that this was the era when Samuel Huntington published his famous and overly optimistic book, *The Third Wave*,[7] on worldwide democratization, and when Francis Fukuyama proclaimed, again over-optimistically, that the "end of history" meant the triumph globally of the democratic idea.[8] An entire cottage industry sprang up centered in the National Endowment for Democracy (NED), its ancillary organizations (International Republican Institute, National Democratic Institute), and the main Washington and international think tanks and NGOs (Non-Governmental Organizations) suggesting, over-optimistically, that democracy was "the only game in town," that the fall of the Soviet Union as well as various right-wing authoritarian regimes meant the U.S. democratic model had triumphed definitively. There were no other alternatives.

By the mid-1990s these views had crystallized into what was called "the Washington Consensus." It was called the Washington Consensus for a reason: it was formulated, written, and promulgated entirely in Washington, D.C., and by the Washington think tanks; no other countries or points of view were involved. The "Consensus," so-called, was based on three basic principles:

- democracy in the political sphere;
- free markets (meaning a capitalistic, modern, mixed economy);
- free trade/globalization which, presumably, would cause a rising tide that would lift all boats.

The "Washington Consensus" would, presumably, apply to all countries, at all times, in all areas of the world.

I was strongly skeptical of the "Washington Consensus" right from the beginning and wrote extensively about it[9] - writings which got me in trouble for diverging from "the consensus" at my own Washington think tanks. First, as a scholar of comparative politics and especially the developing areas, I was skeptical if all the world wanted democracy, or wanted it all that much, or in precisely the same form, as the U.S. Second, I was a student of corporatism and state capitalism; my studies led me to conclude that free markets were unlikely to triumph in a world where the state played such a large role in development. Third, while I generally supported free trade, I recognized that trade and globalization produced losers as well as winners.[10] And, overall, I was quite aware that the so-called Washington consensus and a newly liberalized international political and economic order would – and it was designed that way – mainly favor the one country that was already liberalized and in a position to take maximum advantage of a globalized economy: the United States itself.

For the purposes of this book, it is striking – and no accident – that the two areas of the world, Eastern Europe and Latin America, that, so to speak, came of age politically and economically during this period of the "unipolar moment" both adopted almost *in toto* the main principles of the Washington Consensus. In the early-to-mid 1990s there was, seemingly, no other alternative available. Hence, Eastern Europe threw off the yoke of Soviet oppression, became democratic, joined NATO and the EU, allied themselves with the U.S., and undertook a crash program in market economics. Similarly, in Latin America: nineteen of the twenty countries are now at least formally democratic: by the so-called "democracy charter," having democracy is a requirement of receiving financial aid; and almost all Latin American countries, despite their statist and *dirigiste* traditions, adopted free-market/free-trade policies. Later, both these areas, both Eastern Europe and Latin America, or at least some countries therein, would come to question these political and economic decisions that they'd made in the 1990s, and even to backtrack on them somewhat; but at the time, in the world's "unipolar moment," they seemed to be the only rational choices available, "the only games in town."

But since that time, since the 1990s, the world has changed considerably. For convenience, let us date the new change from the year 2000. Essentially, and at the heart of the analysis in this book, two new and major paradigm shifts have occurred. First, the U.S. or Western developmentalist model is no longer so universally accepted as the "only way"; a great variety of other developmentalist models, as we see in detail in the book, are now available. And second, the entire world system of power relationships, as best put forth recently in Henry Kissinger's new book,[11] has been fundamentally altered. No longer is the U.S. so overwhelmingly powerful – the "unipolar moment" – as it was in the 1990s. And meanwhile, a number of other countries, with their own alternative and often challenging models – Russia China, Iran, and others – have recently emerged to offer alternatives to U.S. hegemony.

Specifically, these new and challenging models and power centers include the following:

- The resurgence of Russia under Vladimir Putin, its new-found unity and sense of purpose as a challenge and alternative to the West, his aggression in the Ukraine and *all along* Russia's present borders, and

Russia's presentation as a successful authoritarian model as distinct from the Western democratic one.

- Autocracy and Corporatism. Putin's Russia is perhaps the most important as well as extreme current case of autocracy or dictatorial rule. But numerous other regimes – Belarus, Egypt, Hungary, Kazakhstan, Kyrgyzstan, South Africa, Turkey – are moving toward a position that combines one-man or autocratic rule with limits on human rights and civil liberties, strict controls on interest group activity (corporatism), and independence, nationalism, or nonalignment internationally.

Understand that we are not here talking of the liberal, social-democratic corporatism of Scandinavia or Germany but of an older form of authoritarian-corporatism as practiced in Franco's Spain, Salazar's Portugal, Vargas' Brazil, Peron's Argentina, or Mussolini's Italy. Authoritarian-corporatism, or what Hungary's Victor Orban (with a bow to Fareed Zakaria) recently called "illiberal democracy,[12] represents a definite challenge and alternative to Western liberal democracy and pluralism; moreover, this model of politics and development is spreading as the number of Western-style democracies is in decline.

- The emergence of East Asia as the most dynamic and successful economic growth area of all world regions. The East Asian model, now spreading to other areas, includes state-led growth, a close alliance between government ministries and the private sector, and limits on democratic participation and civil society.

- The more representative and inclusive versions of this model are in Japan, South Korea, and Taiwan; Singapore occupies an intermediary position; while China is still at the more authoritarian, even Leninist and exclusionary, end of this continuum. Nevertheless, China's impressive growth rate, now slowing, is what attracts most attention worldwide – another alternative to the U.S./Western model. The Chinese model, as distinct from the rest of East Asia, merits its listing as a separate, alternative model.

- In the Islamic world, Iran and ISIS are vying for supremacy, along with Turkey, Indonesia, Egypt, Pakistan, Saudi Arabia, and perhaps others. Nevertheless, Iran and ISIS are the states that most command our attention currently and that most seek to present an explicitly *Islamic Model* of the state, politics, society, and economics.

Iran and the Iranian Revolution, particularly, are products of that period in the late 1970s, early 1980s, when the idea of an indigenous, local, or home-grown (in this case, *Islamic*) model of development was at the forefront.[13] While Iran may not be our favorite regime we must admit that it, and ISIS, offer both a challenge to the Western model of development *and* a challenge on the international front to U.S./Western hegemony in the Middle East.

- "The Rise of the Rest" (after the title of Fareed Zakaria's book).[14] Consider some big, intermediate-level countries: Argentina, Belarus, Brazil, Kazakhstan, Nigeria, Peru, South Africa, and Venezuela. None of these important countries is exactly following the U.S. model, either in terms of their development policies or their international alignments.

Now consider another group of big, intermediate-level countries, Chile, Colombia, India, Indonesia, Mexico, the Philippines, South Korea, and Turkey, which *are* (mainly) following the Western model both politically (democracy) and economically (mixed statist and private sector). It is here, in these countries, that much of the conflict over what development model to apply (statist vs. free-market), what political model (democracy vs. autocratic), and what international alignment (Western vs. independent) is being fought out.

While some of these countries seem to have made a definitive decision one way or another, in quite a number of them the disputes between these very different orientations and world views are being struggled over and are still in dispute. The fact that there is even a disagreement over these important issues in these key countries, all of which are regional powers and maybe something larger than that, tells us a lot about how diverse the world is and how open-ended the questions are that are being asked, as compared to the relative consensus ("the Washington Consensus") of the 1990s. Clearly there are many more options now, many more models open, than was the case twenty years ago.

In this book we test these ideas by exploring all of the major world areas. We begin with "The West," the United States and Western Europe and "the Western Model" that they have advanced globally. We then examine the degree to which that Western model has been exported and absorbed by other global regions: Eastern Europe, Russia, East and

Southeast Asia, South Asia, the Middle East, Latin America, and Sub-Saharan Africa. Each of these regions receives chapter-length treatment; in the Conclusion, we bring all these themes together and assess where the Western Model and Western foreign policy (the Western international system) have been successful and where not.

CHAPTER 2

THE UNITED STATES AND WESTERN EUROPE: THE "WESTERN MODEL" OF DEVELOPMENT

Is there a Western Model of Development? Everyone uses the term and there is widespread agreement that there is such a model, but thereafter the consensus starts to break down. What exactly is the Western Model? What does it encompass? How can such a diverse group of nations as those of Western Europe and North America (the United States and Canada) have a single, developmental model on which they can all agree? Especially since the Western European nations are fragmenting and growing farther apart, and since the U.S. and Western Europe seem to have less and less in common these days, what is there that still ties these two areas together?

So is there still a common Western model? If so, what precisely does it consist of: what are its ingredients? Or is it just a figment of the imagination, an invention that had some utility as a concept in the past but is now so shopworn, frayed, even coming apart at the seams, that it has lost all usefulness?

I think there is such a model. And certainly, those who rail against the Western Model and think that it is colonialist, imperialist, and even racist think so, even while expressing their opposition to it. As the questions above imply, it is possible that the Western Model is a bit of an invention, a construction, a narrative propagated by the West to advance its own power and influence, and that that narrative is now fraying and more open to questioning than before. Thus, we want to know what exactly the Western Model consists of, does it still correspond to the realities of divergence within the Western world, and how successful has been the West in exporting its model to other regions, countries, and areas?

What, then, goes into the Western Model? The following are six components, which are more fully described and developed in the body of the chapter:

1. A certain common cultural history (Greece, Rome, Christianity, feudalism, the Renaissance, the Enlightenment, the industrial revolution, and modernization) with which most Westerners would identify.
2. An emphasis on certain common political values: democracy, human rights, pluralism, the rule of law, and social justice.
3. A modern, mixed economy with sufficient open markets to ensure dynamism but also regulated to ensure fairness and equity.
4. An emphasis on social programs, reform, equality, and sufficient welfare that no person is left behind or excluded.

5. Agreement on basic political institutions: regular elections, parliament or congress, an independent judiciary, and civil society.
6. An agreement on the process by which these desirable goals came about: first, economic growth; which gives rise to pluralism and social change; which, in turn, leads to a broadening and deepening of democracy; then, social justice.

Obviously, not everyone in the West will agree on all these features. Different countries and different groups within these countries will have different priorities, and these will also change over time. It also needs to be said that when there is a common outside enemy, as during the Cold War (but less recently in response to the war on terrorism), there is greater consensus and coalescence around these core values: witness the widespread support for such institutions as the Atlantic Alliance, the European Union (EU), and NATO. By the same token, when there is no common enemy, the consensus starts to fray and loyalty to these institutions begins to wane.

At the same time – and the focus of much of this chapter – fealty to the idea and concept of a single, all-encompassing Western Model has recently been greatly eroded. For one thing, as much of the West continues in recession, the Model itself has not recently delivered much in the way of economic development for its members, and as an export the Model has been severely tarnished in much of the Third World. For another, the Western European nations themselves are frequently at odds over what the Model stands for; witness the current disputes between prosperous Northern Europe and stagnant-if-not-depressed Southern Europe and who is to blame for the present economic crisis. For a third, the United States and Western Europe have been increasingly drifting apart in terms of values and international orientation: "dancing in the dark" as Dennis Bark's recent book title puts it.[15] We need to face the fact that, while the Western Model has by no means disappeared and is still strong enough to galvanize common action, it has in the last two-and-a-half decades been severely eroded.

One final preliminary question: who exactly is included in the Western Model? Here by "the West" we mean Western Europe and primarily Great Britain because so many of our Western institutions – the supremacy of parliament, rule of law, checks and balances, limited government, separation of powers, civil and political rights – derive from there. But also, the Continent – France's bill of rights, for example, and law codes. And then also those "fragments" of the West (Louis Hartz's term)[16] – the United States, Canada, Australia, New Zealand, and South Africa – which were powerfully shaped by this Western European and Anglo-British tradition. But not Latin America, a separate civilization, shaped more by Southern Europe: Spain and Portugal. And not Eastern Europe yet, which can be argued to deserve a separate chapter and separate treatment in our book. Eastern Europe *may* become further integrated into the West but for now, as we see below, it is only part-way there, a separate and distinctive "Second World of Development."

History and Political Culture

Let us assume that we know the history, in its basic outline, of Western, Judeo-Christian civilization. Western civilization first emerged out of the Eastern Mediterranean, the Levant, some four thousand years ago, and had Syrian, Persian, Egyptian, and Hebrew (*The Bible*) roots. Then came Greece, Rome, and the rise of Christianity.

After the collapse of the Roman Empire in 476 AD, the West went through a one-thousand-year history of feudalism (agrarian, two-class, poor, top-down, authoritarian, scholastic, and Catholic) which took additional centuries to overcome. The United States and Canada, however, founded only in the evolving, modernizing seventeenth and eighteenth centuries, were fortunate *not* to have had a feudal past which they needed to overcome – except perhaps in the plantation, slave-holding U.S. South.

Then, in the West, came the Renaissance, the Enlightenment, the industrial revolution, the scientific revolution, the Protestant Reformation, and the rise of capitalism. Vast social change, the rise of the middle class, and then the revolutions of 1689 (Great Britain), 1776 (the United States), and 1789 (France) broke the back of the old, traditional two-class society and ushered in the modern, democratic age. With lots of exceptions – mainly Southern Europe, Eastern Europe, but also for a long time, Germany and Scandinavia – that is the general pattern of Western development. Both Canada and the United States were cultural, intellectual, and political byproducts of this "age of revolution."

Once we reach the modern age, the various countries of the West diverged even more. France, Great Britain, Germany, Italy, Spain, the Nordics, the United States, and the others all went their separate ways. Yet there was sufficient similarity in their pattern of development that we can identify a common Western model. That model, not without its flaws, was elaborated by eminent economic historian W. W. Rostow and in the school of thought known as "Developmentalism."[17]

Rostow posited five stages in the economic, social, and political development of the West: (1) traditional society, (2) the preconditions for take-off, (3) the take-off, (4) the drive to maturity, and (5) the age of high mass consumption.

In the first stage of the model, presumably applicable to today's developing nations as well as the earlier, Western developers, traditional society is characterized by a predominantly agricultural economy, lack of industry and technology, a rural and mainly illiterate society, little upward mobility or social change, a society that is two-class, hierarchical, and family-, clan-, or tribe-based, and no democracy. This is what a traditional, underdeveloped, feudal, or semi-feudal society looks like.

In the second stage, the pre-conditions for take-off are established. In Western Europe and America this period would be roughly the seventeenth and eighteenth centuries, slower in Southern and Eastern Europe, faster in the West. In this stage, markets and trade start to expand, banks are established, entrepreneurial spirit increases, education expands, roads are built and port facilities expanded, economic progress comes to be seen as a societal good, and political authority is consolidated in strong monarchies, militaries, or oligarchies. But traditional society and its values remain in place and there is little or no democracy.

The third or take-off stage now follows. In this stage, agricultural production increases even while peasants start moving to the cities, traditional society starts to give way, industrialization begins and investment starts to come in, banks modernize and use compound interest, technological and mechanical innovation advancement goes forward, and stable oligarchic, elite-dominated government is established. Think of Western Europe or North America in the "long" nineteenth century up to World War I.

The drive-to-maturity, our fourth stage, goes in Europe and America from roughly the turn of the twentieth century through the 1950s. We now have a regularly growing economy. Between 10 and 20 percent of national income is reinvested, new industries proliferate, and the country becomes more urban than rural. The society demonstrates that it can produce almost anything; it becomes more integrated into the global economy. The old elites are supplanted, the middle class grows, and democracy expands – although there may be setbacks. Rostow suggests, which may have relevance to today's developing nations, that the drive-to-maturity may take fifty or sixty years.

The fifth and final stage is called the age of high mass consumption. Clearly, Western Europe, Japan, South Korea, Singapore, North America, and Australia and New Zealand have reached this stage. In this period, affluence, as measured by per-capita income, increases, the middle class becomes dominant, and the work force adjusts to new technological advances. Society shifts from a concern exclusively with bread-and-butter issues to such issues as the environment, human rights, and leisure time. In parallel fashion, the welfare state expands and democratization now includes all groups. That is the stage in which we in the First World of modern, mixed, globalized economies and societies now live

This is the Rostow-developmentalist model, which provides a useful picture of Western economic and societal modernization but which also has its flaws. First, the model pays no attention to distinct cultural differences – Islamic, Asian, African, Latin, etc. – affecting development. Second, it leaves out foreign influences on development, including interventions, occupations, diplomatic pressures, war, etc. Third, it makes the entire process of development seem so nice and easy – too easy, in ignoring revolutions, coups, bloodshed, civil wars, and violence. And fourth, not so important here but more so later on when we talk about the Third World, the Rostow model is based entirely on the particular *Western* experience (Europe and the U.S.) of development and has almost nothing to say about the history, culture, and setting of the non-West.

Even with these limits, however, we find the Rostow model useful in providing an outline of at least the *Western model* of development. And it bears repeating that by "Western" we mean Western Europe, North America, Australia, New Zealand, and, to a lesser extent, South Africa – all countries or regions, as colonies powerfully shaped by this Western tradition and by Western institutions. However, Eastern Europe was peripheral to this model of development so we reserve discussion of that area to a separate chapter. Similarly, Latin America: it is *partly Western* but represents the Southern European, "Latin," or Mediterranean variant on the Western tradition, has its own *indigenous* culture and society and, therefore, merits a separate chapter to itself.

Not only is there a Western model of development but there is also widespread agreement within the West about how the change process and democratization go forward. First, you need a long period, thirty or forty or fifty years, of stability – Bismarck in Germany, Queen Victoria in England – which may amount to *forced* stability or even "soft" authoritarianism, in which feudalism definitively gives way, investment can work its wonders, industrialization proceeds, and rapid economic growth takes place.

Economic growth in turn gives rise to vast social changes: rising literacy and urbanization, an organized working class, and a far larger middle class. These changes help stimulate greater social pluralism and, over time, give rise to demands for free elections and democratization.

We can see that, with the appropriate reservations and qualifications, this process has largely worked its way out in the Netherlands, Great Britain, France, Germany, and Scandinavia. Within Europe, it has been less successful in Eastern Europe and in the Mediterranean countries of Greece, Cyprus, Italy, Spain, Malta, and Portugal. Interestingly, this same model, by extension, has been applied in East Asia in those countries heavily influenced by the West: Japan after World War II, South Korea, and Taiwan. We return to this theme in the East Asia chapter.

Already hinted at in the above paragraphs are *within-Europe* differences of the Western tradition, as well as increasing differences between Western Europe and the U.S. Within Europe the main differences are socio-cultural and regional: the wealthy and historically Protestant

Nordic countries of Denmark, Finland, Iceland, Norway, and Sweden; as well as the "Core" European countries of Great Britain, Ireland, the Netherlands, Belgium, France, Germany, Luxembourg, Switzerland, and Austria; *versus* the poorer and historically Catholic or Orthodox Southern European countries of Portugal, Spain, Italy, Malta, Greece, and Cyprus. Culturally, socially, politically, and economically, North and South of Europe are very different sub-regional areas – and probably becoming even more so. All of them, however, are developed, democratic, industrialized, free, and with a modern, mixed economy which, along with the cultural tradition outlined above, make them *Western*.

The differences between Western Europe and the United States are even greater than these within-Europe differences – and becoming increasingly more so. Of course, the U.S. as well as Canada are similarly developed countries, democratic, industrial, free, and with a modern mixed economy, which gives rise to the notion of common Western purpose and an alliance of "Free World" countries. But these commonalities were most apparent during the Cold War when Western Europe and North America were united by a common enemy, the Soviet Union. Since then, however, with no common enemy to hold the Western Alliance together, the United States and Western Europe have increasingly diverged – with Canada, a story in itself which cannot fully be told here, now perhaps closer to the European systems than to the America one.

The social, cultural, and political differences between the U.S. and Europe are immense. Religiously, 80 percent of Americans believe in God while only 40 percent of West

Europeans do. Forty-five percent of Americans go to church or synagogue regularly, only 5 percent of Europeans do. Americans believe in capital punishment while Europeans do not and condemn the U.S. as "barbarians" for continuing it. Europeans are wedded to their beloved welfare state and are willing to pay 50, 60, or 70 percent of their income in taxes to maintain it. In contrast, Americans pay only 20-30 percent and would much rather have larger take-home pay or what we call "disposable income."

In international affairs, the differences are similarly pronounced. Europeans believe in international institutions and negotiations to settle disputes, and they criticize the U.S. for too often acting unilaterally and relying primarily on military force. Europeans are believers in the United Nations and the International Court of Justice to settle disputes, while Americans tend to be skeptical of these institutions.

Importantly, since the end of the Cold War, Europe has reduced its military budgets and forces almost to the vanishing point, leaving them all but strategically impotent in times of crises. The defense budget cuts have had the effect of rendering NATO (North Atlantic Treaty Organization) weak and leaving the U.S. to shoulder almost the entire burden of peace-keeping in places like Serbia, Afghanistan, or Syria or in the war on terrorism. Western Europe has so emasculated its armed forces and its defense and foreign affairs budgets that it is now only a weak player in international politics, made worse by the fact that, while on some issues there is a common EU policy, on others each country tends to pursue its own national interests.

Socioeconomic Overview

Western Europe, along with North America (Canada, the United States) and Japan, is one of the world's wealthiest areas. It is classified by the World Bank as a "high-income area" with a per-capita income average of $37,153. That puts Western Europe at exactly the Japanese level and slightly below the North American average. Western Europe has clearly reached "developed country" status or what W. W. Rostow called the "age of high mass consumption." For comparison with Russia analyzed in our next chapter, Western Europe is approximately twice as rich on a per-person basis (see Table 2.1).

In Western Europe, you don't see much poverty, disease, bloated bellies (not from too much but from too little food), or malformed bodies (from poor health care) the way you see these things in the Third World. No, Western Europe is long past the stage of underdevelopment. Western Europe, along with the U.S., Canada, Australia, and New Zealand, is instead wealthy, developed, industrialized, highly literate, with good health care and long (eighty years) life expectancy. Of course, it is still possible to see *pockets* of poverty in Western Europe or *individual cases* of poverty and poor health, but no generalized or society-wide situations of poverty.

TABLE 2.1
WESTERN COUNTRIES: POPULATION
AND GROSS DOMESTIC PRODUCT
PER CAPITA, PPP 2014[18]

Country	Population (in millions)	Gross Domestic Product per Capita
Austria	8.5	47,682
Australia	23.4	45,925
Belgium	11.2	43,435
Canada	35.5	45,066
Cyprus	1.1	30,239
Denmark	5.6	45,537
Finland	5.4	40,676
France	66.2	39,328
Germany	80.9	46,401
Greece	10.9	26,851
Iceland	0.3	43,933
Ireland	4.6	49,393
Italy	60.7	35,463
Luxembourg	0.6	98,460
Malta[2]	0.4	29,526
The Netherlands	16.9	48,253
New Zealand	4.5	37,679
Norway	5.1	65,615
Portugal	10.4	28,760
Spain	46.5	33,629
Sweden	9.7	45,297
Switzerland	8.2	59,540
United Kingdom	64.6	40,233
United States (for comparison)	318.9	54,630

Source: World Development Indicators, The World Bank

---

[2] 2013 PPP GDP per capita due to unavailable 2014 value

Western Europe has nice, clean streets and parks, great museums, and wonderful train service. Americans who visit there tend to come away admiring Europe and wondering why we can't have as good public services and facilities as they have. The answer is that Europeans *pay a lot* for these services in the form of steep income and sales taxes that may amount to 50, 60, or 70 percent of their personal income. At the same time, while Europeans have nice parks and public services, they have far fewer personal things: one car (if that) instead of two, an apartment instead of an individual house, and, in general, less furniture, fewer toys, fewer clothes, fewer *things* than do most Americans. Americans and Canadians have generally preferred having more individual disposable income over higher taxes with more government services.

Europeans have opted electorally for what we have come to call the "social" or the "welfare state." That means a shorter work-week than most Americans are accustomed to, longer vacations, generous pension plans, free education, free health care, and free, cradle-to-grave welfare. Of course, you pay for all these "free" things in the form of those exceedingly high taxes referred to previously. Yet most Europeans are exceedingly proud of their generous welfare systems and would not want them to go away. Along with freedom, elections, and basic rights, the welfare state has now become embedded in the European definition of democracy itself.

Hence, European politics and the European policy model tend to be considerably to the left of what the United States has historically considered to be mainstream politics. The European mainstreams tend to be social-democratic and even socialist. Even the Center and Center-Right parties in Europe tend to be to the left of the mainstream U.S. parties. In Europe, the conservative Center and Center-Right parties do not campaign, because it is so popular, on a platform of doing away with the welfare state; instead, they say only that they will manage it better. This leftward orientation of much of Europe as compared to the U.S. helps explain why President Barack Obama was so wildly popular there: because he was seen as being closer to *European* political preferences. To put it another way, President Obama's election was seen by Europeans as the U.S. finally "catching up" to the "advanced" European welfare-state level.

Of course, there are differences within Europe on these issues. The Nordic or Scandinavian states (Denmark, Finland, Iceland, Norway, and Sweden) tend to have the largest, richest and most generous welfare states. Germany, Great Britain, the Netherlands, and Switzerland have larger private sectors, are more free-enterprise oriented, and, even while having generous welfare programs, are closer to the U.S. model of a mixed (state *and* private) economy. Countries like Austria, Belgium, and France are in-between: advanced welfare states, a generally statist economy, but still with a sizable private economy.

Another interesting way to look at Western European welfare systems is according to geographic regions. In this perspective, Nordic or Scandinavian Europe is the richest and most generous; its five countries are regularly listed as among the world's happiest, most socially just, most contented, the nicest places to live. Just a notch below them in wealth and living standards is what we will call "core Europe": Great Britain, Ireland, the Netherlands, Belgium,

France, Luxembourg, Germany, Austria, and Switzerland. These nine countries are also highly developed and, in general, well-managed countries whose per-capita income is in the high $30,000s and thus intermediary in terms of wealth and social welfare. The poorest and least generous welfare states in Europe are all in the South: Cyprus, Greece, Italy, Malta, Portugal, and Spain. These countries have *for centuries* been poorer and less developed than Core Europe with per-capita incomes averaging about half (Greece, Malta, and Portugal) to three-quarters (Cyprus, Spain, and Italy) the West European average.

It is thus no accident, because of its relative poverty, that Southern Europe has more underdevelopment-related problems than either Nordic or Core Europe: crime, corruption, inefficiency, weak infrastructure, high unemployment, weak civil society, a weak and precarious middle class, and frailer democracies. Nor is it an accident that when the global economic downturn set in in 2008 that Southern Europe was the most devastatingly affected, with rising joblessness, a middle class squeezed into poverty, despair, and the potential for political instability.

The focus of international politics in Europe has also, significantly, shifted to the South. It used to be, during the Cold War, that the main focus was East-West: the threat from the Soviet Union, the Berlin Wall, and NATO versus the Warsaw Pact and the Iron Curtain. And then when the Soviet Union collapsed in 1991 and the Wall came down, the main issues became Eastern Europe, EU, and NATO expansion into those countries formerly under Soviet control and the building of democracy and prosperous economies in Eastern Europe.

That task now largely accomplished, attention turned to Southern Europe: instability and ethnic conflict in the Balkans (Southeast Europe), the threat of Islamic violence infiltrating Europe via Turkey and the Middle East, and now out-of-control immigration coming into Southern Europe across the Mediterranean – and all the problem issues that arise when a poor, Third World area (North Africa, the Sahel, and Sub-Saharan Africa) comes in direct contact with a rich and developed area (Europe): disease, crime, illiteracy, discontent, violence, joblessness, envy, and lack of assimilation. Indeed, because of these problems which are remarkably akin to those facing the United States along its southwestern border, I have taken to calling the Mediterranean the "European Rio Grande." Security issues have also refocused toward the South and away from its former location mainly in Germany: NATO has moved many of its functions to the South, U.S. naval operations are headquartered in Italy, and the EU has concentrated its diplomatic and economic/social assistance programs in the South and Southeast.

After the fall of the Soviet Union and, by 2004, with Eastern Europe safely incorporated into the two great Pan-European "clubs," NATO and the EU, bumper stickers began appearing proclaiming "Europe: Whole and Free." That meant that Eastern and Western Europe were now united for the first time and that the entire European continent was free of Soviet control and democratic. However, we have already seen that Europe is still divided into blocs and regions and with great disparities of wealth between them. Similarly, while we applaud Europe's new freedom, we have also seen that democracy and liberty are still precarious in the South, the Southeast, and, as we see in Chapter 4, the East.

Nevertheless, there is, with these qualifications, something to this notion of Europe "whole and free." Europe is, after all, at least its western parts, one of the world's richest, nicest, most prosperous areas. Except for relatively small outbreaks of violence and ethnic cleansing in the former Yugoslavia, Europe has been – a remarkable achievement – relatively free from war for the last seventy years. In that same time period Europe has rebuilt its cities and industries, which had been bombed into piles of bricks during World War II; it has also rebuilt its economy into one of the wealthiest areas on earth, fashioned a parliamentary-democratic model that is the envy of much of the world, and – a matter of great pride in Europe – built up its welfare state to the point where Europe may be the most livable of all world areas. The "European or Western Model" has a lot to offer.

Even on foreign and security affairs, where Europe is weakest, a great deal has been accomplished. As we said, there has been no war in Western Europe for seven decades. Europe has built up its common judicial, consultative, and economic integration institutions to the point where there are common European practices governing all major social and economic issues. Even in foreign affairs, where there is less unity and common purpose, Europe now has a common foreign policy, a single foreign minister, and even a common defense and security policy. All these ingredients and more go to make up what we can call "the European Model."

But let us not exaggerate or romanticize these accomplishments. Over the last one hundred years, since approximately World War I, the United States has considerably surpassed Europe in wealth and power. Former colonies Canada and Australia have also become wealthier than the European average, while New Zealand is somewhat poorer, about at the Southern European level. These other offshoots of Europe are known for their peace-keeping abilities but none of them has the military capacity and power of the U.S.

Within the Western Alliance – if it can still be called that – there is increased divergence between the main allies. Europe and Canada tend to see the U.S. as too individualistic, too militaristic, and too willing to go its own way, while Australia supports a robust U.S. military presence especially in Asia. The Europeans and Canada criticize the U.S. for seeming to prefer unilateral military action before seeking their own favored solutions: talks, negotiations, diplomacy, and multilateral action. Meanwhile, the U.S. criticizes Europe for downsizing its military, being unprepared for war or conflict, and being unwilling to use force even when necessary. By now the U.S., Canada, and Western Europe are so far apart ideologically and culturally that they find it increasingly hard to work together or to mount joint exercises. What the United States likes to refer to for legitimacy and support as "the international community" has been reduced to just a handful of nations; what we call an "alliance" is now only a "coalition of the willing."

Government Institutions and the Role of the State

The United States, Western Europe, Canada, Australia, and New Zealand are all, even with their differences,

Western-style democracies. That means that, unlike authoritarian or communist regimes or some mix of those, there is a common basis of political understanding and operating that makes it easier to function as alliance partners.

But there the similarities end, and that causes problems for a common alliance foreign or security policy. First, the United States is a superpower and none of these other countries is. The U.S. has immense resources and firepower at its disposal which these other countries lack. That means the "Alliance," so-called, is always going to be lopsided, unequal, unevenly weighted, and disproportional, with an overwhelming preponderance of power and influence on the American side. In any alliance negotiations or actions, the Americans are *always* going to be in the lead and with the most power, while the other allies, as British Prime Minister Tony Blair's foes called it, serve as "lapdogs" to the American lead.

Second, the U.S. is a presidential system while *all* these others, including *all* of Western Europe, are parliamentary regimes. The U.S. has also a system of checks and balances: the three-part division of power, a federal system, and powerful domestic interest groups that can strongly influence or even veto policy. Parliamentary systems lack this system of extensive checks and balances because, by definition, the prime minister, cabinet, and a majority in parliament must all be from the same party or a coalition of parties. Hence, you do not see the same internal divisions over policy-making that you see in the U.S. Such divisions are particularly pronounced when the White House, as at present, is in the control of one party and the Congress, or one house therein, under the other's control. It particularly causes consternation among Europeans, who with their parliamentary regimes do not well understand the American system, that the opposition in Congress can frustrate the wishes and policies of an American president, or even carry out a foreign policy of their own. Because in the European parliamentary systems that would *never* be allowed to happen.

A third difference between Europe or these other parliamentary regimes and America is the role of interest groups in politics. America has many more, and larger, and more independent, interest groups than is the situation in Europe. In Europe there are far fewer interest groups and, in Europe's corporatist-style system, the largest groups, labor and business, are often part of the government, not separate and independent from it. They, therefore, have no interest in opposing their own government's policies. Whereas in the U.S. the interest groups are much more vocal and independent. It mystifies our European friends that the Cuban-American lobby can have veto power over U.S. Cuba policy or that the so-called "Israeli lobby" can have so much influence on American Middle East policy.

A fourth difference lies in the role of public opinion. Of course, European governments also listen to public opinion but in general their governments and foreign ministries are more immune to popular shifts of opinion than in the U.S. In the U.S., even foreign and security policy is highly politicized whereas in Europe governments are freer to pursue the national interest independent of the public mood. France, for example, when its secret service blew up a Greenpeace boat seeking to interrupt a French nuclear bomb experiment in the South Pacific, simply cited "reasons of state" and got away with that reasoning, even though France killed twenty-some people in the process. One cannot imagine such a tragic event occurring in the U.S. without public opinion being aroused.

A fifth and most important difference between Europe and the U.S. lies in the sheer size and functions of the state – although that is now changing. In Western Europe, the state and state corporations generate between 40 and 60 percent of GNP – at the higher figure in the more socialized countries of Scandinavia, lower in the more private enterprise oriented economies of Germany, the Netherlands, and Great Britain. In contrast, in the United States the government's share of GNP has historically been far lower than in Europe, in the 20-25 percent range. However, under President Obama and now with Obamacare, the state's share of GNP has shot way up, approaching European levels. The question is, whether Americans with all their earmarks, logrolling, corruption, and special interest groups are getting as much in the way of services from their government as are Europeans with approximately the same state size. The answer, apparently, judging from America's high taxes but poor public services (schools, police, public transportation, etc.), is no.

These differences in the nature and functioning of the main state institutions in the U.S. and Western Europe are wide and important. They lead to a lot of misunderstandings – especially over the role of interest group politics and oppositionist Congress in the U.S. system of checks and balances – between the two. On the other hand, let us re-emphasize that all the nations of North America and Western Europe are democracies. They all, with perhaps slightly different emphases, believe in human rights, freedom, social justice, and the rule of law. It is on this basis of a shared history, culture, beliefs, and fundamental political and economic interests that the United States and Western Europe have maintained the Atlantic Alliance, with NATO as its military arm, for some seventy years.

However, we should not take the Alliance for granted. U.S. and European values and interests since the end of the Cold War, as we have seen, have become increasingly divergent. We are slowly pulling apart. And, as our values and interests diverge, it will become increasingly difficult to keep the Alliance together except on a voluntary and case-by-case basis. What then happens to the notion of a common "Western" alliance and model?

The Western World

The so-called "Western Model" is clearly fraying at the edges and maybe more basically. With Western Europe and the U.S. increasingly pulling apart and going their separate ways ideologically, socially, culturally, politically, and economically, it is hard to maintain the idea of a common alliance or model based on shared values and interests. Some commentators believe these differences between the U.S. and Europe are now so large that the can no longer be bridged. Our own assessment in this book, while acknowledging the widening gap, does not go that far. But before we make our final assessment, it is important to know what exactly is the Western Model that we are talking about here.

The Western Model, by our lights, has two dimensions: the domestic and the international. On the domestic side, if there is one common thing that the United States believes in, it is freedom. Freedom to speak up, to move around the country, to choose your occupation, to exercise your rights and your individualism. And all this without government interference. By European lights, Americans are almost anarchists in their insistence on unfettered individualism; Europeans regularly denounce us for practicing what they call "cowboy" or "gunslinger" diplomacy: going it alone in the world, operating unilaterally, preferring military solutions over negotiated settlements.

Europeans, too, believe in freedom, but their sense of freedom is more circumscribed than in the U.S. That is because Western Europe is much more crowded population-wise than is the U.S., Europe has no frontier as the U.S. has in the West where one can start life over again, and because the realities of state power are much more constraining of individual initiatives and freedoms than in the U.S. Rather than unbridled freedom and individualism, West Europeans tend to have great faith in what they call the European Social Model.

The European Social Model provides a common vision and ideology for Europe that combines the goals of economic growth, high living standards, full employment, social inclusion, social protection (the welfare state), and cooperation between business and labor. This emphasis on social protection, the welfare state, etc. is now so deeply embedded in the European people that it is part of their political culture and even their definition of democracy. The American definition of democracy focuses on freedoms, rights, and procedures (elections, separation of powers, and legislation); Europe includes those things, too, but its main focus, in addition, is now this social model. British historian

Tony Judt argues that the social model is what binds Europe together and gives it unity, in contrast to the American way of life that heavily emphasizes individualism.[19]

The European social model, however, is not everywhere the same, and the differences largely correspond to the regional variations in Europe emphasized earlier. That is, there is a Nordic Model of full and generous social welfare; a Continental Model (France and Belgium) which emphasizes pensions and security; an Anglo-Saxon Model (Great Britain, Ireland, the Netherlands, and Germany) which, like the U.S., is less generous than the previous two and provides social assistance mainly as a last resort; and finally, the Southern European Model which provides far lower levels of social assistance. Even with these variations, however, the European social model is a matter of great pride and provides an attractive goal toward which other areas (Eastern Europe, much of the developing world) aspire.

We see, therefore, a growing divide at the domestic level between what Europe stands for, on the one hand, and what the U.S. believes in, on the other. These gaps are not only becoming wider, they are also coming to encompass a broad range of differences: attitudes about capital punishment, for example, the role of religion in society, drug use, guns, law enforcement, social inclusion, and a *host* of other issues. Europe and the U.S. are becoming so far apart ideologically and politically that it is a wonder that they are still able to cooperate at all, let alone form a single *Western* Model.

Now if we turn to the international side of the equation the differences between the U.S. and Europe are at least as wide as they are on the domestic side. Europeans tend to see the U.S. is a "cowboy society" internationally – shoot first and ask questions later. They perceive the U.S. as preferring to act unilaterally, shunning and denigrating international institutions like the UN, and turning too quickly to military solutions rather than diplomacy. Of course, this is a considerable caricature of actual U.S. policy, a picture shaped particularly by President George W. Bush's imprudent military intervention in Iraq. And we also need to bear in mind that part of Europe's criticisms of U.S. foreign policy is a product of their own weak military position and near-impotence as a force in international security. When you are militarily weak, international law and institutions are your only defense.

Europe likes to say, however, that it has moral standing and worldwide diplomatic influences even if its military clout is constrained. And, let us face it, Europe is not wholly impotent militarily: two nuclear powers (Great Britain and France), small but well-trained militaries, and secret police and intelligence services that are first-rate. But in most larger military actions, if it comes to that, Europe must rely heavily on the U.S. for weapons, transport, and equipment.

Rather than seeking military solutions, however, Europe much prefers negotiations and diplomacy. That, too – the *peaceful* solution of conflicts – has become part of their ideology and political culture. Europe wants to work through the UN, the International Court of Justice, and the EU itself to find resolution for international problems. It believes that talk and negotiations are always better than military solutions. And it often criticizes the U.S. for what it sees as a too-eager opting for military action. Of course, the defense of international law and of international institutions is a reflection, in part, of the fact that Europe lacks military capability. We must also remember that, while diplomacy, discussion, and negotiation are useful, they represent only one arm of foreign policy. Some conflicts involving terrorism, civil war, or war between nations may be beyond the stage where negotiations alone can resolve them.

On both the domestic front – the European Social Model – and the international – diplomacy versus military solutions – the U.S. and Western Europe are very far apart and becoming increasingly more so. These differences make it difficult for the U.S. and Western Europe to work together, let alone to form an Alliance. Remember also that in the world of values, religion, culture, and politics the U.S. and Europe are now poles apart.

And yet, and yet..., even with all these growing differences the U.S. and Western Europe often see eye-to-eye and are able to work together. More than that, there is still something to those hallowed and venerated institutions called "the Atlantic Alliance" or the "Western Model," although these concepts are fading as the generations change. In defense of human rights, for example, the U.S. and Europe, at least for now, are clearly in accord. Similarly, with democracy promotion: not only are the U.S. and Europe dedicated to promoting democracy outside of their home areas but it is inconceivable that any European state would now reject democracy and still remain within "The [European] Club." On terrorism, the U.S. and Europe similarly often work together, although they may disagree on specific tactics. However, with regard to such large issues as sanctions on Russia, policy toward Israel or Iran, or policy toward China, the U.S. and Europe often pursue different policies, or else they are *rivals* and competitors in some parts of the globe.

Especially interesting to us here is a basic agreement between Europe and America on the model that they would export to the rest of the world. That model includes both specific institutions – elections, democracy, parliament, and rule of law – *and* a common understanding of how development is achieved. That process involves economic development first, then social change, then (or concurrently) democratization and social justice. Of course, the reason Europe and the U.S. advocate this particular model is that it echoes and mirrors their own historical experience with development, *and* it serves their interests. This model is what Rostow, Lipset, Almond, and all those early pioneers of development theory wrote about and advocated more than fifty years ago. The question now is whether that model applies or fits the rest of the world where the cultures, histories, and sociopolitical structures are fundamentally different.

CHAPTER 3

RUSSIA: DISILLUSIONMENT WITH DEMOCRACY; RETURN TO AUTOCRACY

Russia has long (always?) been an autocratic, authoritarian regime. Whether under the czars, dictator Joseph Stalin and the communists, and now President Vladimir Putin, Russia has been governed for a thousand years from the top down, authoritatively, from the center of power in Moscow outwardly to distant provinces. Authoritarianism in Russia is so long-standing and so deeply embedded that it has become part of the political culture. And, to complicate matters, Mr. Putin manipulates Russia's authoritarian political culture to present himself as an indispensible man, *the* incarnation of Russian values, and thus to rule out and even suppress Russia's weak but alternative and oppositionist *democratic* political groups.

What is Putin up to? Why is he doing what he is doing in foreign policy? What is the developmentalist model from which Putin is working?

First of all, Putin wants to rebuild Russia, after the collapse of communism nearly thirty years ago, and restore it to great power status. To do that, second, he believes that in such a huge, disperse, and chaotic country as Russia, lacking much civil society, democratic institutions, and basic infrastructure, only a strong, centralized, authoritarian state under strong leadership can succeed. Third, Putin is rebuilding the Russian economy, which similarly collapsed after the fall of communism; with most other industries destroyed and little of either domestic or foreign investment, Putin is exporting the one resource he has, which he also uses as a club against other countries: oil and natural gas.

Fourth, Putin is heavily emphasizing Russian nationalism, the concept of "Greater Russia" (which scares Russia's neighbors including the Baltics, the Ukraine, parts of whose territory Putin has seized), and the need and *obligation* for Russia to again be an aggressive force in the world, a Great Power. And fifth, Putin is rebuilding all those institutions associated not with democracy but with the old regime and with authoritarianism: the army, the secret police (in which Putin spent his early career), the Russian Orthodox Church, and the central state bureaucracy.

So what is the Russian model of government and bureaucracy? Well, it is clearly centralized, authoritarian, autocratic (one man), nationalistic, top-down, and even expansionist. In other words, Putin's regime, in a big, resource-rich, important country (the world's largest) represents a *reversal* of the trend toward democracy that scholars like Francis Fukuyama (*The End of History* guy) predicted some twenty years ago.[20] Moreover, not content with authoritarianism at home, Putin is attempting to *export* this model to other countries, not just those close to home ("the near abroad") such as Belarus, the Ukraine,

Moldova, Georgia, Mongolia, the "Five Stans" (Kazakhstan, Tajikistan, Turkmenistan, Uzbekistan, and Kyrgyzstan) of Central Asia, and the Trans-Caucus (Armenia and Azerbaijan), but also such distant countries as Argentina, Bolivia, Cuba, Egypt, Turkey, Syria, and Venezuela.

Clearly the Russian model, to the degree that Putin succeeds, represents both our alternative and a challenge to American foreign policy *and* to our efforts to build democracy abroad. And perhaps to the entire, existing, Western world order.

History and Political Culture

Russia occupies a huge land mass and is *by far* the world's largest country, *twice* as large (before the collapse of the Soviet Union it was *three* times as large) as the United States, Canada, China, or Brazil. It is so big that Russia stretches over nine time zones (versus three for the U.S.), now arbitrarily reduced to seven by Mr. Putin. Russia is both a European and an Asian power and straddles the entire Eurasian landmass, which a lot of strategic thinkers still consider *the key* to controlling world power.

Russia is not only large, it is also rich in natural resources – the richest in the world in terms of its potential. Russia has *everything* that a modern economy should have: abundant iron ore, coal, oil, natural gas, timber, rare metals, and some of the largest and richest (like the American Midwest or the Argentine *pampa*) areas of agricultural land in the *world*.

With both a huge European and an even larger Asian land mass, and stretching southward into the Islamic Middle

East, Russia is also exceedingly diverse. It has approximately two hundred distinct ethnic, religious, and language groups. In this sense, Russia is like Indonesia, similarly with hundreds of ethnic groups, but in the Indonesian case, obviously unlike Russia, spread over some thirteen thousand islands. At least in Russia its huge landmass is contiguous.

And here lies the great problem in Russian history and culture: how to tie all this huge territory and all these diverse ethnic and language groups together into a single, integrated nation-state. And then, once that is done, how to mobilize, harness, and exploit Russia's vast resources so as to achieve a coherent and workable strategy for integral national development. No government in Russian history – neither the czars, nor Stalin and the communists, nor the short-lived democratic government under Boris Yeltsin that followed the collapse of the Soviet Union – has ever succeeded in this quest, although it remains the goal of *all* Russian governments. We will have to see if current president Putin can succeed in doing so.

So how do we begin to understand and interpret Russia at least preliminarily? Let me offer some tentative suggestions, reserving final conclusions for the end of the chapter:

1. It is a huge country preoccupied with achieving internal stability, the defense of its borders, and securing a rim of allied buffer states all around.
2. A country that is underdeveloped and in many areas, is close to the poverty of the Third World.
3. A separate *civilization* into itself – culturally, religiously, politically. Russia is both a European and

an Asian country, and yet separate and apart from both of these main continents. Russia is intensely self-occupied and wants to develop its own, unique, Russian model.

4. A country that is intensely nationalistic, bitter at its defeat in the Cold War, and that wants to *re*-establish its place as a great superpower.

5. A country with a gigantic inferiority complex and a chip on its shoulder. It wants the *benefits* of the West (greater affluence, investment, a modern country) without becoming *like* the West. At the same time, it wants to leapfrog history to achieve developed-country status, taking shortcuts (authoritarianism, violations of human rights, etc.), if necessary.

6. A country with an authoritarian tradition, with a people used to taking orders. Does that explain Mr. Putin; also, Russia's failure so far to achieve democracy, civil liberties, and the rule of law?

7. British Prime Minister Winston Churchill once described Russia as "a riddle, wrapped in a mystery inside an enigma." Is it still that? Or can we begin to unravel this mystery and advance our knowledge and understanding of Russia?

Let us begin with Russian history. Russia has long been a vast, wild, wooly, violent, largely unsettled territory. It has been invaded and overrun on numerous occasions by conquering, marauding armies from both the West (Europe) and the East (Asia). All these conquests, back-and-forth, and marauding armies help account for the diverse languages, ethnicities, and peoples within Russia, and its historic difficulties in tying all these peoples together and forming a functioning nation-state.

Much of early Russian history took place in what is now the Ukraine. The Russian Orthodox Church was first organized a thousand years ago in Kiev, the capital of the Ukraine, as an offshoot and resurrection of the Eastern Orthodox Church centered in Constantinople but now overrun by Muslim/Turkish armies. The first czars were also crowned in Kiev and the first Russian armies, secret police, and bureaucratic offices were founded there. From Ukraine, these instruments of Russian nationalism and authoritarianism spread northward to present-day Moscow and eventually westward to Saint Petersburg and the Baltics and eastward to the Ural Mountains (the border of European Russia) and ultimately across Asia to the Pacific and beyond – Alaska, northwest Canada, and down the U.S. west coast.

The early centuries of this period of conquest and expansionism were chaotic and violent, reinforcing the Russian idea that only a strong czar, a strong state, and a strong army could hold this immense territory together. Back and forth the Russian czars and their armies went, moving first to expand their borders westward into Europe, then eastward across Asia, and also southward against the Tatars and other Muslims, and to find a warm-water (no ice!) harbor for Russian ships. Meanwhile, the armies of Europe – Poland, Sweden, France, and Germany – also invaded Russia, as did the eastern armies of the Mongols, Mughals, and others, turning Russia into an early multi-cultural, multi-lingual, and multi-ethnic society. Again the theme is: how to turn these disparate ethnic groups and identities into a single, coherent, functioning state.

Modern Russia began to emerge out of this vast, wild, and unruly territory with Peter the Great in the seventeenth century. At the time, Russia was still a feudal, medieval country: poor, untamed, primitive, uneducated, a peasant society with a small elite at the top. Peter, a towering man, managed not only to hold this huge territory together but also to expand it further eastward, westward, and southward. Unlike Europe, Russia's great east-west expanse was not hindered by national boundaries so the Russian state swallowed up thousands of square miles of new territory yearly, unhindered by other nations. At the same time, Peter visited Western capitals and began the process of Westernizing and modernizing Russia, at least among the elite and in the main cities of Moscow and Saint Petersburg.

Peter was succeeded in the eighteenth century by Catherine the Great who continued his policies of expanding the Russian nation and bringing European practices to backward Russia. But she did so, as had Peter and his predecessors, under autocratic, centralized, highly authoritarian leadership. From this point on, all of Russia's great accomplishments would be associated not with democratic development but with authoritarianism. That would be true under the czars, under the communists, and now under Putin. As Catherine herself argued, in such a huge, unruly territory, only a strong state and an absolute government would be capable of holding the country together and achieving national development.

But development in Russia even in the best of times was severely limited. It was limited to a small upper-class at the top and only to Russia's largest cities, which were all in Europe. The rest of Russia, including all of Siberia and Asian Russia, remained poor, backward, illiterate, and malnourished. Serfdom was the condition of 95 percent of the population. Moreover, Westernization was limited to the elite groups; the rest of the population was left far behind. The result was that all the great revolutions which we associate with the modern world – the renaissance, the enlightenment, the scientific revolution, the industrial revolution, the Protestant Reformation, and the revolution of democracy and modernity – either passed Russia by completely or else were very superficial, limited to a handful of Western-oriented aristocratic families but having little effect on the vast mass of the population.

All through the "long" (until the Russian Revolution of 1917) nineteenth century, Russia continued to be ruled by the autocratic czars. Some of the czars were more-or-less enlightened, others, the majority, were completely reactionary. By focusing almost exclusively on retaining their own absolutist power, they held Russia back. All through the nineteenth century Russia lagged further and further behind Western Europe in terms of education, industrialization, social change, and democratization. Meanwhile, a small, arrogant, self-centered elite lorded it over this vast peasant society and prevented reform and social change. When the explosion finally came in 1917 it was violent, chaotic, and bloody; the old elites were eliminated and a new communist dictatorship emerged.

Immediately after the revolution in 1917 Russia was in chaos. The old regime had been destroyed but it was unclear what would replace it. Democracy was tried for a few months, and rejected and overthrown. Civil war ensued between pro- and anti-revolutionary forces. Meanwhile, agriculture ground to a halt, the countryside was in turmoil, and mass starvation set in.

Out of this tumult the communist party under Vladimir Lenin emerged as the strongest force. Lenin and the communists began to pull the country back together, often using the most brutal kind of force. But Lenin died prematurely; after a vicious internal power struggle, he was succeeded by Joseph Stalin, the head of the communist party and a new "czar."

Using even more brutal, totalitarian methods, Stalin restored order to Russia. No one knows exactly how many people died as a result of Stalin's policies: estimates are in the tens of millions. Stalin also restored Russian agriculture (the state farms), began Russia's rapid industrialization, and in World War II elevated Russia to great power status. Staying in power for almost thirty years, Stalin gave Russia the stability it needed to carry through its economic take-off and industrialization; by defeating Nazi Germany in World War II Stalin also elevated Russian pride and nationalism. Once again, as under Peter, Catherine, and the czars, all of Russia's great accomplishments came to be seen as stemming from and associated with strong, centralized, authoritarian (in Stalin's case, totalitarian) rule. Democracy and human rights were nonexistent.

Over the long run, however, Soviet totalitarianism proved to be not very effective or productive. In the short run, Stalin's brutal rule *did* develop the Soviet Union, but in the post-World War II period Russia proved unable to compete with the West. The Soviet regime was woefully corrupt, bloated, bureaucratic, top-heavy, inefficient, and unable to deliver the goods and services that its citizens wanted. The result in the 1970s and 1980s was a growing and multi-pronged crisis: a crisis of the economy which could not produce, a crisis of society which did not change fast enough, a crisis of legitimacy as more and more people came to question the regime, a crisis of leadership as a succession of aging presidents or party chairmen died in office, and a crisis of morality as the regime was revealed to be both brutal and ineffective. Faced with these domestic pressures coupled with pressures from the outside (the U.S., Eastern Europe, and the pope), the Soviet Union imploded and collapsed in 1991. Both Soviet totalitarianism and the long, forty-five-year Cold War ended without a shot being fired!

As the Soviet Union disintegrated in 1990-91, the United States, Western Europe, and the Russians themselves made an effort to rebuild their society on the basis of capitalism, democracy, and greater openness to the outside world. In late 1991 Boris Yeltsin was *elected* as Russia's president, a parliament was similarly elected on a democratic basis, and the Russians invited in outside experts (including the author) to help them rebuild their society, economy, and institutions on a new basis.

But the outside advisers and the Russians themselves woefully underestimated the magnitude of the task. For in the wake of the Soviet Union's collapse the state farms stopped producing, almost all factories closed down, corruption was widespread, and government bureaucracies, since no one was paying their employees, ceased to function. Meanwhile, the feckless President Yeltsin was lost to frequent drinking binges, family members and close associates stole the country blind, foreign capital needed to rebuild the economy pulled out, and Russia plunged into chaos.

We tend to forget that, when a totalitarian regime like the Soviet Union collapses, what is left is also a near-total vacuum. That is the nature of totalitarian regimes: because they control *everything* (hence, the term "totalitarian"), when they collapse there is nothing there to build on. Everything must be reconstructed from scratch. That is not, as the United States government hoped, a three- or four-year effort; it is instead a three- or four-*generation* project. And, at the same time that Russia was collapsing internally, it was also, as the Baltics, Eastern Europe, the former Yugoslavia, the trans-Caucasus, Central Asia, and Mongolia broke away, losing about 40 percent of its population and almost the same amount of its national territory. Russia was not just defeated in the Cold War, it was *humiliated* and *embarrassed*, falling from Great Power status to "just another" (but big!) Third World country.

Russian discontent and unhappiness, with Yeltsin, with democracy and free-market capitalism, with the West and NATO's expansion right up to shrunken Russia's borders, and with their own sorry state internally, rose gradually during the 1990s. It was not that Russia and the Russians wanted to go back to the totalitarianism and brutality of the past or to a renewed Cold War. But they did want a measure of national respect, their dignity restored, and a government, unlike Yeltsin, that was effective and could deliver real goods and services. Polls in the 1990s showed a growing disaffection with the newly imported Western economic and political models and a strong desire to restore

Russian nationalism, strong government, and centralized rule. After all, those traits had been associated with Russia's great leaps forward in the past – Peter the Great, Catherine the Great, Stalin and the communists – and many Russians believed that model could be successful again. And that is precisely what the Russians got in Vladimir Putin.

Thus, Russian history and culture have been more supportive of authoritarianism than of democracy. In *all* of Russian history there has been less than a decade of what could be called democratic government. In contrast, authoritarianism has been the practice for approximately a *thousand years* of Russian history. Moreover, it is a strong if not authoritarian state, a strong Orthodox Church, Russian nationalism, and a strong army and security services that most Russians associate with the best times in their history: growth, expansion, and great power status.

Therefore, we should not expect democracy, pluralism, or liberal, free-market capitalism to be established anytime soon in Russia. Instead, we can most likely expect the continuation of authoritarianism or, at best, a mixed system that combines a strong state with some more liberal and democratic institutions. That likelihood also carries strong implications for the kind of foreign policy we can expect from Russia: tough, aggressive, nationalistic, and uncompromising.

Socioeconomic Overview

Nearly thirty years ago, just before its collapse, the Soviet Union had a population of around 290 million. In terms of population as well as size, the Soviet Union was then bigger than the United States.

Today, Russia's population is down to 150 million. It has lost about one-third of its territory and almost half of its population. Its population is now only one-half that of the U.S., one-third that of Europe. Vast swaths of what were once Soviet territory or under its control have gone their separate and independent ways: the Baltics, *all* of Central and Eastern Europe, the former Yugoslavia, Belarus, the Ukraine, Moldova, Georgia, and the Trans-Caucuses, the five Central Asian republics, and Mongolia. Russia is angry and bitter over the loss of all these territories and people. In addition, since population size provides one measure of national power, Russia has also lost power and its place as one of the world's great superpowers. Russia would *love* to get all these things (people, size, and superpower status) back.

Russia's population has not only shrunk in numbers but also in longevity. Under the socialism of the U.S.S.R., Russia was never a very healthy, long-lived country, but now it is far worse. Life expectancy has shrunk to the mid-sixties for women and the high fifties for men. Those numbers place Russia at Third World levels. The poor figures are the result of the fact that when the Soviet Union collapsed, so too did agriculture (the state farms were abandoned), industry (ripped off by the oligarchs), employment (no jobs!) health care, the education and social welfare programs, everything.

Having toured in Russia at the time (early '90s), the author was convinced that other factors were involved: having lost everything, defeated in the Cold War, shrunk in size and population, and downgraded from superpower status, Russia suffered a gigantic moral and psychological breakdown. It was like the Inca or Aztec empires of the Americas, defeated by the Spanish *conquistadores*: an entire civilization devastated and destroyed and a massive psychologic breakdown suffered as a result. As a result, in Russia, alcoholism, always a problem, massively increased, health standards plummeted, food was scarce, and, hence, gout, liver disease, kidney disease, heart disease, and cancer all increased, thus massively reducing life expectancy especially for men.

After the collapse of the Soviet Union, Russia's per-capita income levels also dropped to near Third World levels. The U.S.S.R. had long lied about the economic statistics, but now in a more open, post-Soviet environment the poverty was there for all to see. Russian per-capita income dropped to about one-quarter of U.S. or Western European levels.

As the state farms shut down in the early 1990s and factories closed, and then as the foreign investment that had come in at that time but fled a few years later in the face of overwhelming Russian corruption, Russia faced extremely difficult economic conditions. As poverty spread and the country slipped backwards, widespread malnutrition set in that led to disease, hunger, and plummeting health and education conditions. One expects to see poverty of this kind in Africa, Latin America, or Southeast Asia, but not in Russia or Europe more generally.

Since coming to power in 1999, Putin has sought to rebuild the Russian economy. Unfortunately, Russian agriculture and manufacturing have still not recovered from the breakdown and devastation of the 1990s. In addition, political and governmental leaders in power at the time used their positions and access to government authorities (primarily former President Yeltsin and his family) to steal and rip off entire industries, land, and concessions from the state. This theft on a massive scale is what gave rise to what we now call the Russian "oligarchy."

Putin has not been able to reverse this corruption or reconstruct the Russian economy, but he has benefitted during the last fifteen years from rising commodity prices for Russian national resources, mainly oil and natural gas. Indeed, the high price of oil and natural gas, until recently, is about the only thing that has kept the Russian economy afloat. In this sense, Russia is like the Persian Gulf oil sheikdoms whose entire national economies are based dangerously on the export of a single product: oil. As long as oil prices remained high, Russia (and these other countries) could stay afloat economically even if it did not thrive; but in a context at present of falling oil prices, and if your economy is so hugely dependent (80 percent of export revenues) on oil, Russia finds itself in bad financial trouble.

Based on these social and economic data, the Russian/ Putin "model" of development does not look very attractive. Russia is a very poor country. Literacy and education levels have declined, disease and malnutrition are widespread, and life expectancy is extremely low. Because of poverty and the economic collapse, Russia does not have a strong middle-class on which a stable, functioning democracy could be built. Official, World Bank figures (2014) show Russia's per-capita income at $13,860, still only about one-third the West European per-capita income. Travels and research in Russia, not just in relatively wealthy Moscow and Saint Petersburg but in Russia's vast, and far poorer, interior, leads one to think the real number is far lower than that. Since

Russia lied about these numbers under the communists, there is no reason to think that Putin's government is being any more forthright. Russia at present simply lacks the socioeconomic base for democratic rule.

However, it is precisely the absence of all these features of a developed country that may make the Putin model look more attractive. Putin, like many authoritarians from China to Latin America, argues that in a vast and poor country like Russia, lacking a strong economy, a strong middle class, and strong institutions, only a tough, centralized, authoritative government (himself!) can hold the country together and stimulate growth. Moreover, he argues nationalistically that Russia should not emulate the West (the U.S. or Western Europe) but should find its own way, a uniquely Russian model as described below.

In addition, Putin is pushing, and sometimes forcing, his system of top-down government on such similarly poor and under-institutionalized countries (and once part of the Soviet Union) as Belarus, Moldova, the Ukraine, Mongolia, and Central Asia, whose similarly authoritarian rulers are often quite receptive to the "Putin model." How successful this model can be, and whether it can be exported to other countries, is a subject we take up at the end of the chapter.

Government Institutions and the Role of the State

One of the key reasons why authoritarianism is strong in Russia is that other institutions are so weak. In a context of a low level of economic development and weak social and political institutions, a strong, powerful, all-encompassing state has emerged to fill the vacuum.

The Russian parliament---nonexistent under the czars, a mere rubberstamp under the leadership of the Communist Party, and only beginning to assert itself under Yeltsin in the 1990s – has never been a strong, representative, and independent body. Similarly, the courts and the justice system: never an independent or third and coequal branch of government, the courts cannot stand up before the power of the army, the secret police, the state, or President Putin. There are few checks and balances in the Russian system, only top-down rule.

Civil society is similarly extremely weak in Russia. By civil society we mean all those groups – political parties, farmers' organizations, labor unions, women's groups, LGBT, student organizations, interest groups, professional associations, local and neighborhood groups, etc. – that take up intermediate and transmission-belt positions between the state and its individual citizens. Such groups serve in a democracy to transmit citizen demands up to the government and to help carry out government policy at lower levels. They also serve ideally as democratic checks serving to limit state power. But in Russia all these groups are exceedingly weak and state power, therefore, is excessively strong.

The reasons for this weakness in civil society are not hard to discern. Under the czars, again, there was no civil society to speak of; under the communists what passed for civil society were just rubber-stamp groups that applauded and enforced everything the leadership said. Hence, it is only in the last twenty-five years, since the collapse of communism in 1991, that civil society has begun to emerge. And that is too short a time for a truly strong and independent civil society to develop.

Civil society in Russia is weak not just because of history and political culture. It is also weak because of Russia's low level of social and economic development, which means Russia lacks the economic base and solid middle class on which civil society can be built. Another reason for Russia's weak civil society is because of totalitarian control under communism. Under the communist system, no independent voices or groups could be allowed, only those groups that echoed the regime's policies. Hence, when communism collapsed, all these stooge groups collapsed with it, leaving Russia once again with a total vacuum of civil society.

During the 1990s, after the fall of communism when Yeltsin was in the presidency, it appeared that Russia might be opening up to a more democratic and pluralist civil society. A host of democracy/civil society advisers and NGOs from Europe and the U.S. flocked to Russia to help the Russians build their new democracy. Invited by Russian universities and supported by the United States Information Agency (USIA), U.S. consultants were to help the Russians build new political science and international affairs departments, and to reform university structures after the rigid, oppressive, stultifying Marxian orthodoxies of the past. To that end, these consultants traveled all around Russia helping to set up these new departments, advising on university reform, and bringing Russian scholars to the U.S. for advanced studies. These endeavors were part of much larger effort to help Russia build a new and democratic political party system, new and independent labor groups, new businessmen's associations, new universities, and a new

Comparative Models of Development

civil society in general. For a time in the 1990s we seemed to be succeeding since Russia then was open to outside advice, the reform effort was going forward, and democracy seemed to be establishing itself.

But Russia's economy had not recovered from the fall of communism, the "shock treatment" formula of economist Jeffrey Sachs (*instant* privatization and capitalism) was ill-conceived and didn't work, and corruption was widespread under the binging Yeltsin. The economy continued in a depressed state and declined still farther, while popular resentments against Yeltsin, the lack of jobs, and all the outside advisers began to grow. At the same time Russian nationalism, humiliated by its losses in the Cold War, the shrinkage in territory and population of the Russian state, and continued underdevelopment, became more intense. Part of this rising nationalism was directed against the many foreign advisers who had come to Russia to help.

Vladimir Putin was both a reflection of and the instrument of these rising nationalistic, resentful, and xenophobic sentiments. He presented himself as a tough guy and, in fact, his early career had been that of an intelligence (KGB) agent. He was also very smart (Ph.D. level), spoke foreign languages, and had extensive experience abroad, especially in Germany. Putin was a nationalist, resentful of all those foreign advisers telling Russians what to do, and was particularly incensed by the expansion of the EU into Eastern Europe and of the military arm NATO expanding right up to Russia's borders ("the gates of Moscow"). To Putin, this meant the West was trying to remake proud Russia – remember, a separate civilization – in the West's image, and was also seeking to surround and contain Russia by countries, led by the U.S., hostile to it.

Putin came to power initially as prime minister through democratic elections and he has been careful to maintain at least the façade of democracy ever since then. Meanwhile, he secured and consolidated his power by building up the power of the Orthodox Church, the Army, the central state, and the secret police. He played on Russian nationalism, the anti-Western resentments of much of the population, and Russia's sense of itself as a great (think Tolstoy, Chekhov, Dostoyevsky, and Solzhenitsyn) – but separate from the West – civilization.

Of course, Putin was also fortunate in that, even though Russia's overall national economy was still chaotic, he benefitted from the rising prices of the few things that Russia did well: the export of oil, commodities, and natural gas. As Putin's popularity, based on his tough-guy image and strong defense of Russian nationalism, began to rise, he asserted his authority over more and more areas of Russian national life. Hence, when Putin traded places with his hapless president, Dmitri Medvedev, it made little difference in the power relations within the Kremlin because everyone knew that, regardless of title, Putin was the one in charge.

It is not surprising, given Russia's history and political culture, that Putin would move in an authoritarian direction and fashion his rule after Russia's great leaders of the past. What is especially interesting for our purposes are Putin's moves to control and restrict Russia's emerging civil society. The model Putin used is in other countries called *corporatism*. Corporatism in emerging societies like Russia often goes hand-in-hand with Putin's political model, authoritarianism, and with his economic model, state- or government-controlled capitalism.[21]

Under corporatism the government controls and restricts pluralism or interest group activity. Interest groups in Russia are now required to register with the government, seek legal recognition from the state (which may also deny or, later, take away such recognition), reveal their membership rolls, and tell also where their finances are coming from. This last restriction is aimed particularly at those pro-democracy, human rights, and LGBT groups financed by the U.S. whom Putin accuses of violating Russia's sovereignty and of creating a "foreign" political model (democracy, pluralism) within Russia.

It is obvious that Putin is here violating what we would think of as basic political rights: of speech, of expression, and of assembly. However, Putin's restrictive policies are wildly popular within Russia even if they are widely criticized on the outside: his political approval ratings are up above 80 percent, ratings that any Western leader would love to have.

Along with restricting the activities of these groups, Putin has moved to encourage and fund those groups and parties that support his government. That, too, is part of corporatism: on the one hand, you restrict the freedom of some groups, usually in the opposition, to operate; on the other, you give favors, patronage, and outright money (rubles!) grants to those that favor your policies. You may even elevate them into the role of *official* interest groups, part of an inseparable from the regime: official (government-controlled) political parties, official trade unions, official student groups, and the like. That way you can play the cooptation versus repression game: play ball with and support us, the Putin government, and you will be rewarded; but oppose us and we will either crush you or take away your financing and right to operate.

Corporatism has long been an effective tool for autocrats and authoritarianism all around the world. Corporatism is obviously not liberalism and pluralism because it denies the basic right to organize independent of the state. On the other hand, corporatism is not totalitarianism either because it is not "total": as indicated, it does allow some degree of freedom of organization, association, and independence outside of the state. It is *authoritarian* but not *totalitarian*. We need to think of corporatism, therefore, as "a third way," a route to development intermediary between liberal-pluralism, on the one hand, and totalitarianism, on the other.

And this path to development, we will find in this book, has become increasingly popular in emerging nations. Nearly thirty years ago, with the collapse of Soviet communism and the displacement of quite a number of authoritarian regimes in Asia and Latin America, social scientists led by Francis Fukuyama and his *End of History* thesis, and in the policy arena the National Endowment for Democracy (NED), were all saying that democracy would be the wave of the future. All countries, the entire *world*, it was famously argued by these optimists, would eventually become democratic. With totalitarianism vanquished in the Soviet Union and authoritarianism seemingly on the wane in Latin America and elsewhere, democracy was seen as "the only game in town." An entire cottage industry sprang up in the social sciences dedicated to studying "transitions to democracy."

We should not have swallowed that literature then,[22] and we certainly should be more than skeptical of it now. Apparently, it occurred to very few people that the "wave" of democracy of that time might peter out, that it might be reversed as in Russia or, most likely of all, that many, even most countries in the world, might stall out, fall short of democracy, and end up with mixed or hybrid regimes that combine autocracy or authoritarianism with democracy. "Illiberal democracy," Fareed Zakaria calls it. But that is, in fact, what is happening not just in Russia but all around the globe.

Russia is, in fact, the first instance in this book of what we will soon see is a general, worldwide phenomenon. And that is either reversals of democracy or, more widespread, regimes that have stopped short of full-throated democracy. Mixed or hybrid or overlapping regimes that combine some elements of democracy (elections, political parties, and parliaments) with strong government, state capitalism, corporatism, and varying degrees of authoritarianism and statism. Think not just of Russia but also of Belarus, the Ukraine, Georgia, Moldova, the five "Stans" of Central Asia, and Mongolia. Now think of big, important China (Chapter 5) which is similarly going not toward democracy but in an authoritarian-corporatist direction. Or of the Arab Middle East and North Africa (MENA, Chapter 7) where not a single government could be considered fully democratic. Or of Turkey, Hungary, Egypt, and others which, after trying democracy for a time, have now reverted to more authoritarian and corporatist models.

The big "success stories" in the transitions-to-democracy literature have been in Asia (Japan, Taiwan, South Korea, Singapore, Indonesia, and the Philippines), Latin America (nineteen of twenty countries "democratic"), and Eastern Europe after the fall of the Soviet Union. But as we see in detail later in the book, many of these countries, including big Russia, are only partly democratic. They incorporate some democratic features – mainly so they can please the big lending agencies who require "democracy" as a condition of their loans – but they also employ many nondemocratic and anti-democratic features: strong states, clampdowns on opposition demonstrators, political imprisonments, curbs on free speech, human rights violations, rigged or one-party "elections," repression against the opposition, restrictions on assembly, and, as we have seen above, corporatism as a means of keeping social change under government control. Many countries who present themselves as "democracies" are really not very democratic at all.

The Russian Model

The Russian model is twofold. On the one hand, Russia presents a *domestic* model that is authoritarian, top-down, and corporatist. On the other, it offers an *international* model that rejects the U.S. view of the world and the collective action and "community-of-nations" approach that goes with it.

On the domestic front, Russia's president Vladimir Putin has reversed the democratic opening that Russia experienced in the 1990s in favor of a more autocratic model that harks back to communist rule and the czars. Putin has clamped down on free speech, the right of assembly, and the opposition. He has put severe restrictions on NGOs and civil society groups and used corporatism to hold social change in check. He has, at the same time, restored the traditional and very conservative wielders of power in Russia: the Orthodox Church, the Army, the state, and the secret police. Putin now rules unfettered by any checks and balances; moreover, his popularity and that of his regime are sky-high: in the 80 percent approval range.

Outside of his immediate region, Putin's "model" is not particularly well-received. Politically, his authoritarianism is well-known, so are his clampdowns on human rights, pluralism, and democratic political activity. Moreover, except for its exports of oil, natural gas, and commodities, Russia has nothing to offer the rest of the world as an economic model.

But remember how big and aggressive Russia is, wanting to get back some of the territories lost when the Soviet Union collapsed. The result is that the Russian model's attractiveness is mainly limited to those countries right on its borders, what Russia calls the "near-abroad" – Belarus, Moldova, parts of the Trans Caucuses, Mongolia Kazakhstan, and Central Asia, Georgia, parts of the Ukraine – who are cowed by Russia's size and power. They may adopt the Russian model both because some of their leaders admire Putin's crackdown on dissent *and* because they fear a Russian invasion if they go too far toward democracy and the West.

Internationally, the Russian model enjoys considerably more popularity. That is because it represents a challenge and an alternative to U.S. hegemony, dominance, and hectoring which many countries resent. At one point in the 1990s, after the fall of communism, there was talk of Russia being integrated into Europe, joining the EU, maybe even NATO; but with Putin in power that talk has been completely silenced. Russia has opted out; it wants to go its own way.

Not only that, it is building its own bloc of supporters independent of and often opposed to the U.S. and its allies – what we often refer to hopefully and mistakenly as the "international community." Russia's "bloc" consists of Belarus, parts of the former Yugoslavia, countries of Central Asia, China depending on the issue, such "outlaw" states as Iran, Cuba, and Venezuela, Brazil on some issues, Syria and other parts of the Middle East, and large swaths of the Third World. In short, Russia has put together a coalition of countries that for various reasons harbor resentments against the United States, "outlaw" countries, and others who challenge the existing international order.

But the discontents go deeper than this. As Henry Kissinger explains in his magnificent new book – published at age ninety-one – *World Order,*[23] whose title really should be *The Absence of World Order,* Russia, China, and quite a number of these others have opted out of the Westphalian system of international relations. That system, centered in Europe and based on a Western Consensus of the rules of international politics, was grounded in balance of power, international equilibrium, and the peaceful settlement of disputes. But Russia, China, Iran, Brazil, India, and others see this "system" as not just excluding them but also prejudiced against the rise of up-and-coming powers like themselves. Therefore, they have opted out and are inventing their own set of international rules, or perhaps having no rules at all. Of course, they maintain their memberships in such organizations as the United Nations, the World Trade Organization, and others so long and to the extent these organizations are useful to them, but that does not mean they are ready to automatically follow or subordinate themselves to U.S. or Western policy.

These trends are, of course, very dangerous and upsetting to the U.S. and of the world order that we champion. The old (Western) rules are not being followed automatically or by everyone any more. The coalition that supports the U.S. is shrinking. Big, important countries (Russia, China, Brazil, et al.) or whole blocs of countries, are increasingly going their own way. In vast Eurasia, the Middle East, East Asia, South Asia, even Latin America and Africa, countries are breaking away from the U.S.-led Western consensus. The result is likely to be not just more and diverse routes to development but a further unraveling of the whole system of world order which the U.S. has championed and stood for so long.

CHAPTER 4

EASTERN EUROPE: BETWEEN EAST AND WEST

Eastern Europe occupies that large land mass – "Eurasia" – that lies between the Russian-speaking territories to the east and the German-speaking lands ("Germania" – Germany, the Czech Republic, and Austria) to the west. Historically, Eastern Europe has been a buffer between Russia, which has long sought to expand its territory westward into Europe, and Germany, which has long sought to grow its lands (*lebensraum*) to the east. As a buffer, long prey to Russian, French, Swedish, Polish, as well as German invading armies, Eastern Europe is also a social, cultural, and political mix, strongly influenced and populated by these invaders as well as by its own home-grown culture, languages, and sociology. Buffeted about by the great and an area of contention between them, Eurasia has been portrayed by geostrategists as a key, maybe *the* key, to world domination. Whoever controls Eastern Europe controls the Eurasian land mass, the argument goes; whoever controls the Eurasian land mass controls the world![24]

It is useful to compare Eastern Europe to Southern Europe. As compared to Core, Heartland, or what we have come to call Western Europe, both Southern Europe and Eastern Europe are relatively poor. Both of these major areas were bypassed by the great revolutions that we associate with the modern age: the Renaissance, the Enlightenment, the industrial revolution, the Protestant Reformation, the scientific revolution of Newton and Galileo, and the democratic revolutions of the seventeenth and eighteenth centuries. Unlike Western or Core Europe which made its great leap forward from feudalism to modernity from the sixteenth to the eighteenth centuries, Southern Europe and Eastern Europe lagged behind, remained poor and isolated, and were locked in the feudal past right through the "long" nineteenth century – i.e., until the old feudal structures and ancient social hierarchies came crashing down in World War I and its aftermath.

What historian Barbara Tuchman called "The Proud Tower" of Old World, quasi-feudal society, culture, and politics in Eastern Europe largely disintegrated with the collapse of the Austro-Hungarian Empire in 1918, like Humpty-Dumpty, never to be put back together again. What followed in both Eastern and Southern Europe can only be described as horrific: war, chaos, economic and political collapse, revolution, fascism, Nazism, slaughter, Holocaust, civil war, communist takeovers, purges, and mass executions. It would require at least fifty years, until the 1970s, for Southern Europe to begin to recover and rediscover its equilibrium, and another twenty to thirty years after that – until the 1990s – before Eastern Europe could become free, democratic, and prosperous.

There are differences between these two areas as well. Both are poor, historically isolated and underdeveloped, and on the periphery (as distinct from in the Core) of Europe. But Southern Europe, which has enjoyed democracy since the mid-1970s (earlier in Italy) and joined the EU in the early 1980s, is quite a bit richer and more developed than is Eastern Europe. Southern Europe per-capita income is approximately three-quarters ($30,000) that of Core Europe, whereas Eastern Europe, which only threw off the yoke of communism in the 1990s and only joined the EU in 2004 and began to participate in Western prosperity, is still at less than half the average of Core Europe and still way behind the South in development and the consolidation of democracy. See Table 4.1.

On the other hand, according to contemporary geostrategists like Zbigniew Brzezinski, Eastern Europe remains the more important of the two areas, at least strategically, because of its location and because it is still caught between prosperous, democratic, and affluent Western Europe and newly resurgent Russia. Hence, for our purposes the key question is, will Eastern Europe follow the Western model of democracy, freedom, and a modern, mixed (both free market and statism, the welfare state) economy, or will it go the corporatist-authoritarian route of aggressive Russia?

TABLE 4.1
EASTERN EUROPE: POPULATION AND GROSS DOMESTIC PRODUCT PER CAPITA, PPP[25]

Country	Population (in millions)	GNP per Capita
Albania	2.8	11,108
Belarus	9.5	18,185
Bosnia and Herzegovina	3.8	10,427
Bulgaria	7.2	17,208
Croatia	4.2	21,635
Cyprus	1.1	30,239
Czech Republic	10.5	31,186
Estonia	1.3	28,140
Georgia	3.7	9,163
Hungary	9.9	25,069
Latvia	2	23,548
Lithuania	3	27,686
Macedonia	2.9	13,523
[26]Malta	0.4	29,526
Moldova	3.6	4,983
Montenegro	0.6	15,055
Poland	38	25,262
Romania	19.9	20,348
Serbia	7.1	13,594
Slovakia	5.4	28,327
Slovenia	2.1	30,403
Ukraine	45.4	8,666

Source: World Development Indicators, The World Bank

Eastern Europe is a particularly interesting case for us. Here we have a large territory, historically poor and underdeveloped, with little experience with democracy, on the periphery of Europe, and battered and devastated by invading armies going back at least a thousand years. Its history in the twentieth century was particularly tragic: destabilized by World War I, beaten down by the Depression, the victim of repressive authoritarian regimes in the 1920s and 1930s, occupied and devastated by Nazi armies in World War II, then occupied and devastated even more by the Soviet Union and its armies from the 1940s on. It was only in the 1990s that Eastern Europe finally threw off its oppressors and ended this near-century-long nightmare.

Now, finally, after a thousand years of struggle, poverty, warfare, and occupation, Eastern Europe has a chance to join the modern, developed, democratic world. The 2004 accession to the EU by most of the countries of the region represented a *huge* step in this direction. Eastern Europe finally had a chance to join two of Europe's great "clubs," the EU and NATO, and to share in the benefits of EU prosperity and democracy. Eastern Europe at that time also became closely allied with the U.S., often closer to the U.S. in its interests than is Western Europe (see Chapter 2).

But just as Eastern Europe seems finally poised, after all those centuries, on becoming affluent, democratic, and a part of the West, a resurgent Russia under Vladimir Putin is threatening to undermine these positive developments. Russia claims not just economic, political, and cultural influence or even dominance in Eastern Europe, it is also running tank exercises up and down Eastern European borders and threatening shutoffs of vital oil and natural gas, thus scaring these new democracies to death right in the midst of their economic and political transitions which are already difficult enough. So Eastern Europe hangs in the balance between East and West; it is one of the great areas of the "clash of civilizations" of which Samuel P. Huntington wrote some two decades ago.[26] Which way Eastern Europe goes is critical both for the area itself *and* for global geopolitics.

History and Political Culture

What is it about Eastern Europe that makes it a distinct and recognizable world region, separate from and different from other regions? The answer is: not an awful lot, or at least not any longer, and therein lies a series of problems. We begin by focusing on the commonalities; after that, we concentrate on the differences, and the implications of both.

`First, there is poverty. All of Eastern Europe is considerably poorer than is Western Europe. To reach Western living standards, Eastern Europe has a lot of catching up to do.

But some countries and some regions within countries are quite a bit poorer than others. Having traveled extensively within the region, the author formulated "Wiarda's Law" to try to explain this. The variation among countries depends largely on the distance the country is from Europe's wealthy core: Germany, France, Belgium, the Netherlands, the Nordics, Austria, etc. The farther each one goes, the farther from the Core, the poorer the country. Thus, Estonia and the Baltics are poorer than Scandinavia, Poland and the Czech Republic are poorer than Germany, Hungary and

Slovakia are poorer than Austria, Slovenia and the Balkans are poorer than Italy.

Wiarda's Law also applies to poverty conditions *within* countries. Thus, eastern Poland is poorer than western Poland; eastern Slovakia, much poorer than western Slovakia; eastern Hungary, poorer than Western Hungary; and some areas in Romania, Bulgaria, and the Balkans, so poor and miserable that they are at Third World levels: poverty, malnutrition, bloated bellies of the children, disease, and malformed limbs. It is often shocking when we observe these conditions in the Third World, even more so, since they are so unexpected, when we see them in Europe.

A second common feature of these countries is that they are often disorganized, chaotic, and dysfunctional. Things don't work very well there. Governments are unstable, the bureaucracy can't deliver goods and services efficiently, schools and especially universities are bad, parliaments are deeply divided, and the infrastructure of a modern society – working telephones, good roads, the internet, transportation, and communications – are generally lacking. Political parties and civil society are similarly weak, government institutions are often unresponsive, and basic state functions often don't work or break down.

These weaknesses may be attributed to two main factors. The first is the historic underdevelopment of Eastern Europe, on the periphery of Europe and historically subjected to repeated foreign invasions. It will simply take a long time for Eastern Europe to catch up. The second factor in explaining Eastern Europe's frequent dysfunctions and underdevelopment is the most recent of these occupations, that of the Soviet Union during the entire forty-five-year length of the Cold War, 1946-1991.

From his work in Eastern Europe, the author took to calling these countries "Second World." Not in the old-fashioned and now outdated sense of that term, as countries that are developed but communist. That phrase – "developed but communist" – suggests that Eastern Europe was on a par with the West (also developed) but only different (communist). However, we now know that was not the situation at all. It was an invention of Soviet propaganda efforts seeking to show Eastern Europe, which it occupied, as just as developed as the West.

But since the fall of the Iron Curtain and the Berlin Wall, and now that we can freely travel and study in the East, we know that was all propaganda, a bald-faced lie. In fact, Eastern Europe under the Soviets was extremely poor, falling even farther behind the West, and, worse than that, drained of its resources and manpower to serve not Eastern European but Russian labor and industrial needs. Hence, the use of the term "Second World" describes a region richer than the Third World but nowhere near First World wealth or standards, with major infrastructure and organizational needs, and facing long-term development problems. Indeed, these infrastructure and long-term development needs are so severe that they may take not three or four years but three or four *generations* (seventy-five to a hundred years) to solve. And in the meantime, Eastern Europe will continue to lag way behind Western Europe and the United States in standard-of-living.

The third commonality that all of Eastern Europe experienced is the rapacious nature of the very Soviet

91

occupation that we have just mentioned. The Soviets devastated Eastern Europe in all sorts of ways. They stole its wealth and resources, stripping these countries dry. They killed, massacred, or sent to labor camps to die (the *gulags* of Siberia) *millions* of people. They set back the natural course of development in Eastern Europe by decades. Their military and secret police crushed not just dissent and opposition but also the will of the people and their cultures. The Soviets relocated millions of East Europeans to remote areas of the Soviet Union, and then relocated millions of Russians into these countries, as a way of curbing East European national, patriotic, and independence sentiment. The Russian occupation, make no mistake about it, was cruel, bloody, repressive, and barbarous. We should not, looking back, have a benign view of what the Soviets did in Eastern Europe.

These commonalities are important in explaining the underdeveloped, non-democratic context, the background in which Eastern Europe existed historically. But at present, what is at least equally impressive are the *differences* between the East European countries. For in a sense there is no "Eastern Europe" beyond the common features listed above. Every country is different; at best, what we can speak of are the several *sub-regions* that have emerged within Eastern Europe particularly since the collapse of the Soviet Union and the liberation of the region beginning in the late 1980s, early 1990s.

Let us begin in the north with the three Baltic countries (going from north to south), Estonia, Latvia, and Lithuania. All three are small countries, three million or under in population. All three have been dominated historically by bigger and more powerful neighbors: Germany, Sweden, Poland, and, most recently, the Soviet Union. With the signing of the Versailles peace treaty in 1918 after the conclusion of World War I, all three enjoyed a twenty-year interregnum of independence, only to be occupied and swallowed up again by Germany in World War II and, after the War, by Soviet armies, and annexed for the next forty-five years as part of the Soviet Union.

All three were liberated from Soviet rule in the late 1980s, early 1990s. With per-capita incomes now above $15,000, about half the West European average, they are among the most successful of the post-Soviet East European states. All three have reformed their economies, become democracies, and joined the European Union and NATO. All three think of themselves as Western countries, with Estonia even considering itself a "Scandinavian country."

But all three live a precarious existence, with small economies, weak political institutions, and the big Russian "Bear" putting the squeeze on them economically (by limiting their oil and natural gas supplies) and militarily, by running military exercises up and down their eastern borders. In addition, both Estonia and Latvia have large Russian minorities, 35-40 percent of the population, within their borders (Lithuania, at 5-7 percent, less so) who are not fully integrated into national life and who may form a separatist, disloyal, "fifth column" element should a revived Russia ever decide to re-conquer these territories. Hence, while the three Baltic countries are primarily oriented toward the West economically, politically, and strategically, their position is still dangerous and it is still conceivable that they could be re-absorbed into the Russian orbit.

Moving south from the Baltics into what has now come to be called "Central Europe," we have four countries: Poland, the Czech Republic, Hungary, and Slovakia. Like the Baltics, these four have experienced successful transitions since becoming independent from the earlier Soviet occupation. They have all reformed their economies to provide for a modern, mixed (statist and free market) system; they have all, with some slippage, become democracies; and they have all joined both the EU and NATO. All four, or at least sizable parts of them, were once part of the Austro-Hungarian Empire centered in Vienna so that gives them a certain unity; all four enjoyed a twenty-year period of independence and democracy after World War I, so that experience ("path dependency") helped them build democracy again once the Soviets pulled out their troops in the early1990s.

All four of the Central European countries lie close to the prosperous German and Austrian economies so that has helped through trade and investment to stimulate their own economic development. They also have the advantage, unlike the Baltics, of never being a part of the Soviet Union, so that once the Soviets pulled out it was relatively easy to resume their national identities. Poland, at a population on nearly forty million, is the biggest of the four and with the resources to become a rich country; the Czech Republic is the most Germanic of the four and is closely tied into the booming German economy. Hungary also received large Western investment and has become a gateway to Southeast Europe and the Balkans. Slovakia, which was once the junior partner of a combined country of Czechoslovakia, is the most undeveloped of the Central European countries and the most fragile politically, still with considerable loyalties to Russia. Overall, however, along with the Baltic countries, Central Europe has been thoroughly integrated into the West and into the European Union and NATO, even though not without its share of tensions, fragilities, and uncertainties.

Quite a number of the Baltic and Central European countries have become strong NATO supporters and are closer to the U.S. politically and strategically than are their better-established West European neighbors. That is mainly because these East European countries still feel threatened by a resurgent Russia and look to the U.S., not to a largely disarmed Western Europe, to provide them with security protection. Some of these countries, to use a popular phrase, have become "more American than the Americans," even while the United States struggles to decide how much it wants to defend Eastern Europe. If Russian forces were to invade Estonia, for example, would we be willing under the famous Article 5 of the NATO treaty which pledges mutual assistance against an outside attack, to come to their defense?

While both the Baltics and Central Europe may be judged to be great economic and democratic success stories for the Western Model, the same cannot be said – yet! – for the Balkans or, as it is now called, Southeastern Europe. This includes the countries of Slovenia, Croatia, Bosnia and Herzegovina, Albania, Montenegro, Serbia, Macedonia, Bulgaria, and Romania. Of these, only Slovenia may be considered an unqualified success: it is richer than the others, it quickly democratized and joined the EU and NATO, and it has the advantage of lying close to and being integrated into the rich Austrian and Italian economies. Croatia, next to Slovenia, is also a majority-Catholic and predominantly Western country, it benefits along its beautiful Adriatic coast (Dalmatia) from large European tourism, and, after some early chaotic and divisive post-Soviet years of civil war and ethnic cleansing, it has gotten its act together sufficiently that it was able to join the EU and NATO.

The farther south and east in the Balkans you go (until you get all the way to Greece), the poorer, less developed, and less Western it becomes. The Austrians have an expression for this: they ask, "Where does Europe end?" and the answer comes back, "Somewhere south of Vienna!" Similarly, the Croatians like to brag, as a Catholic-majority country and long a part of Venice's Adriatic empire, that their country is the last bastion of European, Western, Christian civilization. The "last bastion" before what, we may ask?

The answer is, the last bastion before the culture, history, and sociology change rather abruptly. First, we have three small, majority-Muslim countries – Bosnia-Herzegovina, Kosovo, and Albania – anomalies in mainly Christian Europe, leftovers from the centuries when the Muslim Ottoman Turks ruled Southeast Europe. Next we have three other small anomalies: Serbia, Montenegro, and Macedonia, Christian countries but products of the Eastern or Greek Orthodox Church once centered in Constantinople, now Istanbul the capital of Turkey. Third are Bulgaria and Romania, now part of the EU and NATO (admitted for strategic and not necessarily merit reasons) but among the poorest nations in all of Europe, very corrupt, also Orthodox, and bordering on the Black Sea and trouble – i.e., close to Turkey, the Middle East, and Russia. Finally, there is Greece itself, which we have classified as Southern European but others consider part of the Balkans: Orthodox, similarly occupied by the Turks for many centuries, and the farthest of all European or EU countries from the central core.

Note that all these Balkan or Southeast European countries are not only considerably poorer than is Western Europe, at about one-fourth the West European average, but also poorer than the Baltics or Central Europe. These countries, because of only limited economic or political reforms since communism, have had the hardest time qualifying for EU and NATO membership. Social modernization and economic development have also lagged in Southeast Europe, as has globalization – i.e., integration into the modern, interdependent world. Indeed, this area was still fighting ethnic and religious wars and practicing genocide right into the 1990s – and beyond. Finally, we should say that Southeast Europe religiously and culturally is very different from the rest of Europe and, because of language, alphabet, and ethnic differences, has a hard time fitting in.

One other group of countries needs to be mentioned in this context, although they may not be considered a part of "Eastern Europe," at least as it is presently defined. These are Armenia, Azerbaijan, and Georgia in the Trans-Caucasus and Belarus, Moldova, and the Ukraine along the frontier where the European and the Russian civilizations now meet. Armenia, Azerbaijan, and Georgia are too far away in terms of both culture and distance to be considered a part of Europe, but that has not prevented them from *aspiring* to membership in the EU or even NATO.

Belarus, Moldova, and the Ukraine are interesting cases because they are almost evenly split between their pro-Russian and their pro-Western populations. In fact, the dividing line between West and East runs right down the middle of these countries and illustrates the fact that cultural and political boundaries do not always exactly follow national boundaries. Consider especially the Ukraine, a country that had its pro-Western revolution (the "Orange Revolution") but which remains deeply split between East and West and into which Russian President Vladimir Putin continues to intervene to keep the Ukraine under the Russian sphere of influence and prevent it from joining the West. In fact, all up and down that East European-Russian border there are cultural, political, and ethnic conflicts that are certain to recur.

Well, there we have it with regard to Eastern Europe's several sub-regions. It looks as though the three Baltic nations (Estonia, Latvia, and Lithuania) as well as the four Central European countries (Poland, Czech Republic, Hungary, and Slovakia) have successfully modernized, democratized, and made it into the Western camp. In the Balkans, however, (and excluding Greece from the discussion) the situation is far more precarious. Slovenia and Croatia are probably safely within the Western orbit, Bulgaria and Romania are still iffy, while the other former territories of what was once Yugoslavia – Bosnia-Herzegovina, Kosovo, Albania, Serbia, Montenegro, and Macedonia – have yet to qualify. This is not to say they will not qualify in the future, and all are candidate countries at least in their own eyes; but so far they have not made sufficient progress on the economic or political (democracy) fronts to join the club of Western nations.

Meanwhile, neither the Trans-Caucasus countries of Armenia, Azerbaijan, or Georgia, nor the "borderlands" countries of Belarus, Moldova, and the Ukraine, divided as they are between their pro-Russian and pro-Western populations and orientations, can be considered part of the West. And to force the issue in their cases may produce both civil war and, as in the Ukraine, prolonged international conflict.

Socioeconomic Overview

Only a few short years ago, Eastern Europe was much poorer than it is now. Of the twenty-five countries listed in Table 4.1, only two of them, Cyprus and Slovenia, had per-person incomes above $20,000 per year. It is worth noting that these were among the first countries in Eastern Europe to be admitted to the EU and NATO, and that in the 2014 figures these two countries remain the two wealthiest countries in the East, although quite a number of other countries have closed the gap.

In addition to these two, six other countries – Croatia, Czech Republic, Estonia, Hungary, Malta, and Slovakia – had per-capita incomes ten years ago above $11,456. That qualified them to be what the World Bank identify as High Income Countries or HICs. It also made them eligible for admission to the EU and NATO in 2004 on the first round of new admits. Note that all six of these plus Latvia, Lithuania, and Poland, now have incomes above $20,000 and are competing with Cyprus and Slovenia to become the wealthiest countries in Eastern Europe. These growth figures show that a total of eleven countries have moved up from a position where their per-capita incomes were only about one-fourth the West European average to one where the per-capita incomes are about one-half (or higher!) the West European average, in only a few short years. These eleven countries have been remarkably successful at achieving economic growth. Being *inside* the EU now for a decade and, therefore, qualifying for a variety of EU grants, loans, and subsidies has been enormously helpful to these countries in achieving development.

Seven other countries – Azerbaijan, Belarus, Bulgaria, Macedonia, Montenegro, Romania, and Serbia – now occupy the range between $10,000 and $20,000 per-capita income. Of these seven, only two, Bulgaria and Romania, are presently members of the EU and NATO – i.e., the two great clubs of the Western Alliance. They were admitted mainly on political and strategic grounds (they had military bases and airports useful in the Iraq and Afghanistan wars), not necessarily because the qualified on economic or merit grounds. The other five see themselves as, or are actual, candidates for admission to the EU. Even though poorer than present members, they argue that they ought to be admitted, even with serious problems, because they are now at the same level the other East European countries were when they were admitted a decade ago.

That leaves seven countries – Armenia, Albania, Bosnia, Georgia, Kosovo, Moldova, and the Ukraine – at under $10,000 per-capita income. Poverty in these areas is more widespread than the numbers show and that the figures may have been inflated to advance their argument for EU admission. Be that as it may, these are all countries that remain unsettled politically and whose poverty would require massive subsidies from the EU which the current members in today's economic circumstances may not be willing to provide.

There are other issues involved on which we ought to briefly comment. Azerbaijan, Armenia, and Georgia are so far away that it is difficult to consider them "European," but Azerbaijan has oil and that may make a positive difference in its candidacy. Armenia is Christian which may help its application to the European club, while Georgia had a democratic revolution that may eventually make it eligible. Belarus, the Ukraine, and Moldova have historically been part of "Greater Russia" so their joining the Western clubs of the EU and NATO is problematic and may trigger a counter-reaction (as already in the Ukraine) from Russia. Albania, Bosnia, and Kosovo are majority-Muslim but they are such small countries (compared to Turkey, another possible candidate) that the EU may admit them just to "prove" it is not "racist" or anti-Muslim.

There are lessons here regarding European and Western expansion to the east, and for the other countries that have aspirations to join the EU and NATO. First, it helps to be rich or at least wealthier than your neighbors; rich countries tend to get in. Second, you need to be democratic and have a good human rights record. Third, you must have embarked on a nationwide reform program to eliminate corruption, improve social programs, and develop infrastructure, in accord with the Action Plan of NATO and the *Acquis Communautaire* of the European Community. And fourth, it helps if you can be a net strategic contributor to NATO, even if your "contribution" is only a single airfield or helicopter.

There is also a clear regional aspect to European enlargement. Note that the three Baltic countries of Estonia, Latvia, and Lithuania, all members of the EU and NATO for over a decade, are also among the richest countries in Eastern Europe, each with a per-capita income climbing rapidly. They have been among the prime beneficiaries of EU grants, loans, and subsidies over this period, enabling them to *more than double* their per-capita incomes in this short time frame. The same for the Central European countries of Poland, Czech Republic, Hungary, and Slovakia: as full members of the EU and NATO for just over ten ears, they have doubled their per-capita incomes in that time period and are now fully integrated into Europe. It is highly improbable that *any* of these countries would abandon the EU or NATO in favor of an independent existence outside the European tent, and even more unthinkable that, after having been liberated for the last twenty-five years, they would now go back to living under Russian hegemony.

The same cannot be said for the Balkans or Southeast Europe. Their situations, both internally (divided, chaotic, and conflict-prone) and with regard to the EU, NATO, and the West, are still uncertain. Some of the countries – Slovenia, Croatia – are safely in the Western camp. Bulgaria and Romania are another matter. Though they joined the EU and NATO over ten years ago along with the Baltic and Central European countries, corruption remains high, reforms have lagged, their economies remain stagnant, and Russia continues to muck around in their internal affairs with the hope of pulling them back into the Russian orbit.

The other Balkan nations – Serbia, Bosnia, Kosovo, Albania, Montenegro, and Macedonia – are even more problematic. Not only have reform and democracy lagged but so has economic development: there is real poverty here. In addition, these are countries still torn by ethnic and political strife and who are not yet entirely clear which way they want to lean: toward the West or toward Russia and the East. There are forces pulling them in both directions.

As for Belarus, Moldova, and the Ukraine – the divided "border countries" – one does not see them joining the EU and/or NATO anytime soon or maybe ever. They are too conflictual, too un-reformed, and too poor for that; they would all require massive subsidies from the EU which are unlikely to be forthcoming. In addition, Russia considers them part of its domain, its sphere of influence, and, as in the Ukraine, would be unwilling to let them go. The same and more – too poor, too unreformed, too divided, too far away, and too much still a part of Russia's sphere of influence – applies to the Trans Caucasus: Armenia, Azerbaijan, and Georgia. None of these countries can look forward to joining the West and its institutions anytime soon.

Government Institutions and the Role of the State

Within a relatively short period of time, two-and-a-half decades, most of the Eastern European countries have successfully transitioned from being puppets and satellites of the Soviet Union to full-fledged Western democracies. The word "successfully" once again applies more to the three Baltic countries and the four Central European nations than it does to the Balkans.

All of these countries now hold regular and democratic elections, have developed parliamentary systems of rule, have built up the full apparatus of democracy (political parties, interest groups, and the like), and seek to govern themselves democratically. In almost all of them the conditions of human rights and civil liberties have improved dramatically. Democracy, albeit sometimes with rough edges, has become "the only game in town." However, democracy is "safer" and more secure in the Baltics and Central Europe than it is in the Balkans or Southeast Europe.

Western political institutions, with the exceptions noted above, are secure, well-established, and functioning in Eastern Europe. Eastern Europe, or at least most of it, is safely in the Western camp. The main alternatives – autocracy, authoritarian corporatism, communism, or some combination of these – have been discredited, although in some countries there is still nostalgia for the generous pensions and free health care and education that communism provided. At this stage, however, it is unthinkable that Eastern Europe would want to go back to the closed systems, inefficiencies, restrictions on freedoms, and widespread human rights abuses of their communist pasts. Once again, these comments about the viability of democracy and the discrediting of communism apply more to the Baltics and Central Europe than they do to Southeast Europe.

Economic reform in Eastern Europe has been far more difficult than democratization. It seems to be harder to go from communism to free markets and a modern mixed economy than to go from communism to democracy. The latter, the political transition, requires mainly a change in institutions which, it is believed, will also result eventually in a change in the political culture toward democratic values and practices.

In contrast, economic reform requires an *immediate* change in the culture, which is much more difficult to achieve than a change in institutions. After forty-five years or two generations under communism, where are all those risk-takers, those markets, those entrepreneurs, the spirit of capitalism, and a free economy to come from? In the absence of any background or experience with free, competitive markets, much of Eastern Europe was an economic wasteland for a time after communism collapsed. There were few jobs, little investment, no functioning stock markets. Agriculture, commerce, and industry were in chaos, often neglected or abandoned. At this stage, EU subsidies helped a lot. Eventually foreign direct investment as well as local entrepreneurs turned the economic situation around. But as we have seen, some countries have been more successful at economic development than others.

A unique feature of post-communist transitions as in Eastern Europe, as distinct from post-authoritarian ones in Latin America or Southeast Asia, is the need to massively downsize the state. Under authoritarianism the state's control of the economy is still limited and there is a dynamic private sector, but under communism the state controls *everything.* So when the communist state disappears, there is nothing – at least for a time – to fill the void: no markets, no businessmen, no investors, no employment. How then to create a modern open-market economy when there is no base, no economic institutions, no entrepreneurships on which to build? It is a long and difficult process and requires outside assistance: hence, the crucial role of the EU.

Even now a quarter-century after the fall of communism, it is still necessary to recall the designation of most of Eastern Europe as "Second World." That term suggests two major gaps or fault lines in Eastern Europe. The first is the woefully underdeveloped state of Eastern Europe infrastructure: railroads, highways, electric grids, transportation, education, universities, housing, water supplies, health care, sewerage, etc. *All* of these must be rebuilt, reformed, updated if Eastern Europe is ever to make it to First World rank. Once again it is EU subsidies that have been instrumental in building all those new superhighways, bridges, hospitals, etc. that are now visible all over Eastern Europe. But there is still a long way to go in all the countries of the region.

The second major problem is the corruption, inefficiencies, and lack of work ethic within state institutions. This fault is also a legacy of the earlier communist regimes because under communism there was no incentive to work hard, serve the public, or efficiently deliver goods and services. But under democracy and today's free-market economic requirements, you cannot get away with such inefficiencies and incompetence. You *must* deliver real goods and programs – or else! But how to achieve all these reforms, how to change the bureaucratic culture of inefficiency and lack of caring, how to downsize the state and get rid of all those old-school and old-generation bureaucrats when the unemployment rate is already too high? It is a terrible conundrum throughout Eastern Europe, one that has not been solved yet even in the more-successful-than-most Baltic and Central European countries.

Another and closely related problem is weak political parties and civil society. We said earlier that it was relatively easy to change political institutions, rewrite the laws and constitutions, and hold democratic elections; that every country in Eastern Europe has done. Far more difficult it is, as with economic reform, to change the political culture, create and build new political parties, and weave the country together through a web or vast network of civil-society organizations. Those are all, in the main, still lacking or in their infancy in Eastern Europe, once again more so in Southeastern Europe than in the Baltics or Central Europe. The absence of strong parties, civil society, and political infrastructure in general is another long-term problem that, like other infrastructure weaknesses, will take generations to solve.

Given the weak infrastructure, the underdeveloped economic and political infrastructure, and the weak civil society throughout Eastern Europe, the temptation is strong for the state to step in and try to manage and run it all. But that is what communism was all about – the state running everything and doing it badly – precisely what Eastern Europe has been seeking to get away from for the last twenty-five years. In addition, remember the "Second World" designation: it is exactly these massive problems of infrastructure and the state's inability to reform and modernize them that is at the heart of the problem in Eastern Europe. Moreover, in the absence of much employment and with huge gaps in social services, politicians will be tempted not to downsize but to *add* to the bureaucracy's ranks and expand the state still more – precisely what Eastern Europe does *not* need.

The one area where Eastern Europe so far has been unambiguously successful is in the security arena. All of the new members of the EU have also opted to become members of NATO. Quite a few of these countries feel more comfortable with the EU because that means riches and affluence than they are with NATO because that means military obligations and expenditures on equipment and manpower; but the argument has generally held that you can't have the benefits of the one – the EU – without the obligations of the other – NATO. And with that they have also come under NATO's and the U.S.'s security umbrella.

At first, that did not seem so important but now, with Russia's resurgence and aggressiveness, Eastern Europe values its NATO membership more than ever as a form of protection from outside (real, Russian) interference and possible occupation. Indeed, with its automatic collective security provisions, under which an attack on one country requires all the other members to come to its defense, Eastern Europe, with only a couple of exceptions, has come to value NATO even more than the U.S., which founded the institution.

Is There an East European Model and of What?

About twenty-five years ago, Eastern Europe, because of the collapse of the Soviet Union and its control over these countries, began making a transition away from communism. Up to this point, until the 1990s, most of the democratic transitions we had seen in Africa, Latin America, and Southeast Asia, were from right-wing authoritarianism, not from communism. So, the East European *post-communism* transitions were something new, to be both experienced and studied.

By this time, we can say that almost all – only a couple of exceptions – the East European countries are safely in the democratic, Western camp. They have, for the most part, embraced not just democracy but also free markets, free trade, and a modern, mixed economy. They have joined both the EU and NATO, the two great European "clubs." Their human rights and civil liberties records are, again with a few exceptions, outstanding. Both the Freedom House and the Polity Surveys rate them highly on their democracy and freedom indices. Plus, they have been successful economically, doubling their per-capita income in a few short years and then *doubling it again* after joining the EU a decade ago. It would take something extraordinary – a complete national breakdown or an invasion by Russia – for these countries at this stage to change direction or veer from the democratic Western path. Neither of these is likely to happen.

But what can these countries offer as a model to the rest of the world of the transition from communism to democracy? Not very much, because there are so few (only four) communist regimes – China, Cuba, North Korea, and Vietnam – left. But these countries are all, by comparison to Eastern Europe, non-Western; in addition, they are far distant from Western Europe and have no possibilities of reaping the advantages of joining the EU or NATO. Plus, Big China, treated later in this book, and maybe the other three, too, has no intention of joining the Western, democratic world; indeed, as we will see, China is taking strenuous pains to *avoid* a democratic and Western outcome.

Hence, the only place where the East European model may be applicable is in those other post-communist countries – Belarus, Moldova, the Ukraine, Azerbaijan, Armenia, Georgia, Central Asia, and Mongolia – which were once part of the Soviet Union. But keep in mind the differences: (1) none of these countries is a member of the EU or has access to the EU's wealth; (2) they are far poorer and less developed than most of the Eastern European countries; (3) culturally, they are, for the most part, only partially Western; (4) their democratic institutions and civil society are even weaker than in Eastern Europe; and (5) Russia still considers these countries part of *its* territory, part of Greater Russia, and, therefore, the Russians argue, as in the Ukraine, the West should keep hands off. Hence, it's unlikely that we will see Eastern Europe being used as a model by many more countries in the future.

Indeed, that is precisely our argument here. Eastern Europe may be unique, *sui generis*. Its experience is unlikely to be repeated elsewhere. That is because it undertook its post-communist transition in such special circumstances that they may be completely unique: (1) the Soviet Union had just collapsed, thus freeing them to join the West; (2) they lie close to Western Europe, one of the richest areas in the world; (3) the U.S. and the EU were willing to absorb and spend money on them; (4) they were already mostly Western in their culture and sociology; (5) they had a prior history – "path dependency" – with democracy from between the two world wars of the twentieth century which made it easier to transition a second time; and (6) and maybe most important, at the time Eastern Europe began its transition, there were no other models for them besides the Western democratic one. They certainly didn't want to go back to Communism, authoritarianism, or totalitarianism;

China had not emerged as a major alternative model; and Russia was not yet resurgent. Democracy was truly, at that time, "the only game in town."

Hence, Eastern Europe was integrated *fully* into the West and the Western model: democracy, membership in the EU and NATO, an open economy and free markets, globalization, the social-welfare state. Interestingly, Latin America, undergoing a democratic and economic reform transition at roughly the same time, embraced almost exactly the same elements of what was then the Washington consensus: democracy, open markets, and free trade. Because, at the time, no other possibility, no other *model*, seemed feasible. Indeed, one could argue that Eastern Europe and Latin America, transitioning when they did, may have been both the *last* and the most *successful* in embracing entirely the Western model. They accepted the Western model all but completely and in all its aspects.

By now, however, there are other models out there: China; Japan; the East Asian "Little Tigers" of South Korea, Taiwan, Hong Kong, and Singapore; Iran, and other Middle East radical regimes; resurgent Russia; other indigenous models emanating from the Third World. The range of options is now far wider than it was twenty and thirty years ago when Eastern Europe and Latin America began their transitions. Would they make the same choices today? Probably Eastern Europe would, for the most part, because they have been successful and membership in the EU has greatly increased their wealth. Probably Latin America, too, in the last analysis, although it has by now moved a considerable distance away from the Washington consensus and, in Argentina, Bolivia, Brazil, Chile, Ecuador, Uruguay, and Venezuela, is experimenting – not always successfully – with new forms and new policies.

Today, the conditions are much different than they were for Eastern Europe and Latin America in the 1980s- '90s time period. Not only are the conditions different now but there are many more options and choices available. It may be, therefore, that the experiences of that earlier period, when *entire regions* of the world embraced a single Western consensus and model, may not be repeatable. Diversity is now the name of the game, a pluralism of options, or *many* modernizations. We will have to see how these newfound policy options and the greater pluralism of models are working out in the remaining areas of the world.

CHAPTER 5

EAST AND SOUTHEAST ASIA: THE ASIAN MODEL OF DEVELOPMENT

East Asia is today clearly the most energetic and dynamic area of the world. Even though we are used by now to comments touting Asia, the importance of the previous sentence needs to sink in. Because for the previous five hundred years it was Europe, and then its extension in America, the United States, that led the world – remember "the *American* Century." Now, *everything* is Asia. Asia is the future, the model to which – not so much to Europe or the U.S. – everyone looks for guidance and instruction.

The question most of the world is asking is, how did Asia do it, the "it" in this case meaning lift itself up from poverty, become among the richest areas in the world, and serve as a model for other countries to emulate. For most scholars in the West, if we had our careers to do over again, we would choose Asia as our specialization, not Africa, Europe, Russia, Latin America, or the Middle East. Asia is currently where the action is.

In this chapter, we deal specifically with East Asia. Not South Asia (India, Pakistan, Bangladesh, Sri Lanka), which is the subject of the next chapter, nor, in the main, Southeast Asia (Indonesia, the Philippines, East Timor, Vietnam, Laos, Cambodia, Thailand, Malaysia, Myanmar, Papua New Guinea) which is briefly treated as a subsection later in this chapter. East Asia includes the first "Asian Tiger," Japan, which is now one of the world's richest countries, comparable to the U.S. or Western Europe, with the world's longest life expectancy, and the third largest economy in the world. It includes the four "Little Tigers" – South Korea (not North Korea; that is in a separate category), Taiwan, Hong Kong, and Singapore, all similarly dynamic and with living standards and per capita incomes either approaching or already having passed that of Japan (or the U.S. or Western Europe). And now the East Asia category of success stories must also include China, equally dynamic, the world's biggest country (1.3 billion people, four times as large as the U.S.), and soon to be, if not already, the world's biggest economy, even though on a per-capita basis still quite a bit poorer than these others.

More recently, the "Asian Model" of growth and development has spread to other countries, which is why we include a briefer discussion of Southeast Asia within this chapter. For, using one or another version of the Asian model, countries like Indonesia, the Philippines, Malaysia, and Thailand have begun to take off economically and have reached middle-income levels. Similarly, although starting at a lower base, Laos and Vietnam have also begun their take-offs. That leaves only a few Asian countries – East Timor, Myanmar, Cambodia, Papua, and New Guinea – that remain locked in poverty and underdevelopment, and even they are changing albeit slowly. We exclude Australia and New Zealand from this discussion – basically European countries and cultures that were, because of history and colonialism, plunked down in the South Pacific but that are now discovering they, too, are "Asian countries."

We have spoken here of an "Asian Model" as if there actually were a single Asian path that all these countries are following. But there is not; in fact, Asia is exceedingly diverse. It makes a huge difference in talking of the "Asian Model" if we are speaking of democratically governed Japan, South Korea, Taiwan, or Singapore; or if we are referring to autocratic, Leninist, top-down, authoritarian China. Both these versions of the Asian Model are alive and well, not just in Asia itself but as an example for other countries to follow. In fact, almost daily there are delegations from Africa, Latin America, and other developing areas passing through Singapore, Hong Kong, Tokyo, Seoul, Beijing, or Shanghai to try to learn the keys to Asia's success.

TABLE 5.1
EAST AND SOUTEAST ASIA: POPULATION
AND GROSS DOMESTIC PRODUCT PER
CAPITA, 2015 (CONSTANT 2010 US $)

Country	Population (in millions)	GDP per Capita
Australia	23.4	54,717
Brunei Darussalam	0.4	29,138
Cambodia	15.1	1,020
China	1357.4	13,206
East Timor	1.2	987
Hong Kong	7.2	36,117
Indonesia	254.5	3,834

Japan	127.1	44,656
Korea, South	50.4	25,022
Korea, North	25	NA
Laos	6.7	1,537
Macao	0.6	55,860
Malaysia	29.9	10,876
Myanmar	53.4	NA
New Zealand	4.5	36,463
Papua New Guinea	7.5	790
Philippines	99.1	2,635
Singapore	5.4	51,855
Thailand	67.7	5,774
Vietnam	90.7	1,684

Source: World Development Indicators, The World Bank

We need, therefore, to be very careful in distinguishing and sorting out the Japanese, the Chinese, and the "Little Tiger" variations of the Asian Model. We will want to know what, if anything, *all* these Asian countries have in common. In other words, is there truly a single Asian model and what does it consist of? Then, secondly, within that single Asian model, we will want to know the individual and country variations: what makes Japan different from China, how are the "Little Tigers" different from both of these, and is it possible for the other Southeast Asian countries to follow this same model – and then, which one among these several variations. It is a fascinating discussion and an especially important one, particularly since so many other countries are now looking to Asia for guidance.

History and Political Culture

Asian culture and civilization go back for three and four thousand years and more. These are very ancient civilizations. Obviously, they are far older than is the United States; the Asian civilizations, we may be surprised to hear, are older than most Western European countries as well.

Long before there were centralized nation-states in Europe, China had already been centralized as a more-or-less unified, coherent unit. China's unity and centralization go back at least twenty-five hundred years. Among the factors explaining China's early emergence as a centralized state were a certain cultural and ethnic unity, political power centralized in the emperor, unquestioned top-down authority, a centralized bureaucracy ruling efficiently, a system of laws and rules exercised universally over China's vast population, an hierarchical social and political order either accepted by or enforced on all, and an underlying ethical or value system that helped unify the population around certain shared beliefs.

This unifying ethic or value system has come to be called Confucianism, after the philosopher, sage, sociologist, and political scientist Confucius who lived twenty-five- hundred years ago. Confucius's thought provided the deeply rooted cultural "glue" that helped hold China together through all the intervening centuries. During that long period, two-and-a-half millennia, from Confucius's time to the present, China has frequently been divided, torn by civil war, badly governed, and occupied by foreign colonial powers. But through all this strife, the Confucian ethic and belief system is what held China together as a single culture and civilization.

From China, the Confucian culture and values spread to other nearby countries. These include the two Koreas, Japan, present-day Taiwan, Hong Kong, Macao, Singapore, and even Vietnam. All of these countries were shaped powerfully by the Confucian ethic, and sometimes directly by Chinese invasions and occupations. Of course, in these other countries the Chinese variant of Confucianism was reshaped and modified by local conditions, cultures, and belief systems, such as Taoism, Shintoism, and Buddhism. That, plus geography, resources, history, and sociology help explain why, within this overarching Confucian culture area (virtually *all* of East Asia), Korea is different from China, Japan is different from both Korea and China, and Vietnam is different from all of these. Nevertheless, within this vast and diverse East Asian area, there is also a certain common core of beliefs, values, and behavior.

More recently in the form of what are called the "overseas Chinese" – Chinese communities that have migrated over the decades to other countries – we find the Confucian ethic taking root in such countries as Malaysia, Indonesia, the Philippines, Thailand, and others. However, in these Southeast Asian countries the Chinese communities and their Confucian-based value systems are still a minority (for example, Malaysia is 25 percent ethnic Chinese; Indonesia and the Philippines, less than that), whereas in the East Asian countries already mentioned the Confucian value system is not only the majority value system but virtually the only one.

What are the main elements of this Confucian value system that is so important in shaping these countries? And in constituting the East Asian Model of Development? The main ingredients include:

- A belief in centralized, top-down, unifying authority.
- A common system, if not of law in the Western sense, then certainly of beliefs, ethics, and rules.
- Government that rules for the common good.
- A centralized bureaucracy that provides honest, efficient public administration.
- A hierarchical social order, with clear rules and customs, where everyone knows and accepts his or her place in society.
- A common ethic of behavior based on honor, diligence, and hard work.
- Violation of this ethic brings shame upon you and your family – in the most egregious cases, obligating you to commit suicide (harakiri) to uphold family honor.
- An emphasis, as we see in the U.S. in high Asian-American SAT or GRE scores, on education, studying, doing well, getting ahead, succeeding, honoring the family and society by one's achievements.

Of course, not everyone in East Asia shares all these political-culture values, or shares them so intensely, or holds these values – which can and often were used to justify an authoritarian political system, culture, or family relations (i.e., the "Tiger Mom") – to the exclusion of all others. In East Asia, as in most areas of the world, these Confucian values are overlapping with other imported ones, being undermined by social media and the worldwide web, and giving way under the impact of globalization and generational change. Nevertheless, for centuries and even millennia this Confucian ethic has undergirded East Asian society, culture, and politics, and even today remains the overwhelmingly dominant force throughout the area.

It is to be emphasized that Confucianism is not a religion or a system of religious beliefs. Rather, it is a set of ethical and behavioral injunctions that undergirds the entire social order and culture. You adhere to these injunctions out of respect, belief, and moral obligation.

The rest of Asia – South Asia, Southeast Asia – except for the minority "overseas Chinese," does not necessarily follow the Confucian ethic. That is why this chapter is focused mainly on East Asia – China, Korea, Japan, Taiwan, Hong Kong, Macao, and Singapore – where the Confucian ethic is powerful. However, when you get to Laos, Cambodia, Thailand, Myanmar, Malaysia, Indonesia, the Philippines, Brunei, East Timor, etc., to say nothing of India, Pakistan, Bangladesh, or Sri Lanka, the culture completely changes. These countries do not share the same ethical beliefs and behavior as those countries shaped by the Confucian ethic.

Look at a map: it is said that the island nations of Indonesia, East Timor, Borneo, and the Philippines, even as far as the indigenous population of Taiwan, are culturally and ethnically really extensions of the culture of the mainland Malay Peninsula, and were populated over the centuries by people in effect "island hopping" from present-day Malaysia and Singapore down through and across the islands. Some say these peoples are less well organized, less disciplined, less driven, and less hard-working than those countries shaped by Confucian values. That may or may not be valid; what we do know is that East Asia, Southeast Asia, and South Asia were shaped by very different value systems that importantly influence their cultures and developmental prospects even to this day.

For a long time, East Asia lagged behind the West. Even though China, Korea, and Japan emerged as separate cultures and as centralized kingdoms centuries and even millennia ago, they were not able to harness their resources, bureaucratic institutions, and Confucian culture into an integrated project to achieve national development. From the fifteenth through the nineteenth centuries, the West, including Great Britain, France, Germany and eventually the United States, too, passed Asia by. We don't know exactly why the West was able to do this; in a wonderful book on this theme, Harvard University historian David Landes argues persuasively that it was Western *culture* that made the difference. That the West's emphasis on education, science, independent learning, exploration, printing, empiricism, the enlightenment, the scientific revolution made all the difference.[27]

Meanwhile, East Asia remained locked in its rigidities, its social hierarchies, its elaborate norms and rules, all of which hindered growth. Europe not only forged way ahead of Asia during these five centuries but, through colonialism and war it subjugated much of Asia. Asia would require, as it began to grow and achieve in the twentieth century, initially in Japan and then spreading to other countries, a new, updated, more modern interpretation of its Confucian ethic before it could forge ahead – and eventually arrive at a par or even surpass the West.

Early students of East Asia and the Confucian value system, therefore, before this revolution in the culture had taken place, such as the great German sociologist Max Weber, thought that the Confucian ethic would *not* be conducive to economic growth. That is because the emphasis on order, authority, hierarchy, rules, and top-down bureaucracy in Confucianism, Weber thought, would snuff out individual initiative and entrepreneurship. He, therefore, predicted that China and *all* of Asia would always lag behind the West.[28]

But Weber was writing a hundred years ago; he did not see the future very clearly. He did not comprehend that all that emphasis on order, hierarchy, authority, rules, and the obligation to obey could be converted, as Japan, China, and the Asian Tigers have done, into a system not of private-sector capitalism but into a very efficient system of *state capitalism* (more on this important model below). Nor did he see that the emphasis on honor, education, diligence, pleasing your parents, hard work, and never bringing shame upon your family could be turned into a system in which Asian children excel in school, on tests, and in professional (especially science, medical school, engineering, mathematics, and computer science) careers.

These two elements – state capitalism, which is a structural or institutional condition, and the cultural traits of hard work, diligence, honor, education, etc. – go a long way toward explaining the Asian Model, as well as why those countries mainly in East Asia that share the Confucian ethic were able to forge ahead so impressively. They also explain, especially the cultural factor, why their neighbors in South and Southeast Asia, which, of course, have their own cultures but not necessarily the Confucian one, have lagged behind. It is *culture*, specifically the Confucian ethic, that is important here, the crucial element that has enabled East Asia to have so much dynamic growth, helping it to surpass all other global areas. After all, other countries, in Asia and elsewhere, have state capitalism; but only East Asia has the Confucian ethic.

Does the Confucian ethic last forever? Some scholars say no. That at most it lasts only two generations. After that the children have too many things, get lazy, don't study or work as hard, and start to disobey and dishonor their parents. Japan already has a colorful term for that: "McDonald's kids." That means that they eat too much, lose their drive and ambition, become obese, hang out all day and waste their time, and neglect their studies. Other scholars, focused on Japan especially, which was the first Asian country to take off and reach full maturity as a developed nation, say that Japan has now entered a "post-Confucian" period where, as in other developed countries, most issues are now decided pragmatically rather than on the basis any longer of any overriding Confucian ethic or behavioral pattern.[29]

We will leave that for the sociologists to determine. Meanwhile, although Japan has indeed slipped from its top position over the last two decades, East Asia remains the most energetic and fastest-growing area in the world.

Socioeconomic Overview

East Asia has been the world's great growth area for the last forty to fifty years. Starting with Japan, then the "Four Little Tigers" of South Korea, Taiwan, Hong Kong, and Singapore, now China, Malaysia, Thailand, Indonesia, the Philippines, and others as well, East Asia has boomed ahead while other countries and areas (the U.S. and Europe) have stagnated or shown only modest growth. Asia seems to be the continent of the future.

We need to remember that fifty years ago most of Asia was thought of as part of the Third World: poor, bedraggled, backward, and traditional. But then Asia took off and became, within two generations, among the most dynamic and energetic areas of the world. Some Asian countries – Japan, South Korea, Hong Kong, and Singapore – are right up there in the rankings with the globe's richest countries; others are fast catching up. That is what makes Asia so attractive and interesting to other, still-poor, Third World countries: how did Asia do it and what can we learn and absorb from their experience?

Unlike Western Europe, Asia has no European Union (EU) so there is no sharing of resources, nor are there subsidies to its poorer members. Each Asian country must, therefore, make it on its own, which makes the Asian countries' accomplishments all the more remarkable. Nor is there an Asian version of NATO, a mutual security arrangement pledging that an attack on one country requires a response from all the others. The absence of such a mutual security treaty makes Asia vulnerable, except for the longstanding U.S. security presence in the area, to conflict between states or aggression by the bigger countries against the smaller.

Without an EU and all the 120,000 (at last count!) rules and regulations that go with it, each Asian country must find its own path to development. For that reason, in the discussion that follows, each of the Asian countries is treated individually. But we will want to be alert to the patterns that we see and that, together, go to make up the Asian Model of Development. Theme and variation: that is the approach we take here.

Japan was the first Asian country to develop into a modern nation. Japan's developmental breakthrough came in 1868 with the restoration of the Meiji dynasty, the rejection of a more traditional and feudal form of society, and the desire to modernize and industrialize. However, Japan's growth suffered a severe setback and massive devastation because of its defeat in World War II.

After the war, Japan was occupied by U.S. military forces who wrote Japan's new constitution, made Japan into a democracy, and to help it recover, gave it special access to U.S. markets. Using a model that included the state, the private sector, and the famed Ministry of Trade (MITI) all working closely together, Japan got back on its feet and then began to prosper. At first Japan produced cheap toys and plastic products, but by the 1970s and 1980s, it was producing high-tech electronics and automobiles that were better than those produced in the U.S. or Europe. Japan was growing so fast that analysts were predicting it would soon surpass the U.S. to become Number One in GNP in the world; its per-capita income at the end of the 1980s climbed to the point where it matched and then surpassed both the U.S. and Western Europe. Japan blended its traditional culture and practices with the requirements of a modern, high-tech world.

But in the 1990s Japan fell into a slump, a recession from which it has not yet fully recovered. Its economy (see Table 5.1) fell back to where it is "only" 90 percent of the U.S. or Western European average. But make no mistake about it, Japan is still a very rich and comfortable society: high income, high life expectancy, universal literacy, excellent health care, and good schools and universities. It should not take much – bringing in foreign laborers, bringing more women into the work force – for Japan to resume its upward growth.

Japan was the first "Tiger" economy, *South Korea* and *Taiwan* came next as part of the four "Little Tigers." There are some fascinating parallels between these two. During the Cold War both were either occupied militarily (South Korea after its own civil war of 1950-52) or became a protectorate (Taiwan) of the U.S. Both started off in the 1940s and 1950s as quite traditional, poor, quasi-feudal regimes. Then they both almost exactly followed the Rostow or Western model of development, although with their own East Asian variations: first an authoritarian regime that provided twenty to thirty years of stability during which foreign investment came in and growth took off; that, in turn, gave rise to vast social changes, the emergence primarily of a large middle class; and ultimately social change and pluralism helped usher in democracy which came to both countries in 1987.

Since then, South Korea has continued to forge ahead and is on the verge of achieving a living standard on a par with the U.S., Japan, or Western Europe. With its ambition, frenetic energy, high education standards, numbers of Ph.D. per capita, and numbers of patents, South Korea promises to be one of the leading countries in the world in the next decade. Taiwan ran parallel in growth to South Korea for half a century, but recently has fallen back over fears of instability in its relations with big, mainland China which considers Taiwan part of "Greater China." Nevertheless, Taiwan is still up there with Greece or Portugal as among the less-well- off Western European countries, a remarkable achievement. Both South Korea and Taiwan, in addition to being protected by the U.S. and given special access to U.S. markets, have generally followed the Japanese model of a close alliance between the state, private business, and certain key ministries such as Trade and Planning.

Both Hong Kong and Singapore (and Macao, too) are tiny islands; really, small city-states; ethnically Chinese; part of the "Four [now Five] Little Tigers" which have managed to become very wealthy. Hong Kong, a former British colony, is a Special Administrative Region (SAR) of China and is gradually being absorbed into its huge neighbor. Without agriculture or industry, it became wealthy on the basis of trade and commerce out of China, as well as now of banking, real estate, finance, insurance, and shipping. By now, Hong Kong has surpassed both the U.S. and Western Europe in per-capita income and is up there in the rankings with the wealthy Scandinavian countries.

Macao, across (twenty miles) the mouth of the Pearl River from Hong Kong, similarly a Special Administrative Region (SAR) of China, and likewise being absorbed into it, was long a more traditional, torpid, and run-down former Portuguese colony. But it has been revived almost exclusively on the basis of the gaming industry (like Las Vegas), a strange and unusual way to achieve growth, and is now one of the richest places in the world, with almost *three times* the per-capita income of the U.S. or Western Europe. This is, however, a distorted and precarious figure because it is based on gambling alone, its wealth is very unevenly distributed, and it is subject to the changing whims of policy coming out of Beijing.

Singapore is one of the most successful and fascinating countries in the world. Beginning in the 1960s as a poor,

Third World country, Singapore has in two generations leapfrogged up to First World rank and beyond, to become one of the world's most prosperous countries. With a per-capita income of around $85,000, Singapore is up there on the list with Norway, Qatar, and Luxembourg, as among the richest nations on the globe, at *almost double* the U.S. and European levels.

Singapore "did it" on the basis of stable government, strong leadership (the late Lee Quan Yew), and an honest, efficient, no-nonsense bureaucracy or public service for half a century. Like Hong Kong, the main ingredients in its phenomenal success are trade, commerce, insurance, banking, shipping, finance, and international business. And like the others already mentioned, its formula for success is a close alliance between the state, private business, and government ministries that promote trade and development. Note how far all five of these Asian countries (Japan, South Korea, Taiwan, Hong Kong, and Singapore) are from the private-sector dominated or free-enterprise system of the United States.

Now we come to China, the acid test of the Asian model. China is a special cast, first and obviously, because it is so big compared to these others; second, because it has recently attracted worldwide attention by passing the U.S. in GNP to become Number One in the world; and third, because China, unlike the other East Asian countries, had a full-fledged revolution in the 1940s that led to a communist regime under Mao Tse Tung. Mao was an ideological communist whose policies killed *millions* of Chinese people, almost destroyed China, and failed to lift China up economically. So the Maoist Model, although popular among some Marxist ideologies five and six decades ago, is no longer what interests us here. Rather, our interest is in the more pragmatic policies followed by Mao's successors, which have succeeded in completely transforming China, lifting it up out of poverty, achieving phenomenal growth rates (10-11 percent per year for a time), and making China into a possible model for other countries to emulate.

Since it is so important, we need to be very clear what the Chinese model is and what it is not. First, most countries do not want to go through all the destructive, chaotic, revolutionary changes, ushered in by Mao and the later "Cultural Revolution," although many Third World leaders still harbor the idea that only a thoroughgoing revolution can destroy the oligarchy and the old order before a new and modern one can be established. Second, while China is no longer a totalitarian state as it was under Mao, it is still top-down, authoritarian, and Leninist, in the sense that a single-party regime, the Communist Party, monopolizes all political power. Third and related, it is corporatist, meaning that the state seeks to monopolize and control all interest group and civil society activity through its official, government-created interest associations. More on this important subject below.

A fourth and extremely important feature of China, and one that relates to the other East Asian modernizes is that in the economic sphere it allows considerable entrepreneurial and business activity, even while the state, its ministries and bureaucracy, and the Party still exercise ultimate control. In other words, China practices a new form of state capitalism, although without the economic and political freedoms allowed by the other East Asian tigers. A fifth feature is the somewhat more open society allowed in China – although still subject to the whim of the Party – including its opening up still in limited ways to globalization. Sixth, China has rediscovered Confucius and thus unleashed the work-hard, study-hard, get-ahead, honor-your-parents (and the regime – Chinese nationalism) ethic of its people. And finally, seventh, the present Chinese leadership is considerably more pragmatic, and less ideological, than it was in the early decades of Mao's communist Revolution.

The Chinese model is of considerable interest to other Third World countries. Obviously, these countries are interested in how China achieved those miracle growth rates for so long (now slowing) of 8, 9, 10, 11 percent. Some of these Third World leaders are tempted by China's political model, a top-down, one-party state that suppresses the opposition and keeps any dissent under control. But there are drawbacks to this political side of the equation as well: no democracy, no independent civil society, no elections, terrible pollution, a bad human rights situation. Hence, if you're looking for a model that combines China's economic growth with a more liberal political system, you travel to South Korea or Singapore, which many Third World leaders are presently doing.

Note that in Table 5.1 China is still *way* below Japan, Hong Kong, Singapore, South Korea, Macao, and Taiwan in per-capita income. With all the attention devoted to the "Chinese miracle," we forget that it is still a very poor country. China still has a long way to go to catch up to these others, a fact that is not always understood by China's admirers. Even Malaysia, which no one ever hears of except when its airplanes crash, has *double* the per capita income of China. Yet no one speaks of the "Malaysian miracle," although probably we should.

Once we get below these Asian "high flyers," there is quite a sharp drop-off before we reach another cluster of countries. Yet, look at Indonesia, the Philippines, and Thailand, all *Southeast Asian* countries that, though still poor (in the $7-$13,000 per capita income range) have significantly improved their standard of living in recent years. They have combined an opening to democracy with an effort to emulate the East Asian model of a close alliance between the state, the private sector, and relevant government economic ministries. But these countries are not part of the *East* Asia culture area and not part of what we call "the Confucian zone"; they are less well organized, less disciplined, less efficient, and more corrupt than their East Asian neighbors. Nevertheless, we applaud their efforts within *their own cultural context* and institutional arrangements to lift themselves up and inspire the living standards of their peoples.

The next cluster includes Laos, East Timor, and Vietnam, at about the $5-$7,000 per-capita income level. Vietnam is especially interesting to us because it shares in part the Confucian work ethic, but it was long held back because of civil war, foreign military interventions (including the U.S.), a rigid communist leadership, and disorganization and destruction following the 1960- '70s conflict. But now Vietnam is industrializing and, ironically, luring foreign business from China because Vietnam's wage rates are even lower than China's.

Laos is still poor but it is picking up steam from the general Southeast Asian rise in prosperity and, specifically, the spillover effect from new investments in neighboring Thailand and Vietnam. East Timor is an anomaly: it is one of the poorest and most miserable places on earth (like Haiti) but benefits from the income from recent oil discoveries in the waters between it and Australia. Nevertheless, in terms of developing the infrastructure for development, East Timor is at the lowest end of the totem pole.

That leaves Cambodia, Myanmar, and Papua New Guinea as the poorest, least-developed countries in Asia. We should probably add East Timor to this list since, except for the "accident" or "dumb luck" of those oil finds, it has experienced little or no development. None of these countries has even begun the process of development or, because of war, conflict, dictatorships, and internal impediments, has yet fashioned the infrastructure for economic takeoff. With neither the Confucian ethic nor the infrastructure for development, these four countries are only at the beginning of the modernization process and with only modest future prospects.

Government Institutions and the Role of the State

East Asia and Southeast Asia have a great variety of government systems. Here we have parliamentary regimes, presidential systems, monarchies and sultanates, democracies, a big (China) communist country, military-authoritarian regimes, and countries that are at some levels still tribal in nature. No one kind of regime is overwhelmingly predominant, although in recent decades there has been a trend toward new Asian or "Confucian" (top-down, state-centered) democracies. That leads us to conclude that, while, of course, you want to get your country's laws, constitutions, and governing institutions right, institutions *per se* are not the key factor in explaining why some countries develop rapidly and others do not.

Because of defeat in and then occupation by the U.S. after World War II, Japan has a constitution and political system patterned after that of its American occupiers. Similarly, in South Korea, Taiwan, and the Philippines: because of either U.S. occupation or major influence, these countries have laws, constitutions, and political systems that, though a little more raucous, are patterned on and greatly influenced – at least initially – by the U.S. But China is a communist regime, completely different institutionally at least from its East Asian neighbors. And Singapore has been for fifty years a strong, authoritative (if not authoritarian), one-party, one-man regime (Mr. Lee) which has regular elections and civil liberties. Under a variety of regimes and institutional arrangements, thus, *all* of these East Asian countries in recent decades have enjoyed phenomenal growth.

Moving to Southeast Asia, we find even greater variety. Thailand and Malaysia are aspiring parliamentary democracies but they have, as a hangover from their earlier histories, sultanships. Brunei, however, remains a sultanship where the sultan actually rules and keeps order, thanks to vast oil wealth. Vietnam is a communist country, now opening up to capitalism for the first time, while Myanmar is just emerging from military dictatorship and opening up to the world. East Timor, because it remained a European (Portuguese) colony longer than any other country in the region, has a European-like constitution providing for both a president and a prime minister. Cambodia, Laos, and Papua New Guinea are struggling to establish efficient, centralized government, but they are plagued by divisive, even breakaway tribalism. Once again, as in East Asia, the main theme here in Southeast Asia is diversity, a variety of regimes whose success depends more on their locations, cultures, and resources than on any particular institutional arrangements.

This last point requires greater emphasis. The main division here in Asia, accounting for greater success versus lesser success, is *cultural* rather than institutional. That is, East Asia (Japan, South Korea, Taiwan, Hong Kong, Singapore, China, and now also Vietnam and Macao) is *Confucian*, in terms of both its value system and its centralized, bureaucratic state, while Southeast Asia is ethnically and culturally something else – Malay (?), Indochinese (?) – definitely more diverse and lacking East Asia's common cultural background. In the absence of East Asia's common cultural tradition which we have seen has been a stimulus to unity and economic development, Southeast Asia is both more varied in its regime types *and* with a culture that, at least until recently, has been less conducive to growth.

While we have quite a variety of regime types in both East and Southeast Asia, there are some commonalities among all these countries as well. Here, Japan was the original model, followed by the four Little Tigers of South Korea, Taiwan, Hong Kong, and Singapore, and now big China. And those commonalities include a centralized, efficient, bureaucratic state, a dynamic private sector interacting closely with the state, and government ministries that actively promote trade, exports, and economic development while also coordinating the actions of both the state and private entrepreneurs. In this effort, an honest, centralized, efficient public sector is absolutely necessary. It also helps if there is a common agreed-upon ethic – Confucianism – underlying these efforts. Obviously, East Asia has such a get-ahead ethic, while in Southeast Asia it is either weaker or, in some of the least-developed countries, mainly lacking.

In East Asia, it is striking that in both communist (China) and noncommunist (Japan, South Korea, Taiwan, Hong Kong, and Singapore) regimes, it is the state, its ministries, and a private sector tied in with the state, that are the driving forces in achieving development. Having a modern, efficient state seems to be the key to success. In East Asia, we have such strong states, along with a strong private sector. But in most of the states of Southeast Asia, the state is mainly weak, inefficient, or limited in its reach: i.e., too limited to deliver goods and services to its own population.

In countries where the state is strong, interest groups and civil society tend to be weak. That is obviously true in China because of its authoritarian, Leninist regime; interest groups, as we think of them in the West as free and independent actors, are not allowed in China or they are completely subordinated to the state. But in noncommunist Japan, South Korea, Taiwan, Hong Kong, and Singapore, interest groups and civil society are also weak. Or else, where they exist, they engage mainly in "safe," non-political activities such as beach cleanups, rescue missions, or humanitarian efforts. But they do not do lobbying in the American sense, nor – and that is why they are weak or involved only in non-political actions – can they interfere in the decision making of the powerful state-private sector-government ministries nexus. It is one of the paradoxes of East Asian development and the bane of U.S. democracy-promotion efforts, that the countries that have been among the most successful modernizers and democratizers in the world are also the countries that have the weakest civil societies.

One other common feature of these East Asian success stories must be mentioned here, and that is corporatism. Corporatism means government control and regulation of all interest- group activity. Interest groups (labor, business, and agriculture) are not independent actors under corporatism; rather, they are subordinated to state interests. In these respects, corporatism stands in opposition to liberal-pluralism à la Madison, Tocqueville, and the American model of democracy.

Corporatism in East Asia enhances the independent power of the state. The state in these countries is not hampered by lobbying, interest group pluralism, or a strong civil society. Instead, just the opposite is true: strong states (in accord with the Confucian-East Asian model) with weak or nonexistent civil society and pluralism. Corporatism thus reinforces the preferred East Asian formula already in existence of strong, centralized, top-down, bureaucratic state structures.

China is a special case, at variance with the other, at least nominally democratic, states of East Asia. China is a one-party, Leninist regime that allows *no* independent interest groups or lobbying. The only interest groups in China are official ones, appendages of and wholly subordinate to the ruling Communist Party. As China has modernized, the regime has created a whole network of these official, government-dominated organizations: business groups, labor unions, women's groups, peasant associations, student groups, etc. That way, in a time of social change, the Party can adapt to modernization by bringing all these groups *into* the regime, but keeping control over them and without giving up any state power and certainly not moving toward democracy.

Interestingly, and making China's situation more complicated, some Chinese workers, women, students, and others are riskily organizing outside and independently of the official state groups where they may invite government repression. Similarly, outside actors largely based in Hong Kong or the U.S. are also seeking to organize independent civil society in the mainland. But so far, the Chinese regime has been able to maintain absolute control even in the face of these efforts toward greater pluralism and maybe even democracy.

As development has come to Southeast Asia, these countries, too, have been attracted to the corporatist model. We can appreciate the attractiveness of that model to the leaders of these countries even if we do not like its anti-pluralist and anti-democratic aspects. For that way the state or the regimes in power can, at one and the same time, stimulate development, give off the *appearance* of having pluralism, and yet maintain the power and longevity of the state. In countries as diverse as Indonesia, the Philippines, Thailand, and others, corporatism, or perhaps a mixed form of corporatism and liberalism, has proved to be very attractive to state interests.

The Asian Model

The Asian Model of development is enormously attractive. It now rivals, but for different reasons, the American or Western Model. It has helped provide for phenomenal growth. There is so much energy and dynamism in Asian society today that it is nothing short of spectacular. Other countries throughout the world are flocking to Asia to see how the Asians did it, how they achieved such miracle growth rates.

The Asian Miracle did not happen all at once nor did the Asian Model come to fruition out of any one person's fertile imagination. Japan was the first Asian country to modernize, to learn how to blend Western technology and know-how with local Japanese culture and ways of doing things. Japan was followed by the four "Little Tigers": South Korea, Taiwan, Hong Kong, and Singapore who emulated, in their own setting, the Japanese model. By now, two of the Little Tigers, Hong Kong and Singapore, have passed Japan by in terms of per-capita income; South Korea is about to do so. In all these countries what was required was a long period of experimentation, trying out, and back-and-forth before they got the Model right and fitted to their own local circumstances.

By now, the Asian Model has spread all around Asia; it has become truly "Asian." For example, we tend to think of Malaysia as still a Third World country, but it is very dynamic and has in fact climbed to a level where its standard of living is equal to that of Portugal or Greece. Indonesia, Thailand, and the Philippines have similarly begun to take off. Reaching further down on the development scale, the

Asian Model is being employed in such heretofore laggard countries as Vietnam and Laos. Even the least-developed countries in Asia – Cambodia, East Timor, Myanmar, and Papua New Guinea – are waking up to the new possibilities.

And then, of course, there is China. BIG China of 1.3 billion people and, just recently, the world's largest gross national product. China had a revolution which devastated the country; it was down there with the poorest of the Asian countries. But then China got its act together, liberalized its economy, and opened up to global trade. However *not* (yet?) to democracy. China retains its top-down, Leninist, authoritarian political model even while it has liberalized its economy. China is, therefore, different from the other Asian success stories because it is approaching the Asian Model from a beginning on the revolutionary Left rather than the conservative or authoritarian Right. And by retaining its authoritarian political structure, China raises the question already faced and resolved by the other Asian countries: whether you can have one without the other. That is, whether liberalism in the economic sphere can survive without the country also moving, as the rest of Asia has done, toward liberalism politically – i.e., democracy.

What is, precisely, this vaunted Asian Model of which we have been speaking? There seem to be three main components:

1. A strong and effective state. A state system that is honest, efficient, and able to deliver real goods and services.
2. A private sector – banks, financial institutions, shipping, industries – closely tied in with the state,

either by common culture, family background, "old school ties," or a common understanding of how to do things.

3. Planning, finance, and trade ministries – in Japan the famous MITI – that bring together the state and the private sector in a coordinated focus on national development.

Most economists are agreed on these three factors as being crucial to explain Asian development. Note that all three of these are *institutional arrangements*; hence, an *institutional explanation* for Asian development. But I think other factors are also involved. First, Japan, the Little Tigers, the newer success stories in Southeast Asia, and, of course, BIG China have all had remarkably free access to U.S. markets, unhindered by high tariffs, and thus with the ability to take off using an *exports-oriented model.* Second, the most advanced economies – Japan, the four Little Tigers, now China, too – all form part of the Confucian cultural or civilizational area and are part of its ethic of hard work, diligence, honor to family, and obligation to society. Culture may thus be as important in explaining East Asia's success as are institutional explanations. Culture also helps explain why other countries outside the Confucian area have not done as well as East Asia.

A third and very important factor is political. And this goes back to our old "friends" Rostow, Lipset, and the developmentalist school whom we spent some time discussing at the beginning of this book. It is striking how closely the East Asian countries, China excepted, have followed the Rostow-Lipset sequences of development. That is, moving out of traditional society, they all, initially, employed an authoritarian political regime to ensure stability, attract investment, and get development started. But economic development soon gave rise to social change and greater social pluralism: a large middle-class, new business groups, an organized working-class, and so on. And social change in all except China then gave way to demands for greater freedom, elections, and, hence, democracy.

This is exactly the sequence provided for by Rostow, Lipset, *et al.* in their famous books. It is the sequence now being followed in most of Southeast Asia as well: Thailand, Malaysia, Indonesia, the Philippines, even Myanmar. The big question remaining is whether that same sequence will eventually be applied in China as well, especially the last step, from development and social change to democracy.

But if democracy is the end product in many of these countries, it is a very Asian form of democracy, and thus in keeping with the special Confucian culture of East Asia and perhaps *not* exportable. First, Asian democracy tends to be top-down, centralized, authoritative if not authoritarian. Second and related, it is democracy that is directed if not controlled by the state, and, therefore, not always participatory or genuinely competitive. Witness the near-monopoly control exercised by the Liberal Party in Japan for most of the last sixty years, or the Kuomintang Party's dominance in Taiwan, or by Lee Kwan Yews People's Party in Singapore.

And third, East Asian democracy tends to be corporatist. That is of particular interest to us here, in part because it helps make East Asian democracy distinctive and, in part, because it points back to Asia's Confucian ethic. Recall that in Japan and the other East Asian countries, civil society tends to be weak while the state is strong. More than that, there is no real equivalence in the main East Asian languages – Japanese, Korean, and Chinese – for such Western concepts as "public interest," "civic responsibility," "civil society," or public involvement."

Hence, not only is civil society weak in East Asia but there is inadequate language to describe it. The terms used tend to imply "obedience," "state interests," "obligation," or "doing what you are told," not what Westerners mean by civil society – participation, active engagement, citizen voices, and protests. It is, therefore, no accident that most East Asian civil society groups confine their activities to such non-political or neutral activities as beach cleanup, environmental concerns, or humanitarian activities.

As a substitute for genuine civil society activities, the East Asian countries have created a system of official state-regulated or state-controlled civil society. Thus, in contrast to liberal-pluralism where almost anyone can launch an interest group, a protest group, or a civil society association at almost a moment's notice, in East Asia much of what passes for civil society and interest-group lobbying is carefully regulated, controlled, and even created by a top-down state. The state, often in alliance with the private sector, creates official or semi-official businessmen's associations, labor unions, farmers' associations, professional groups, etc. that closely collaborate with the government and its ministries in the development effort.

These are not fully independent organizations as in a liberal polity but closely tied in and coordinated with government policy. This way there are no disruptions in government policy, everyone is on the same wave length, and policy goes forward by consensus. Under corporatism, these official and semi-official bodies fill the organizational space, serve as transmission belts to help implement government policy, and prevent protests or opposition to state policy. All of this – a top-down, hierarchical system, enforced consensus, official, state-directed groups – is very Confucian. Of course, within this corporatist framework and model there is room for considerable variation, ranging from the mixed liberal-corporatist form of Japan, South Korea, and Taiwan to the authoritarian, almost totally state-controlled system of China.

It may be of particular interest and importance that this corporatist aspect of the Asian Model has now spread to Southeast Asia. It has missed the attention of most analysts that, while much of Southeast Asia has democratized over the last thirty years, it has also become more corporatist. That is, with a system of official interest groups, often carefully regulated and controlled by the state, to go along with its more liberal aspects. Hence, the existence of liberal features – elections, parliaments, representative democratic governments – alongside a corporatist or mixed system of interest associations, business-labor relations, and policy implementation.

And all these corporatist arrangements, like those in East Asia, designed to keep the new groups that emerge with modernization under state direction and control and part of a coordinated development policy. While political scientists have extensively studied elections and democratization processes in this part of the world, they have largely missed the growing corporatism that has accompanied it. But, like many things in Southeast Asia, its corporatism is less extensive, less efficient, less state-controlled, in short less Confucian, than it is in East Asia.

The success of the Asian countries and of the Asian model has increasingly drawn the attention of other countries. Almost every day in South Korea, China, Singapore, and others there are delegations of African, Latin American, and Middle Eastern officials coming through to see how the Asians did it. Not just how the Asians are achieving miracle economic growth but also how they are avoiding, through corporatism, the consequences in the form of strikes, descriptions, and breakdowns that often accompany rapid social change. Most analysts have focused on the economic success of Asia and secondarily on democratization but they have largely missed this other and equally important component of the process: corporatism.

We may conclude, therefore, that there are three, maybe four, aspects to the East Asian Model and success story. The first is economic and institutional: a strong state, featuring state capitalism, close cooperation between the state and the private sector, and with government ministries such as MITI, coordinating trade, exports, and overall economic policy. Access to U.S. markets for long periods also helped. The second is cultural: the Confucian ethic, with its emphasis on order, hard work, honor, accustomed ways, education, and accepting one's place in the social order and not rebelling against it. And the third is political: top-down authority, coupled with weak civil society, and a corporatist system designed to prevent the disruptions that accompany social change. Of course, within this framework Asia can accommodate many variations, from the relatively open and free democracies of Japan, South Korea, and Taiwan, to the stricter and more authoritative system of Singapore, to the Revolutionary-Leninist and still authoritarian structure of China.

The fourth aspect of this Asian Model is international. For all these decades, since the late 1940s, East Asia has been protected by the U.S. security umbrella. It helps enormously in the development process if you never have to worry about outside military attack or internal revolution. For decades, the U.S. has provided this protection to Japan, South Korea, Taiwan, Indonesia, the Philippines, Malaysia, Thailand, and others, enabling them to concentrate on internal development rather than external threats. Obviously, communist China, North Korea, and Vietnam lay outside this U.S. security perimeter, and in many ways still do. Indeed, BIG China as an emerging, twenty-first-century global power is now challenging the U.S. conception of world order, and the U.S. model of America's hegemonic position, growth, and all the assumptions on which they are based.

Indeed, this is happening throughout Asia. Not just China but other Asian countries as well. They are, first of all, moving away, or have already moved, from the U.S./Western model of growth, in many of its dimensions. And second, they are moving away from U.S. dominance and the U.S. system and concept of world order and to a system of greater independence. We shall have more to say about these momentous shifts in the world's cultural, political, economic, and tectonic plates in the Conclusion.

CHAPTER 6

SOUTH ASIA: A MULTILAYERED APPROACH TO DEVELOPMENT

Carolin Maney Purser

South Asia, and especially India, is often seen as one of the "hottest" regions for us to watch out in international affairs. The reasons for this international importance are varied, ranging from the struggle between two rivals (India and Pakistan) with nuclear weapons, an average of 6 percent per annum economic growth for the past two decades, proximity to multiple countries of strategic interest for world politics, and cultural diversity. Though the region consists of eight countries including Bangladesh, Sri Lanka, Nepal, Bhutan, Afghanistan, and Maldives, India and Pakistan receive most international attention. It is crucial for policy makers and students of global politics to understand how the governance, political and social cultures in the various South Asian countries vary, and how different international policies might influence various aspects of the domestic and international relations within these countries.

How are South Asian countries faring economically and politically in the global community? Are there patterns in the economic and political policies that are adopted in these countries? Does India, with its population, geographic size, and global presence lead the way for other countries in the region? How would an Indian model compare to other models of development that have been discussed by scholars and policy makers? Would such a model be useful in bringing political and economic development to other countries?

Firstly, some South Asian countries have seen steady, high growth rates of between five and ten percent in the past decade, whereas others such as Pakistan and Afghanistan have had less impressive growth rates. Despite some setbacks due to the global recession, South Asia has suffered fewer losses and even thrived in some areas, faring better than many other regions of the world.

Secondly, despite some similarities in terms of religious and cultural diversity in the South Asian countries, their economic and political models are rather different from each other. Comparing the types of governments, including constitutional monarchy in Bhutan, a federal republic with state religion of Islam in Pakistan, and the secular federal republic in India, demonstrates this diversity. Similarly, despite the proximity of Bangladesh to India, the major export of the former is from the garment industry, whereas that of the latter is much more diversified but mainly from the information technology industry.

However, India, being the largest and more geopolitically salient in the region, creates ripples in the policies of the different countries in South Asia and even of the world. Similarly, successes and failures of policies of these neighboring countries have serious implications for each other due to possible spillover of insurgents, terrorists, and displaced individuals. India has large groups of refugees from the Tibet region in China, Sri Lanka, and Myanmar. Bangladesh has a large refugee population from Myanmar. Most countries in the region also have territorial disputes over their shared borders.

The most striking shared feature of the region yet, is the confluence of the cultures of various empires and kings that ruled this region that consisted of disparate kingdoms, the latest being the British influence on the region, which mobilized the region to act almost unitedly against the colonialists. The types of government, the territorial disputes, and the successes of South Asia in outsourcing due its English-speaking population are all different manifestations of the region's colonial past. However, the different countries in the region have taken very different paths to development that cannot be captured by a model based on the legacy of British influence alone.

The tensions between Pakistan and India continue to be a security threat to the region and the world. The United States has found a strategic partner in India due to its location in the neighborhood of Northwest Asia (Middle East) and China. India is the second most populous country in the world and has continued to demonstrate its capacity to be an important global actor. Therefore, though international policymakers may be aware of the differences among South Asian countries, most of the international attention to South Asia has been focused on India and Pakistan. Secondarily, however, Bangladesh and Sri Lanka also receive international attention in select policy areas, especially in international human rights. Afghanistan is often clumped together with the politically and economically unstable states in Northwest Asia also referred to as the Middle East than with the rest of South Asian countries. In effect, international actors, especially the United States, have looked to India as a regional hegemon that could influence other countries in the region and the world, resulting in the India's policies and development to be seen as the "South Asian model". Since the appropriateness of India's policies and development being seen as a model of all of South Asia is contentious, I will discuss whether there is an Indian model of development, and what the different elements of such a model might include. I will discuss how such a model would compare with both other Western and non-Western models of development, and whether such a model could be generalizable to the development trajectories of other countries in the region and the world.

History and Political Culture

South Asia is home to hundreds of languages, with at least fifty languages that are spoken by large populations. However, Hindi and Bengali are the most spoken languages in the region, while English, advantageous in a globalized world, is an important secondary language. South Asia is also the birthplace of Hinduism, Buddhism, and Sikhism, and is now home to sizeable populations of Hindus, Muslims, Christians, and Sikhs.

The Subcontinent, as many refer to South Asia, is called so due to the countries in the region being situated on a different tectonic plate than the rest of Asia, separated by the majestic Himalayas, the world's highest mountain range. The ancient civilization around the Indus River that can be traced as far back as 7500 BCE was only the beginning of a long series of invasions and settlements of various ethnicities and religions.[30] These invasions and settlements have, in turn, resulted in countries in the region sharing aspects of religious beliefs, cultural customs, and linguistic roots.

Ashoka, the greatly successful Mauryan emperor, united large parts of the subcontinent under his rule before 232 BCE. The Turks' conquering of parts of the region by the 1200s led to settlement of Muslims. Later, the Mughals consolidated large parts of India until the 1700s. The Mughal Empire exercising control over large parts of the South Asian subcontinent was crucial in the conceptualization of India as being a united country. This conceptualization was particularly important for British colonialization of "India", which included present-day India, Pakistan, and Bangladesh. Sri Lanka, then known as Ceylon, was also colonized by the British Empire. India was colonized by Britain, France, and Portugal over the course of four centuries. In the seventeenth and eighteenth centuries, the English and French companies competed against each other to colonize South Asia.

After the eighteenth century, the British East India Company came to dominate much of present-day India, Bangladesh, Bhutan, Pakistan, Sri Lanka, and Myanmar. Though there were multiple attempts from the local South Asia population, the revolt of 1857, referred to as the "Sepoy Rebellion" (and as "the First War of Independence" in Indian history textbooks) shook the British Empire. The

British state took over the governance of India after the revolt of 1857. Though the British rule brought railways, road systems, and a language that could unite individuals from all parts of India, there were many aspects of the British Raj that were illiberal and exploited the natural and human resources of the region. Afghanistan and Nepal, though forced to engage in wars or treaties with England, were not under its governance as were the other countries of the regions.

The early twentieth century saw increasing resistance against British governance of India. The Indian Congress Party, founded in 1885, was greatly influential in determining the path of India's independence. Under the presidency of Mohandas Karamchand Gandhi (also known as *Mahatma* Gandhi), the Indian Congress Party made significant headway in their quest for the country's autonomy and independence. Gandhi led several non-violent campaigns such as non-cooperation movements, boycott of foreign goods (*Swadeshi* policy), the Salt March (Salt *satyagraha*), and the *Quit India* movement, which contributed to the eventual power transfer from the British Government to an independent Indian government led by Prime Minister, Jawaharlal Nehru.

The Indian Independence Act of 1947 passed by the British Parliament also separated India and Pakistan, due to a demand for a separate state for Indian Muslims led by Muhammad Ali Jinnah. The Pakistan that gained independence on August 14, 1947 included East and West Pakistan, present day Bangladesh and Pakistan respectively. The 1965 Indo-Pakistani war impacted West Pakistan's economy and public approval negatively. These negative circumstances, paired with East Pakistani discontent with the predominantly West-Pakistani governance and the war of 1971, led to East Pakistan gaining independence as Bangladesh.

Socioeconomic Overview

South Asia, which consists of a mixed group of independent, newly independent, and monarchic administrative styles, also has wide variance in its socioeconomic indicators. This wide range of starting points within the region reflects the differing political and economic histories of the countries, despite their geographic proximity. Sri Lanka, Bhutan, and India have the highest GDP per capita within the region (see table 6.1). Sri Lanka, after more than two decades of conflict with the Liberation Tigers of Tamil Eelam (LTTE), has recently experienced strong economic growth. The government's efforts to strengthen industries that increase growth, revenue from Sri Lankan workers abroad, and the tea, textiles and tourism industries have been pivotal to Sri Lanka's economic performance.

Bhutan, with the second highest GDP per capita, primarily relies on hydropower, agriculture, and forestry for its revenues. However, its economy is not only very small but also lacking in development. While diversification of the economy has been at the top of the policymaking agenda, Bhutan is cautious is expanding its tourism and international trade. Bhutan's strong trade and monetary relations with India dominates the country's connections to global markets.

India, which follows Sri Lanka and Bhutan, is not comparable in scale or population to the previous two countries in this section. With a staggering 1.2 billion people, the largest country in the region and the world's largest democracy dominates international discussions on the growth of South Asia. India's GDP per capita has seen a steady increase over the course of the past twenty years. This growth has been attributed to the economic liberalization that began in the early 1990s. The major sector that drives the growth of the country has been the service sector (57.9%), with India's ability to export information technology services, provide cost-effective business outsourcing, due to its large English-speaking population. Industry (24.2%) and agriculture (17.9%) sectors complement the Indian economy. Political turmoil, low levels of foreign direct investment, and lack of effective economic policies have left Afghanistan, Bangladesh, Myanmar (Burma), Pakistan and Nepal behind in steady and stable economic growth.

TABLE 6.1
GROSS DOMESTIC PRODUCT PER CAPITA IN SOUTH ASIAN NATIONS

Country	2014 GDP per capita, PPP (current international dollar)	2014 GDP growth (annual percentage)
Afghanistan	1,933	1.3
Bangladesh	3,123	6.1
Bhutan	7,816	5.5
India	5,701	7.3
Myanmar	NA	8.5

Nepal	2,374	5.4
Pakistan	4,855	4.7
Sri Lanka	11,110	4.5

Note: Based on data from the World Bank

Despite the varying levels of GDP and economic growth, two phenomena obstruct the economic development in all South Asian countries: corruption, and income inequality. Table 6.2 demonstrates South Asia's poor performance with respect to corruption. Corruption and lack of transparency not only results in suboptimal policy implementation, and entrepreneurs facing many obstacles in starting new small businesses, but also in many corporations having greater say in policies or government bids. The pervasiveness and seriousness of the problem of corruption has recently received enough attention in India to cause widespread protests, non-governmental organization advocacy for transparency and anti-corruption legislation, as well as the creation of a new political party, the *Aam Aadmi* Party, which translates to the Common Man's Party. However, much more legislation and reforms need to be implemented before India and neighboring countries can overcome the problem of corruption and transparency.

TABLE 6.2
SOUTH ASIA'S CORRUPTION PERCEPTION SCORES AND GLOBAL RANK WITH RESPECT TO ANTI-CORRUPTION PRACTICES IN OTHER COUNTRIES

Country	Corruption Perception Index Score (0-100)	Global Rank (out of 175)
Afghanistan	12	172
Bangladesh	25	145
Bhutan	65	30
India	38	85
Myanmar	21	156
Nepal	29	126
Pakistan	29	126
Sri Lanka	38	85

Note: Based on data from Transparency International Corruption Perceptions Index 2014

An Indian Model of Development?

Acknowledging the wide range of paths that South Asian countries have taken with respect to economic and political development, any attempt to claim the existence of a South Asian model of development would be fraught with problems. Therefore, considering the population size and global impact of India's economic and political development, a focus on the developmental trajectory of India, which shares a lot of the challenges such as poverty, corruption, and income inequality with other South Asian countries since it gained independence in 1947, would be a more efficient exercise to look for a model that could also serve as a regional benchmark.

Being a pioneer of the non-aligned movement, India did not take sides with either bloc during the Cold War. India continues to distinguish itself as an independent actor, and building diplomatic relations across global power rivalries, though its voice has become much more important in the global arena since the end of the Cold War. While India has made big economic leaps and risen in international status, it continues to struggle with many of the problems that have haunted it right from its birth as a new country: education, health, sanitation, infrastructure, widespread poverty, malnourishment, and population explosion.

The patchwork of cultures, languages, and classes that India is, paired with corruption, and dominion of the government by a single party for decades, has resulted in slow, uncoordinated reforms to the policies in this country. While some politicians at the state level have very poor educational records or no high school education, others, especially at the national level are highly educated, well-traveled politicians and policymakers. This creates a schism in the way many policies are formulated and the way in which they are implemented. The chief bureaucrats who implement executive decisions are chosen into the Civil Service through a highly competitive, meritocratic process. However, the civil service personnel are greatly outnumbered by lower-level government employees that they oversee. In this way, India has struggled with paradoxes at every level of its governance. A closer look at the different institutions of the Indian political system will not only help readers to understand what drives or hinders development in India, but also to think about what other regional or national contexts would be conducive to effective implementation of India's approach to development.

Pieces of the Indian Political System

India is a federal republic, i.e. power is divided between the federal government, also known as the central government, and the state governments. India currently consists of twenty-nine states[31] and seven union territories[32], many of which are drastically different in linguistic and cultural practices from their neighbors. The capital, New Delhi, serves as the seat of all major central government offices.

The legislative branch at the national level, the Parliament of India, is bicameral in nature with an upper house, known as the *Rajya Sabha*[33] (Council of States) and a lower house, known as the *Lok Sabha*[34] (House of the People). Members of the *Rajya Sabha* are elected indirectly by the lower house of the state legislatures (*Vidhan Sabha*). Members of the *Lok Sabha* are directly elected by the citizens through a first-past-the-post electoral system, i.e. the candidate with the most votes in each of the constituencies wins the parliamentary seat.

The Prime Minister of India is determined primarily by the party or coalition of parties that wins the majority of the nation-wide Lok Sabha (lower house) elections. The head of government of India, at the apex of the executive branch, is the Prime Minister, and the head of state of India is the President, with mostly ceremonial powers. The Prime Minister appoints Cabinet Ministers to lead the various ministries. Ministries in India include, but are not limited to, Home Affairs, External Affairs, Finance, Defence, and Agriculture.

The constitution of India, the supreme law of the country, is the longest of any sovereign country, and has been amended many times since it came into effect on January 26, 1950. India has a common law legal system, where judicial cases are considered the most important source of law, as opposed to codes and statutes[35]. The Supreme Court in New Delhi, is the highest constitutional court in India, and has the power to review the constitutionality of laws (constitutional review). The legal system accommodates the incredible religious diversity in India with its separate personal laws that apply to Muslims, Christians, and Hindus, with matters related to marriage, divorce, and succession.

State governments consist of the legislative branch with a bicameral or unicameral legislature, the executive branch led by the Chief Minister of the state, and the judicial branch with a hierarchy of subordinate courts that fall under High Court of the state.

Though not one of the three branches of government, political parties are an integral part of the Indian political system. India has a multi-party system, with many parties running for open seats at the state and national levels. Though the Indian National Congress (INC) and the Bharatiya Janata Party (BJP) are the most dominant national parties currently, the past two decades have seen the government being formed by coalitions led by the INC or the BJP. There are also over sixty political parties that contest for seats at the regional levels, representing the economic, social, and cultural diversity of the country. The large number of political parties provides for an interesting collection of party symbols that are used on the ballots. Party symbols in India include a broom (Aam Aadmi Party), a rising sun (Dravida Munnetra Kazhagam), an ink pot and pen (Jammu and Kashmir People's Democratic Party), an umbrella (Sikkim Democratic Front), and a ladder (Indian Union Muslim League).

Another important component to the Indian political system is its large civil society. The 1.2 billion population and the immense diversity within India make the country a perfect petri dish for civil society. Rajesh Tandon, the founder of a leading non-governmental organization in the field of governance, Society for Participatory Research in Asia (PRIA), defines civil society as individual and organizational initiatives for the public good[36]. Tandon and Srivastava[37] note that in 2002, despite the nearly 1.2 million organizations in the non-profit sector that is an important aspect of India civil society, nearly half of them were unregistered and invisible. The various kinds of civil society organizations in India include religious and faith based networks, civil society organizations such as the National AIDS Control organization that are government-promoted, and self-help groups where individuals voluntarily contribute small amounts of money regularly to a common fund to help emergency needs of individuals in the group. Some temporary and long term social movements, corporate social responsibility initiatives, and other community based organizations also contribute to the Indian civil society.

The role of civil society in India has changed significantly before and after the implementation of economic liberalization policies. During the years of the *license raj,* civil society organizations focused on increasing the salience of certain social and environmental issues, raising awareness of these issues, and empowering socially and economically disadvantaged groups of the population. However, since the 1990s, civil society organizations not only continue to fulfill the roles they previously filled, but also emphasize the promotion of good governance, including means to increase citizen participation and transparency of government policies and procedures.

Some civil society organizations also collaborate with central and state governments to implement new and innovative programs based on research and analysis. Today, civil society in India serves to monitor the efficacy of the government at the local and national levels, advocate for various issues, collaborate with the government to formulate better policies, and to mobilize citizens to call for reforms in policies. Significant improvements in many social indicators such as disease awareness, literacy, and economic empowerment, are as much a function of civil society, if not more than, as that of government efforts.

The Thali Approach to Development

In India, *thali* (plate) is a term that is often used to refer to a meal that showcases anywhere between five and thirty side dishes from the region, along with rice and local breads. Despite many of the side dishes being very different from each other, they share at least a few common ingredients. Furthermore, the cumulative experience of the various side dishes being combined with each other and with the rice or breads is greater than each part that forms the *thali*. It is also sometimes the only way in which travelers visiting India can try a wide range of dishes representative of regional cuisine. Keeping the image of a *thali* in mind may be beneficial in understanding India's incredibly complex, diverse, and pluralistic society and development.

Given the complex circumstances of a population with at least 150 different languages, twenty-two of which are recognized as official, six major religions, vastly different political and social cultures, in its 29 states and 7 union territories, and varying state and local governance models, it is no surprise that despite vast leaps in technological and social development, the social indicators from one state to the next are starkly different. Kerala and Delhi have much higher human development than the average level of human development for India. However, Bihar and Odisha perform much worse in indicators such as life expectancy, education, and per capita income, when compared to the India averages. At any given time, India attempts to balance spurring economic and social growth, countering issues such as poverty, income inequality, and population explosion, and upholding the values of a democracy.

Many scholars of development look to the case study of Kerala as a model for social development due its achievements in social development despite relatively low per capita incomes[38]. The Kerala model of social development consists of provision of easy access to health clinics, budgetary and socio-cultural emphasis on education, and high levels of grassroots political participation. The high levels of literacy and education paired with low levels of infant mortality have inspired the Indian government and the other Indian state government to take notice and emulate the model. While the political institutions and the linguistic legacy of British colonialism continue to influence India, home-grown models of development (such as the Kerala and Gujarat) have been crucial in India's recent rise to the top.

The past decade saw higher-than-average growth rates in the state of Gujarat. The impressive economic growth in the state through what is now referred to as the Gujarat model of development has received much national and international attention, in the light of the 2014 national elections which featured the former Chief Minister of Gujarat, Narendra Modi, running a national campaign highlighting his record of improving Gujarat's economy through better governance. The Gujarat model is more focused on improving the ease of doing business by streamlining the procedures for licenses, permits, and other clearances necessary to start a business. However, this model is not focused on social development. India attempts, not always successfully, to bring together the Kerala and Gujarat models of development, for a well-balanced development that brings prosperity and potential for social mobility for all strata of India's society.

India, as we see it today, is an integrated reflection of its rich history from the Indus Valley Civilization, Maurya Empire, Mughal Empire, British colonialism, and the more than sixty years of independence. Political scientist, A.K. Somjee's (1999) description of India's development model as multilayered and integrated continues to hold true, even more so in the past sixteen years, since Somjee's original work on the Indian model of development[39]. As an important member of the G8+5 and G20 international forums, Asian Development Bank, the World Trade Organization, and

International Monetary Fund, India has been recognized as an emerging country as well as a leader and proponent of the developing countries. India's policy of not picking sides between the powerful countries and pursuing its strategic foreign relations regardless is a central element to India's developmental path. India has continued to foster its decades-long relationship with Russia despite its closer alliance with the United States and the European Union in more recent years.

Somjee discusses the theoretical implications of India, a non-Western democracy, being the largest democracy in the world. He notes that India exemplifies a mixed approach to development in that it adopted Western, liberal, legal, and political institutions, but also infused these with pragmatism, when there were incompatibilities between the structure dictated by Western models and the circumstances on the ground, given the history and culture of the country. He also highlights that India defies the Western model of development in multiple ways; by focusing on state-building, consolidation of democracy, and central planning in the four decades after independence, and gradually liberalizing since the end of the Cold War, as a response in part to the parallel growth in its Eastern and South Eastern neighbors. India defies the traditional five stages of development presented by Rostow[40] in that it had democracy not as a result of, but preceding economic take-off. However, the liberalization and growth of the economy in the past two decades have led to more political activism and demand from the educated, middle classes for anti-corruption legislation, greater transparency, and accountability of government leaders and agents, which in turn has further strengthened India's democracy.

The spread of capitalism and globalization has had very different effects in India than in countries like the United States. The high levels of competition brought about by telecommunications companies as well as ease of local and long-distance traveling within India have been greatly instrumental in stimulating upwards mobility. Indian politician and writer, Shashi Tharoor refers to the phenomenon of low-wage laborers, street vendors of owning inexpensive phones with affordable text plans as a transformation that has been crucial in the past decade of India's development[41]. Similarly, the low costs of seeking healthcare make it possible for a large majority of the population to access medical care at early symptoms of diseases, even without health insurance. This element of widespread access of technology, education, and healthcare could be seen as being at the core of the Indian model of development, allowing upward mobility for many individuals from middle and low income families.

As is often the case in newly independent countries, the government that came after India's separation from the British Empire focused on avoiding anything that might further exploit its resources. The leaders at the time, who were influenced by Fabian socialism, formulated policies that emphasized equality and protectionism. The state played an important role in the functioning and budgeting of the various industries. Centralized planning, through the Five-Year Plans, was crucial in guiding the economic and social development of the country. The *License Raj*, where every aspect of the economy was planned and controlled by the government using selective provision of licenses to private entrepreneurs and regulation of production, provided stability in the early years of independence, but eventually led to low growth rates and stunting of social development.

In 1991, in accordance with conditions laid out by International Monetary Fund to financially assist India in its time of economic crisis, the Indian government took measures to open the economy to foreign investors and competition. Though the concept of liberalization and openness of markets was part of a model of development pioneered by many developed countries, the key to the model's success in India was the country's ability to not only have the resources to manufacture the goods, but also the ability to compete in terms of quality and price on the global market. The large market that country has with its huge population and a fast-growing middle class is another advantage that India has had over many other countries that try to emulate the liberalization model. Though there is disagreement on the exact size of the middle class in India, estimates range to up to 300 million, not much smaller than the population of the entire US. The ability of many Indians to speak English also gives the country untold advantages in a fast and ever-globalizing world market. The unprecedented success of liberalization has made all national parties prioritize liberal economic policies, paired with protectionist measures in the agricultural and dairy sectors to safeguard the interests of the large percent of the workforce that is employed in the agriculture sector.

Indian citizens have been increasingly enthused and sometimes concerned with India's role as an emerging power in the world. Citizens are skeptical of the leadership of the

Indian National Congress (INC), a historic political party that continues to be one of the most important in Indian politics, being closely tied to the Gandhi family. The legacy of Jawaharlal Nehru, Indira Gandhi, and Rajiv Gandhi has continued after each of their assassinations through the INC's leadership by Sonia Gandhi, and Rahul Gandhi. The systemic corruption at every tier of government is also receiving nationwide pushback. As a result of the nationwide demand for reform of the Indian politics and bureaucracy, India has seen a rise in the number of new political parties. The competition among parties has allowed for, at least to some extent, debates over policy stances, significant reforms, and increasing accountability.

Social welfare schemes have been an important aspect of India's efforts to improve various social indicators. These welfare programs include Midday Lunch Scheme, which provides free lunch on all weekdays for students in public schools, and National Social Assistance Scheme, which provides assistance to citizens in case of unemployment, old age, sickness, and disability. The recently passed National Food Security bill provides heavily subsidized wheat and rice for families that live below the poverty line, and the Mahatma Gandhi National Rural Employment Guarantee Act guarantees a hundred days of employment each financial year to adult members of rural households. While many of these welfare programs are much-needed given the demographics and social issues of India, they often fail to reach their full potential due to lack of public awareness and existence of overlapping programs at the central and state level that are not well-coordinated. The efforts of the Indian government to provide biometric cards that allow for direct deposits to qualifying citizens of the various schemes may help improve the effectiveness of the social welfare programs, and decrease welfare fraud.

As this overview of India's social and economic development demonstrates, there are a series of factors that have contributed to India's economic development in the past few decades. Though India adopted liberalization measures, it has continued to protect certain sectors. Though the state has reduced its influence on the market in favor of laissez faire, it still continues to play a major role. The large market that the country provides for both domestic and foreign investors has also been an important component in India's rise. However, despite the high levels of economic growth, India still struggles to achieve high levels of social development.

Applications of the India Model

Given the multilayered approach to development as well as the mixed results of development in India, could the Indian model be emulated in other countries in South Asia or other parts of the world? Is the Indian model guaranteed to bring development to other low-income countries? Both of these questions are hard to answer, just as it is hard to answer questions about the applicability of any model of development. It seems plausible that low-income countries could adopt some of the elements of the Indian model of development, such as cautious and gradual liberalization, developing strategic trade and diplomatic alliances that are not severely constrained by any one partner, and utilizing human capital to push the economy forward. However, there are also aspects of the Indian model that were uniquely functional in the Indian context.

One such aspect is the 1.2 billion citizens, a large number of which serves as a huge domestic market for many products. Another element of the Indian model was the societal norm that education, especially the pursuit of degrees in engineering, medicine, or computer sciences, can serve as a ladder out of poverty. Once again, this norm, along with the large population of the country, results in large graduating classes of engineers, medical doctors, and computer scientists, and therefore, an abundance of the necessary human capital for economic and social development. In addition, consolidation of democracy in the first four decades since gaining independence gave India a stable political environment for economic development in the 1990s and after, just the reverse of usual predictions of the Western model of economic development first, and then democracy.

Given these conditions, the application of the India model to other countries in South Asia or other regions of the world, should take into consideration the unique circumstances of the country in question, and consider how the various aspects that fostered growth in India could be adapted to fit the economic, social, and cultural context of other countries. All the other countries in South Asia are significantly smaller than India. The primary sources of income of the various countries in South Asia are also very different from each other. However, India serves as a hopeful example for countries experiencing widespread corruption and poverty, that despite pervasive problems that hinder development, a country can achieve high levels of economic growth. Most importantly, the Indian model demonstrates the need for country-specific innovation when existing models have failed to bring expected development.

CHAPTER 7

THE MIDDLE EAST AND NORTH AFRICA (MENA) FRUSTRATED DEVELOPMENT

Of all the global areas of interest to us here – North America, Western Europe, Russia, Eastern Europe, East and Southeast Asia, South Asia, Latin America, and Sub-Saharan Africa – the Middle East and North Africa (MENA) has to be the most disappointing. Let us say "disappointing" rather than "failed" (although this area also has its share of failed states) because the MENA area could do so much better in terms of both democracy and development.

After all, this area of the Fertile Crescent was one of the cradles of history, it is the homeland of some of the world's greatest civilizations (Egypt, Persia, Hebrew, Assyria, Babylon, and Mesopotamia), the Garden of Eden was located here along the Tigris and Euphrates Rivers, three of the world's great religions – Judaism, Christianity, and Islam – began here, it has rich natural resources (not just oil) and an energetic, creative people, and for a long time during the West's "Dark Ages" this area was the *world's* center for philosophy, mathematics, astrology, architecture, and learning. Given this rich history and all these advantages, it is one of the world's enduring mysteries why the MENA is so troubled and why it has lagged behind not just the U.S., Western Europe, and East Asia, but also, increasingly, such other developing areas as Southeast Asia, South Asia, and Latin America. What is *wrong* with the Middle East and North Africa?

Much of the MENA is exploding in violence, revolution, chaos, terrorism, and civil war at the moment. Afghanistan, after the Americans and other NATO members left, is degenerating into violence and strife; ditto for Iraq; Syria has exploded into civil war; Yemen and Libya have become failed states; Israel and the Palestinians are at each other's throats; Egypt is under unstable rule; the chaos is spreading to heretofore hopeful Jordan and Lebanon; and the king of Saudi Arabia had just died, throwing the future of the entire Persian Gulf area into doubt. The spread of the Islamic State's territory, radical ideology, and violence has posed not only a threat to any hope of stability in the Middle East and North Africa, but to a sense of security all around the globe. Iran still has tense relations with its neighbors and many major powers. *Not one* of the Arab states has become a democracy (Turkey is a partial exception but it is not Arab) nor has the MENA modernized its society and culture as other societies and cultures have done. Something has gone radically off-track with Middle Eastern modernization and development.

For Westerners, and for the Western Model, the modern Middle East is a very difficult area to comprehend and come to grips with. Very few of the theories and concepts that we use to study comparative politics and international relations work out as expected there. The Middle East is full of riddles, anomalies, mysteries, and puzzles. The correlations that are supposed to help us understand when democracy emerges do not correlate very well; the causative factors that are supposed to explain social change and modernization often in this area carry little causative explanatory power. In short, it is hard for Westerners and their social science models to penetrate and comprehend the Middle East or to draw any hard-and-fast conclusions from it.

Not only do our usual social science models not apply there very well, but our international relations literature is not up to the task either. We only weakly, if at all, understand the rage and violence sweeping the Middle East, and we are still not able to answer the question posed after the terror attacks of 9/11/2001: "Why do they hate us so?"

More than that, and rather like Russia and China, much of the Middle East rejects the Western notion of world order, like these others seeing the present international system as a reflection of U.S. hegemony which the Middle East cannot accept. Indeed, the Middle East and North Africa seem intent on establishing *their own* system of global relations with their own region at the forefront. On both the domestic development level and at the level of foreign policy, the Middle East is determined to go its own way. And yet, and yet . . ., even with all the upheaval in the Middle East in recent years there are hopeful signs both of broad-scale development and social modernization, *and* that some countries at least are ready to take their place in the modern global scheme of things.

Here, preliminarily, are just a few of the anomalies, ironies, questions, and paradoxes with which we begin our analysis of the MENA countries:

- Israel, the Jewish state, is the only fully modern and Western-oriented country in the entire Middle East and the only one that is both developed and democratic. Israel's per-capita income, viewed comparatively, is about at a Spain or Portugal level.

- Turkey is the only mostly democratic country in the Islamic Middle East, and it is not an Arab country.

- The richest countries in the Middle East – Bahrain, Kuwait, Qatar, Saudi Arabia, and the United Arab Emirates (UAE) – are all autocracies; there is no correlation between wealth and democracy.

- These same five countries are also the most literate, best educated, and most urban; according to S. M. Lipset and an entire *library* full of Western social science, they should be the most democratic. But, as above, they are not.

- The Middle East and North Africa these days seem to be consumed by violence and terrorism. But is that true, or is it just confined to a few countries?

- Of all world areas, the MENA seems to be the *least* successful in securing either democracy or development. Why is that? Is it culture, history, society, politics, resources, geography, religion, or colonialism? What? Does the Middle East even *want* U.S. or European-style democracy?

- Much of the Middle East appears to reject Western culture and civilization. Will we begin to see an *Islamic model* of change and development alternative to the Western one? And what are the implications of *that*?

- In the conflict between the Islamic Middle East and the West, will we be, or are we already, seeing the beginnings of Huntington's *Clash of Civilizations*? Are the West and the Islamic countries fated for conflict?

- Should we give up on the MENA countries? Are they hopelessly antagonistic to us and we to them? Where do hope and possibility lie?
- If there is such a thing as an Islamic or Middle Eastern model of development, what would such a model look like? Will it look like theocratic Iran, more democratic Turkey, Monarchist Jordan, or traditionalist Saudi Arabia?
- Can anything be done to stem the current violence in the Middle East? Is violence and bloodshed endemic in Islamic culture and society, or can it be dealt with and resolved as modernization goes forward?

Clearly, as we examine the Middle East, there are numerous interesting themes to discuss. Let us try to make some sense of it all.

Background and Political Culture

What we now call the Middle East or the MENA has a very long history. Some of these countries and civilizations – the Egyptian, the Hebrew, the Cretan, the Assyrian, the Babylonian, the Persian (Iran) – go back six and seven *thousand* years. Compared to the United States (the first "New Nation," only 240 years old), these are ancient, often proud civilizations who resent being called "emerging," "developing," or "Third World" nations.

Indeed, it could be said, with all due respect to China which claims to be first in everything, that civilization, even modern and Western civilization, began here, in that arc, usually called the Fertile Crescent, that begins along the northern Nile River in Egypt, sweeps northward up the fertile, coastal area of present-day Israel and Lebanon west of the Jordan River, then around to the east and southeasterly down the fertile valleys of the Euphrates and Tigris Rivers until they join at Basra, Iraq, and empty into the Persian Gulf. It is here that the Garden of Eden is supposed to be located; from which Abraham, the father of all three monotheistic religions (Judaism, Christianity, and Islam) emerged; and in which some of the world's first and greatest civilizations developed. Long before "the West" (Europe and North America) was settled and civilized, this area circling around the west, north, and east (check your maps) of the Arabian desert was a thriving, booming, advanced set of early civilizations.

These civilizations were almost constantly at war with each other and with outside, invading powers. The area that we now think of as Israel/Palestine was the setting for most of these wars. Invading Egyptian armies came from the south up the coastal plain that is present-day Israel, while invading Phoenician, Assyrian, Babylonian, Syrian, and other armies came from the north and east; they met in Palestine. Meanwhile, from the West, Macedonia, came the army of Alexander the Great who conquered the entire Fertile Crescent and drove his army all the way into India, while from the east came Nebuchadnezzar, from Babylon, and Darius the Great from Persia. These conquering, marauding armies devastated the lands they fought over while simultaneously providing the spark and the innovation that got modernization and civilization in the Middle East started.

Two thousand years ago Christianity began in the Middle East with the birth, preaching, and miracles of Jesus of Nazareth. In the next three hundred years, Christianity spread throughout the Roman Empire, around the Mediterranean, and around the Fertile Crescent and all the way to India, eventually becoming the official religion of the Empire and giving rise to those sizable Christian communities throughout the Middle East that struggle to survive under Muslim domination even today. By this time the knowledge and philosophy of Greece, carried initially by Alexander, had spread to the Middle East; under Roman rule the center of gravity in world power and domination shifted away from the Fertile Crescent and toward the West.

In 570 A.D. there occurred one of those historic events, the birth of the Prophet Mohammed, that would forever powerfully influence the entire Middle East. The Prophet's teachings and converts were initially limited to his home towns of Mecca and Medina on the Red Sea side of today's Saudi Arabia; in the next decades they spread throughout the vast Arabian Peninsula. But in the following centuries the Islamic beliefs spread like wildfire throughout the entire Middle East and eastward to today's Pakistan, Bangladesh, and India (India, with over 170 million Muslims out of a population of 1.2 billion, has the world's largest number of Muslims), then down and throughout the Malay Peninsula, and reaching all the way to Indonesia, the world's largest Majority-Muslim nation and the southern Philippines. Westerly, the Islamic tide carried along the entire coast of North Africa, thus encompassing Egypt, Libya, Tunisia, Algeria, and Morocco, and carrying across the Straits of

Gibraltar to encompass for seven centuries Spain, Portugal, and the southwest of France.

As Turks from Central Asia migrated west into and conquered Asia Minor, they adopted the religion of the people they conquered (usually it's the other way around: the conquered adopt the religion of the conquerors), and in the ensuing centuries the Turks, or Ottomans, spread Islam northward into the Caucuses and southern Russia, northeastward back into the Central Asian countries (Kazakhstan, Turkestan, Uzbekistan, Kyrgyzstan, and Tajikistan) from which they had come and even into Western China, and northwesterly into the Balkans (Bulgaria, Romania, Greece, Serbia, Bosnia, Albania, Montenegro, Kosovo, and Hungary) and all the way northward to the gates of Vienna where the Muslim thrust was eventually blunted and then reversed. These vast conquests, incidentally, explain why in southeastern Europe we still find small, Majority-Muslim countries (Albania, Bosnia, and Kosovo) not yet admitted – in part because they are Muslim – into the ranks of the EU or NATO.

As Islam expanded over the centuries and became institutionalized, Muslim culture also crystallized. By the twelfth century A.D., when Western Europe was still locked in the Dark Ages, Islamic culture was flourishing. In art, architecture, music, science, mathematics, philosophy, and astrology, the Islamic world was way ahead of the West. We sometimes forget that during almost the entire thousand-ear length of the Middle Ages when Aristotle, Plato, and Greek philosophy were completely lost to the West, the Arab world had rediscovered, translated, and was reading the Greek classics. It is one of the great wonders of early modern development why this initial lead by the Islamic world in culture and the sciences was lost while the West, which started later, flourished and passed the Arab world by.

Meanwhile, Turkish tribes from Central Asia had begun invading the Middle East. Over the course of three or four centuries, these Turkish tribes moved across Iran, Iraq, and Syria before settling in Asia Minor – present-day Turkey. The Turkish or Ottoman Empire was vast, reaching northward into Russia, southerly into the Arabian Peninsula, and westerly into southeastern Europe. The Turks, curiously, adopted the Islamic religion of the peoples they conquered, although it needs to be emphasized – and it is one of the basic splits in the Middle East – that the Turks are not Arabs and that the two groups or ethnicities, despite their common faith, do not always get along well together. While flourishing at first, the Turkish Ottoman Empire also failed to modernize and reform itself. Known as "the sick man of Europe," the Ottoman Empire went into long-term decline and eventually disintegrated in World War I.

While the Ottoman Empire was on its back and in decline, the European colonial powers – France and Great Britain principally – were busily carving up the carcass. France took much of the Levant – present-day Lebanon, Syria, and for a time Egypt – while Great Britain controlled Iraq, Afghanistan, also Egypt for a time, Palestine, and the major sea routes. European colonialism did not develop or modernize the Middle East; instead, it provided a way for the European powers to advance their economic, trade, and security interests, especially after the completion of the Suez Canal connecting the Mediterranean and Red Seas in 1869.

When they left after World War I, the colonial powers divided the Middle East artificially into the countries that we see today: Jordan, Iraq, Syria, Lebanon, Palestine, Saudi Arabia, and the Gulf States. Few of these borders have anything to do with the realities of tribal, ethnic, or even geographic divisions within the area. In this sense, the Middle East is similar to Africa after the colonial powers withdrew following World War II: Artificial borders, unreflective of local tribal or ethnic realities, and creating new nations that were completely unviable. That is why some current analysts are predicting that, with the Middle East today in crisis and ISIS marauding across borders, we are likely to see in the next few years a complete re-drawing of the borders of the entire region.[42]

As the colonial powers pulled out of the area, most of the Middle East was left under the control of kings or the newly created national armies. In Egypt, after a fifty-year period of monarchy and a British protectorate, the military took power to ensure order and stability. The United States and the Western Alliance aided and abetted these armed forces dictatorships because, in the midst of the Cold War, they offered not just stability but also anti-communism in a region known for its volatility. Or else, the West worked out agreements, in Saudi Arabia, Kuwait, and the Persian Gulf states, to support the ruling families, sultans, or kings in return for oil. In Iran, it was the dictatorship of the Shah that we supported as part of the same Cold War calculation.

These military-authoritarian regimes remained in power for years, even decades. In some countries they were challenged and even overthrown by civilian Baathist (Islamic socialist) political movements and parties, but the Baathists often proved as corrupt, as undemocratic, and as ineffective as their military predecessors. Nor did these regimes, the authoritarians, the monarchies, or the Baathists, do much to stimulate Middle Eastern development and modernization. Indeed, during this entire period from the 1950s to the present, the Muslim Middle East continued to lag behind not just the West but now Asia as well. In most countries but especially those without oil, the reaction was frustration, disappointment, and anger.

That brings us up to the present and the angry, frustrated, disappointed, failed, and self-absorbed Middle East that we find today. Middle East scholars, religious leaders, government officials, and the general public are all debating the questions of where did we go wrong, what is wrong with us as a people and nation, why have we lagged behind, why did the West and other areas pass us by, what can we do about our under-development and lack of democracy, what model will work for us? Is it to be the Iranian model of the mullahs, the Turkish democratic model, military dictatorship, Russia, China, what?

Here are some of the questions that come to mind as we think about this past history as well as the current political culture of the MENA countries:

1. Is there something in the *Koran* or in Islamic culture that has prevented democracy from emerging in the area?

2. Why does the MENA lag behind other areas in terms of economic development?

3. As social change (rising literacy, urbanization, middle classness) goes forward, will the MENA

countries also undertake a transition to democracy as in the Rostow/Western model? Why or why not?

4. What should be done about the current wave of violence and terrorism in the Islamic community? Is this inherent in Islam or are there other causes?

5. The *Koran* prohibits usury, which has been interpreted to mean it also prohibits interest. Is this prohibition a hindrance to MENA economic growth; how have countries of the region gotten around this prohibition to justify Islamic banks, insurance, and financial institutions?

6. The *Koran* tends to justify authoritarian and top-down government; could the same flexible reinterpretations that are used to justify banking now also be used to justify democracy?

7. The Islamic world is not monolithic; be prepared to discuss differences between countries and within the Muslim community. What percentages within that community are peaceful, "normal" citizens, versus the percentage that sympathize with, or may participate in, terrorism?

8. Do Muslims assimilate into other countries and cultures as well as other groups? Stick to the facts but answer: why or why not?

9. What is the future, or the future model, for the MENA? Does it lie in Turkey, in Iran, in Tunisia, in Saudi Arabia, or Egypt; or, alternatively, does it lie in breakdown à la Yemen, Syria, Libya, Iraq, or Afghanistan?

Socioeconomic Overview

Part of the problem of the Middle East are the huge disparities in wealth and poverty. These immense disparities are present both between countries and within countries. It is one of the key reasons why resentments and anger in the MENA are so high.

Take a look again at Table 7.1. Countries such as Afghanistan, Eritrea, Sudan, and Yemen are among the poorest countries in the world. The bulk of their people must eke out a meager, often starvation existence on only a few dollars per day. On the other hand, Bahrain, Kuwait, Qatar, Saudi Arabia, and the United Arab Emirates (UAE) are among the richest in the world, with their wealth based almost exclusively on oil. It is sometimes said that the main dividing line in the Middle East is not the religious one of Sunni-Shia but between those countries that are oil-rich and those that are oil-poor. And that is not very far from the truth.

In addition to these between-country differences, there are also within-country differences. Along with Latin America, the Middle East is the region with the widest gaps between rich and poor. Take note of the five wealthy countries listed above: *all* are monarchies. The royal families in these countries live very well, enjoying a level of opulence (palaces, cars, diamonds, and bank accounts) that is almost unimaginable to the rest of the world. These are all large, extended families where the numbers of princes and princelings and their families may number in the hundreds, if not thousands. Often these princelings get in trouble, drink too much, live too high, cause scandals, and are a disgrace to their own families. In *all five* of these super-rich oil sheikdoms, there is often deep, simmering resentment toward not just these wastrel princes but toward the royal family in general. Some serious social scientists have predicted that in the long run all these quasi-feudal, Gulf-oil sheikdoms are doomed to revolution and overthrow.

TABLE 7.1
THE MIDDLE EAST AND NORTH AFRICA
(MENA) POPULATION AND GDP PER CAPITA[43]

Country	Population (in millions)	Per-capita Income
Afghanistan	31.6	1,933
Algeria	38.9	14,193
Bahrain	1.4	45,500
Djibouti	0.9	3,270
Egypt	89.6	10,533
Eritrea	5.1	NA
Iran	78.1	17,303
Iraq	34.8	15,057
Israel	8.2	33,703
Jordan	6.6	12,050
Kuwait	3.8	73,246
Lebanon	4.6	17,462
Libya	6.3	15,597
Morocco	33.9	7,490
Oman	4.2	38,630
Qatar	2.2	140,649
Saudi Arabia	30.9	52,010
Somalia	10.5	NA

Sudan	39.4	4,069
Syria`	22.2	NA
Tunisia	11	11,436
Turkey	75.9	19,788
United Arab Emirates (UAE)	9.1	67,674
Yemen	26.2	3,785

Source: World Development Indicators, The World Bank

It is not just their own lower classes, Bedouins, and others who are resentful, but also the many foreign workers that these countries have imported to do manual labor: construction, garbage collection, street-cleaning, custodial, and service work in general. It is not well known that the population of countries like the UAE consists of 80 percent foreign workers – Filipinos, Indians, Pakistanis, Bangladeshis, Indonesians, etc. These foreign workers earn high salaries – that is why they are there – but they cannot bring their families along, they live in poor conditions in desert barracks, they are completely isolated from the local population, and they have *no possibilities* of ever acquiring citizenship. No "path to citizenship" here. Instead, they work in the rich Gulf states for five or ten ears, build up a nest egg, and then go back eventually to their home countries to marry and start a life. They also, as well as the locals, harbor deep resentments toward the ruling families in their "host" countries. It may not be possible in these Gulf monarchies to maintain a viable country if you exclude 80 percent of the population from any participation in the national life.

The ruling families of these countries recognize these festering resentments and have taken steps to relieve them. For the foreign workers, they provide high salaries and extremely close police supervision and the right to expel from the country anyone who steps out of line or commits the most minor infraction. For the local population, the main strategy of these regimes is to provide rich benefits to head off the possibilities of rebellion: free education, free health care, a free apartment once you marry, and a yearly subsidy that may range up to $50,000 or more. If you are a Saudi or an Emirati, you can work if you wish but you will do so only at non-hand-labor or civil service jobs, hand-labor being too demeaning. Why would anyone revolt against a government that gives you so many benefits? The oil-rich states have effectively bought off both their foreign workers and their domestic populations, thus heading off the possibilities for revolution while diversifying their economies away from oil.

Only countries that are extremely wealthy – the five listed above – can afford to play this kind of peace-through-wealth distribution and cooptation game. The other, poorer countries cannot afford this luxury. However, their populations demand the same kind of benefits as the rich countries and their governments seek to put pressure on the wealthy oil kingdoms to share the wealth with them. If they do not, it breeds both domestic and regional resentments.

Look again at the numbers for those five rich countries: Bahrain, Kuwait, Qatar, Saudi Arabia, and the UAE. The first three of these far surpass the U.S., Western Europe, and the Asian Tigers in per-capita income, and Qatar is one of the richest countries in the world. Saudi Arabia and the UAE are at high European (Scandinavia) levels. All five of these are also highly literate and urban societies. In other words, by most of the criteria used in the social sciences, these are modern societies. Yet *none* of them is a democracy. Nor have any of them even *begun* the process of or the transition to democracy.

The conclusion we must draw is that the correlation and even causation that all the early scholars of development posited – Lipset, Rostow, Almond, et al. – between social modernization, economic development, and democracy are, in the Middle East, not correlating at all. In fact, one can say that these rich countries are among the *least* democratic in the entire MENA. Only two conclusions are possible from this: either our usual social science models don't apply in the Middle East environment, or else there is something radically wrong with the Middle East countries that they are able to defy the usual trajectories – economic development to social change to democracy – of developing countries. Or maybe both of these.

As we move down the scale from wealthiest to least wealthy in the Middle East, the correlations do not get any better. Additionally, there is a sharp drop-off from the rich oil states at over $50,000 per capita to the next country, Turkey, at $20,500[44]. Turkey is a democracy, for the most part, but it also has autocratic tendencies. It is probably the country in the Middle East, but remember it is also non-Arab, that comes closest to the Western model: traditionalism and quasi-feudalism give way in the 1920s-1930s to a Western but authoritarian government, which gives rise to vast social change, which over time produces a more or less democratic state. But still only partially so and, in 2016, seemingly moving back to a less democratic and more Islamic model.

Quite a number of countries – Algeria, Egypt, Iran, Iraq, Jordan, Lebanon, and Tunisia – are clustered in a bloc just below Turkey in which the per-capita income is between $10,000 and $17,000 per year. Using the Rostow-Lipset model of national modernization and development, one would expect these countries to be, like Turkey several decades ago, at least *beginning* the transition to democracy. But Algeria has been battered by violence and instability over the last sixty years, Egypt had a revolution and then a military coup, Iran is a theocracy, Iraq is consumed by civil war, Jordan is a monarchy but has a parliament with limited powers, Lebanon is strife-torn and has gone backwards from the emerging democracy of forty years ago, Tunisia is just emerging from a long dictatorship, and Yemen is in chaos, a failed state. *None* of these provides a good example of the Western model although, if you're an optimist, you may find hopeful prospects in Egypt, Jordan, and Tunisia.

The bottom tier of countries includes Afghanistan, Djibouti, Eritrea, Morocco, the Sudan, and Yemen. Some of these countries are in northeast Africa but they have *large* Muslim populations and are often considered part of the MENA. None of these countries has oil. None, except perhaps Morocco, a monarchy, has even begun to put in place the infrastructure for development, although in *all* of them the first stirrings of social modernization – greater literacy, urbanization, and social change – are beginning to take place. None of these is a democracy nor have we even begun to see the stirrings of a democratic transition. All these countries, again Morocco excepted, plus the others for which we have no data – Libya, Somalia, and Syria – are closer to the "Failed State" category than they are to the "Successful Development" category.

With the possible exception of Turkey, there are no examples of the success of the Western development or democratization model in the Middle East. Of the countries that are the most economically successful – Bahrain, Kuwait, Oman, Qatar, Saudi Arabia, and the UAE – *none* of them is a democracy. Nor do they show any signs of moving in that direction. They have used cooptation as well as repression to keep their populations in check. Meantime, as we move farther down the scale of development, few if any of these countries show signs of following the Western path either. It is clear that the Western development model has little applicability in the MENA except in very limited ways and in very few (five or six out of twenty-four) cases.

Meanwhile, Iran has sought to fill this space with its own Islamic Model of development. The Iranian-Islamic Model includes: (1) a theocratic state ultimately controlled by the mullahs or Islamic holy men; (2) strict controls on civil and political rights in accord with Islamic principles; (3) a top-down and authoritarian political system under civilian rule but ultimately responsible to the religious leadership; (5) state regulation and control of the bulk of the economy – Islamic state capitalism; (6) the Shia version of Islam – i.e., rule by those who are *direct descendants* of the Prophet Mohammed; and (7) Iranian nationalism and cultural pride which goes back thousands of years to Persian civilization.

Until recently, Iran has had difficulty expanding its model to other nearby countries. But now, with the U.S. pulling out of Afghanistan and Iraq, with Syria in chaos, a Shiite movement bidding for power in Yemen, large Shia minorities in Bahrain, Qatar, and Saudi Arabia, and weak

Oman and the UAE only forty miles away across the Persian Gulf, Iran thinks that this may be its moment.

The trouble with Iran's strategy, however, is that, first of all, while it is a good-sized country of seventy-seven million, it is not big enough or powerful enough to dominate an entire continent or subcontinent – although Iran's development of nuclear weapons could change all that – the way China or India do. Second, Iran has yet to convince the Muslim world, let alone such other big, majority-Islamic countries as Egypt, Indonesia, Pakistan, Turkey, or Bangladesh, that *its* Islamic model is the one that all Muslim countries must follow. And third, before Iran can reconstruct the grand Persian – but now Islamic – empire of Darius the Great, stretching all the way from Egypt and the Mediterranean Sea to India and Central Asia, it must contend not just with other powers in the region – e.g., Saudi Arabia is armed to the teeth – but also with the U.S. fleet which with its immense firepower continues to patrol the Persian Gulf, the Red Sea, and *all* the countries of the region.

We will return to this possibility of an Iranian or more broadly Islamic Model, at both the domestic and international levels, later in the book.

And yet, and yet . . . travels around the Middle East demonstrate vast social, if not yet political, changes underway. Understand, we are talking here not of the strife-torn countries of North Africa, Afghanistan, Iraq, Syria, Lebanon, or Yemen, but of the more stable countries of the Persian Gulf. Perhaps surprising to many, that list also includes Iran. In all these countries literacy is rising, wealth is increasing, urbanization is accelerating, modernization is going forward, and women are taking their rightful place in society. A strong middle-class has emerged, prosperity is widespread, the housing is excellent, and people shop and spend money at the many malls just like you or I. People go to work, ride the metro, and worry about their families; in short, even in some of the most rigidly closed and authoritarian *political systems* of the Middle East, vast economic and social changes are nevertheless going forward.

These *facts* should prompt us to be more cautious and guarded about our assessments and predictions for the MENA. These are more complex, ambiguous, and mixed societies than our television coverage usually portrays. While the Middle East has more than its share of terrorists and suicide bombers, the vast majority of people are seeking to live their lives, go to work, and raise their families. While political development and democratization are often stymied, economic development and social modernization are going forward so rapidly that they may ultimately *force* political change as well. At the least, we should recognize the unpredictability of current Middle East events and try to understand the area within its own dynamics: old societies breaking apart, new ones being formed, accompanied by both violence and anti-Westernism, on the one hand, and by moderation, modernization and – perhaps most surprisingly – Westernization on the other.

Government Institutions and the Role of the State

At present, there are four types of governments, or regimes, in the MENA: absolute monarchies, theocracies, struggling and uncertain governments, and countries in varying degrees of chaos or breakdown: Failed States. Israel is the only stable, settled democracy in the entire area, and it is obviously a special case.

The absolute monarchies include Bahrain, Jordan (but with a parliament), Kuwait, Morocco, Qatar, Saudi Arabia, and the United Arab Emirates (of which there are seven, held together in an economic, political, and security federation). Absolute monarchies – the category includes kingdoms, emirates, and sultanates – are opaque: it is hard to see into them and, because they are "absolute," that makes them even harder to penetrate. These regimes are ruled by a single, but usually large, ruling family, who govern through the use of retainers, a small bureaucracy, patronage, and a strong military.

Remember that absolute monarchy was one of Max Weber's forms of traditional authority; it is based not necessarily on merit but on inherited power and wealth. Recall also Prof. Anwar Syed's prognostication more than fifty years ago that "in the long run all these Middle Eastern sheikdoms are doomed." On the other hand, that was before the skyrocketing price of oil enabled these regimes to not just survive but also to prosper, modernize at some levels (but not politically), diversity their economies away from oil, and even become globalized. So the jury is still out on these absolute monarchies and their ability to survive; but most likely they do not constitute a "model" for the other countries. Absolute monarchy is probably a thing of the past, able to hang on for some time as long as the oil keeps flowing, but likely to give way eventually as the pressures of social change, modernization, and for democracy continue their relentless course.

Iran, since 1979 and the overthrow of another monarchy, that of the Shah, is the only theocracy in the region. The *mullahs* or Islamic religious leaders rule through a largely civilian government and public administration, and they even hold regular elections; but it is the clerics who have final judgment. They rule in accord with the *Koran* and *Sharia* law; the country is called, formally, the *Islamic Republic* of Iran. In some other countries, the mullahs are powerful behind the scenes, ISIS would likely want to establish a similar theocracy but we still don't know the outcome of its efforts.

The Iranian Revolution of 1979 attracted widespread attention initially. It was thought in some quarters that here at last was an Islamic model and answer to the West, to (then) Soviet and Chinese communism, and to the East Asian model of development. So, there would now be an Islamic form of government, an Islamic social science as distinct from the West, and an Islamic model of development.[45] But after nearly forty years of rule by the mullahs, the Iranian model – closed, religious, authoritarian, intolerant, top-down, and theocratic – looks less attractive, both to outsiders and to its own people. On the other hand, Iranian foreign policy and influence in today's turbulent Middle East appear to be making enormous headway in such countries as Afghanistan, Iraq, Syria, Lebanon, Yemen, and the sheikdoms of the Persian Gulf. Unfortunately for Iran, it is not big enough or powerful enough (but what if it gets nuclear weapons?) to be a regional hegemon able to dominate all of the Middle East.

A third category is that of struggling, uncertain, possibly unstable states. This category includes Algeria, Jordan,

Lebanon, Egypt, Oman, Tunisia, and possibly even Turkey. But Turkey is at the high end of this group – modernizing, *mainly* democratic, with emphasis on the "mainly" – while Tunisia looks hopeful at present and Jordan has the advantage of a relatively stable monarchy. But the entire MENA is so uncertain and unstable these days that any or all of these countries could be caught up in the whirlwind.

The final category is countries in varying degrees of chaos, civil war, and violence possibly leading to failed states. In this category, we need to put Afghanistan, Iraq, Syria, Libya, and Yemen: countries that have fragmented, broken down, and are virtually ungovernable. Unfortunately, there are quite a number of these chaotic or failed regimes in the MENA; and quite a number of those countries in the previous group could rather easily fall down into this category. When a country is in the Failed State category, it usually means that all efforts at democratization and economic development are largely hopeless until other, even bigger issues are settled. You can't build democracy or lure investment in the midst of revolution, civil war, and chaos. It also means, when a country breaks down into chaos or civil war, that it is useless to talk of distinct *models* of development. Only when the existing civil war is resolved or the underlying causes of chaos dealt with can the country resume the dialogue of what model (or models) is best for it.

Note that in this discussion of the MENA countries we have so far said nothing about the form or *institutions* of government: parliamentary versus presidential systems, unitary or federal, etc. Of course, a country must eventually get its laws and constitution correct and establish the rule of law. But the Middle East is, in the main, not at that stage yet, as America or Western Europe are, where the debate is limited chiefly to institutional issues. No, the Middle East is consumed by more fundamental, even existential, questions than that: war, revolution, chaos, civil strife, and regime survival. In this sense, the MENA countries are much like Latin America forty and fifty years ago, similarly consumed by civil wars, revolutions, military coups, and chaos.

When the issues are as deep, fundamental, and existential as that, talk of whether to have a parliamentary or a presidential system is premature and beside the point. Fortunately, Latin America over time resolved this existential or "system" problem in favor of democracy; but the Middle East is not yet in a position (and may still be deteriorating even further) where it can begin to worry about what seem to be these lesser problems. For the record, however, given the Middle East's current disintegrative, fragmenting, and unraveling tendencies, it is likely that a presidential system, with strong centralizing and authoritative power, is the most likely and the most appropriate form of government.

It hardly needs saying, then, that in this uncertain context courts in the Middle East, parliaments, or congresses, the rule of law, the judicial system, police and law enforcement, and public security tend to be weak. These are usually viewed as secondary problems as compared to the larger existential issues mentioned earlier of war, conflict, and regional survival. It would be nice if foreign aid, human rights, and other reform-minded groups could work on all these issues at once and look forward to gradual, incremental development on all fronts, but unfortunately much of the MENA is so torn by strife that not only can such a Western-style reform agenda not go forward under today's conditions, but it is often dangerous and even deadly for practitioners to talk about or lobby for them.

There is a sharp split between those countries struggling for Western-style reform and those struggling to implement their own forms of Sharia law. The issue is freighted with importance because it relates to even larger issues of whether the Middle East can develop its own, indigenous form of government, independent of Western models. In this quest for local, home-grown solutions, the modern Middle East is not unlike Russia, China, East Asia, India, and others similarly looking for their own workable model. Or else, seeking to blend imported Western ways with their own indigenous cultures and ways of doing things.

In this search for a unique, Middle East-based plan for governance and development, the *Koran*, *Sharia* law, and a theory of the Islamic state and society will have to be involved. If your idea is that human rights, civil liberties, and democratic governance are all universal and that they of necessity must take a Western form, this idea of an Islamic model of the state will be disconcerting. Today, Iran is the main example of an Islamic theocratic state, a regime whose practices leave many of us uncomfortable. But countries such as Egypt, Saudi Arabia, Jordan, and Turkey are also, each in its own way, experimenting with ways to import the best of Western practices while also preserving their own traditions and cultures. Whatever the outcome of these quests, few of the MENA countries, given the immense cultural differences between them and the West, are *ever* likely to mirror exactly the Western model.

Much the same applies to considerations of civil society. Historically, civil society in the MENA consisted of the *mullahs* (religious leaders), the *bazaari* (small businessmen and commercial elements), and rural Bedouin or tribal leaders. Periodically, the king or emir would venture out into the desert to consult with the tribal leaders, to receive their petitions, and to grant their requests or act on them expeditiously. This consultative process, which we came to know in Afghanistan as the *Loya Jirga*, has elements of democracy in it – Islamic "democracy."

As modernization (rising literacy, greater urbanization, economic development, an organized working class, and a new middle-class) has gone forward in the Middle East, civil society in the Middle East has become more differentiated and complicated. Alongside the traditional religious leaders, bazaari, Bedouins, etc., there are now labor unions, business associations, professional groups, farmers' associations, and others. Strikingly, however, since it runs so contrary to the Western world, the impact of these new groups has not necessarily been toward greater pluralism and democracy. Instead, governments and ruling elites in the MENA countries have moved toward greater corporatism. That is, official, government-controlled or closely regulated civil society and tied in with the state.[46]

In opting for the corporatist solution and form of state-society relations, many of the MENA countries – those that are not in chaos and still have a functioning system of governance – are not all that far away from how Russia, China, East Asia, and other developing countries are dealing with modernization. If that is indeed a global trend – and we have first encountered it as a global phenomenon in this book – it begins to validate our original hypothesis that in much of the world the Western liberal-pluralist-democratic model is in decline even while other culture areas and countries are beginning to devise their own ways of dealing with modernity.

An Islamic Model?

Today's Middle East appears to be enveloped in chaos, bloodshed, civil war, and violence. Or at least that is the image that is conveyed on our television screens. We tend to view the MENA countries as not very successful with development (except for oil) and certainly not successful with democracy. And we shake our heads in wonder and horror at the beheadings, the stoning, the cutting off of hands, and the burnings of persons while still alive. What kinds of societies are these, we ask; where are the elements of civilization?

It is not our purpose here to refute that image of a violent Middle East. The violence of today is a major component of MENA society, politics, and even culture. Nevertheless, two points are worth noting. First, not all of the Middle East is locked into this pattern of violence. In this sense, our television and news coverage distorts because that is dramatic, attention-getting, and riveting.

But, in fact, violence is not the only thing that is happening in the Islamic world. Actually, in most countries and communities of the MENA, people go to work, they raise their families, they struggle to get ahead, life goes on. Meanwhile, at a broader level, societies as well as individual circumstances are changing, modernization and globalization are going forward, prosperity is spreading, a new middle-class is emerging. Such changes are going on all over the world; the Middle East, though presently more torn apart and violent, is *not all that different* from other societies undergoing rapid, even revolutionary change. Older and more traditional societies are being challenged and torn apart, while new ones are beginning to emerge. It is not at all unusual – think of the French revolution or the U.S. Civil War – that violence accompanies this process.

The second thing to say is that, out of all this violence, tumult, and change, a new Middle East is beginning to emerge. That is difficult to comprehend in the midst of all the chaos, and it is by no means certain what the final outcome will be. Nevertheless, if we go beneath the surface of violence, beheadings, and conflict, we can begin to discern a new order. This Middle East will not look like the one that went before or that exists today. At the same time, we must recognize the realities: that it will not bear much resemblance to the preferred U.S. model of development either.

The main ingredients in this new model of the Middle East (leaving aside those states that are in complete fragmentation and breakdown – failed states) will be the following:

1. States in which Islam will be at the core of their religion, politics, and culture. Unlike in the West, modernization in the Middle East has not led to either secularism or religious pluralism. Instead, the Middle East demonstrates that a person can be both modern and religious at the same time, without a contradiction between the two. We should, therefore, not expect that the American/

European concept of the separation of church and state will take hold in the MENA. Rather, state, society, politics, culture, *everything* will continue to be infused by Islam. The great question, of course, is which type of Islam will prevail: Shia, Sunni, Saudi Wahhabism, or ISIS fundamentalism? The answer: *all* of these competing for dominance, sometimes peacefully, other times violently.

2. In the political sphere, we will continue to see a variety of states: kingships, sultanates, military governments, theocracies, and probably a few democracies. But in all of these there will be some common features: strong government often verging on authoritarianism, top-down rule, strong states with weak civil societal organizations, and, if democracy, then centralized, limited, illiberal democracy.

3. The economic realm will follow from the political. And that means mainly statist or state-capitalist economies. The state will make most major economic decisions, not the marketplace or individual entrepreneurs. These statist regimes will not look all that different from those in Russia, East Asia, or Latin America. The main political-economic models will not at all look like the U.S. system of democracy, free markets, and pluralism.

4. Society in the Middle East will continue to modernize. That may be surprising to some readers given the chaos enveloping the region that we see on television every night. Modernization – rising literacy, urbanization, economic development,

growing middle-classness, and education (including for women) – will go forward despite the violence and sometimes even because of it, in the sense that the violence may uproot peoples and villages from their traditional ways and drag them whether willing or not into the modern world. More and more people will be educated, will shop at big malls, will acquire cars and appliances, will try like the rest of us to make a better life for themselves and their children.

But here, as in the political and economic realms, the state will again be a major, dominating presence. As modernization goes forward, the state will try to capture, coopt, and control these changes by creating official, state-controlled associations for all these new groups: the working-class, farmers, and the middle-class. This is called corporatism: not pluralism as we know it but societal groups submissive to the state. And, of course, the effort of the state to monopolize and control societal activity will lead in some countries to a real tug-of-war between the state seeking to control everything and societal groups trying to preserve their independence. Sometimes this tug-of-war may produce real pluralism and even democracy, but usually only for a short period of time; more commonly corporatism produces authoritarianism.

5. The Middle East will continue to feel the pressures of, and seek to adapt to, globalization. Already, mainly in Turkey, the Persian Gulf, and North Africa (just across the Mediterranean from wealthy

Western Europe and the EU), the globalization of trade, business, banking, airline connections, tourism, commerce, finance, and even education (as U.S. and European universities establish branches there) is well underway. In these countries and regions, we have a fascinating paradox: even as they seem to reject the West and Western influences at some levels, they embrace Western culture and ways of doing things – Western dress, Western sports, Western television and movies, Western travel, Western hotels, and others. This is another tug-of-war that will continue: the desire to distance itself from Western ways and preserve its own Islamic religion and culture, on the one hand, and the wish to embrace and be like the West (wealthy, powerful, and even democratic), on the other.

6. The Middle East is ambivalent about the modern world system. On the one hand, we have Iran, ISIS, and the followers of their positions in many other MENA countries who reject the Western system (North America, Europe, and Japan) of world order and believe it is contrary to the interests both of their countries and of Islam. On the other, we have countries like Jordan, Lebanon, Tunisia, Morocco, probably Egypt, the UAE, and others who desire the West's (NATO, the U.S.) protective security umbrella and see that their peace, stability, and possibilities for development all depend on maintaining, with some adjustments, the present global system. Finally, there are countries like Turkey, a UN and NATO member, who would

like to have it both ways: tied to the West through business, investment, and security alliances, but also following an "Eastern" policy that gives them a bigger role in an emerging, but also dangerous, Middle East.'

All of this – advancing development, modernization, and globalization, and readjusting the world order – is hard to do in the best of times; it is obviously even more difficult to do in the chaotic conditions of the MENA today. Yet the change process goes forward inexorably even in the midst of all the tumult and violence of the present. Out of this will likely come over time a new and more modern Middle East in accord with the six criteria and characteristics set forth above. In this vortex of change, no one single country (Iran, Egypt, Turkey, or Saudi Arabia) is likely to emerge as dominant; at the same time, across the region we are likely to see a growing rejection both of the U.S./Western model of domestic development *and* an increased effort on the part of the Middle East to continue to go their own way internationally.

The Arab and Muslim model is not one that is seen desirable by the majority of those not Arabic or Muslim themselves. One of the major challenges of the model is the lack of cordial relations between the two major branches – Sunni and Shia – that have struggled with religious, political, and social contestations both within and between countries in the Middle East.

There are several limiting factors for the model to be viable elsewhere. It is basically based on interpretations of the Quran. The accuracy and legitimacy of various interpretations of the Quran by religious and political leaders and groups have been challenging both for citizens, and especially international actors, to grapple with. An important aspect of this challenge is demonstrated in who is considered an infidel by religious law. Given these limitations, the application of the Islamist model elsewhere seems complicated. Many of the states of the Middle East do not answer the question of whether democracy and Islam are truly compatible. We will need to wait and see which of these countries stabilize and thrive, and which of them change the power distribution within their governments significantly in the next twenty or thirty years.

CHAPTER 8

LATIN AMERICA: A MODEL
FOR ANYONE?

Latin America, along with Africa, is one of the world's great neglected areas. It is not high priority in terms of our national interests or security concerns. We do not pay it much attention or read about it. We do not know much about it though we may have strong – mostly negative – prejudices and stereotypes. As far as the U.S., Europe, and Asia (except China) are concerned, Latin America may have fallen off the map. Certainly, it is off their radar screens.

The reasons for this neglect are various. Latin America is mainly *mestizo* (a mixture of Indian and white) or mulatto (black and white) so probably race prejudice has something to do with it. Nor, unlike Europe, do we often travel to Latin America except maybe Mexico and the Caribbean; Latin America is off the main east-west travel routes. Third, we harbor other prejudices about Latin America, perhaps relating to the fact that the area is strongly Catholic, and that it is still underdeveloped after five hundred years and, seemingly, unable to consistently govern itself democratically. A fourth reason for our neglect of Latin America in a foreign policy sense is this: when an American secretary of State wakes up in the morning he/she already has forty-seven other problems accumulated overnight on his plate, mainly related to the Middle East, Asia, Russia, or Europe. The last thing the secretary wants to hear during the day is that number forty-eight dealing with some obscure issue in Latin America has just been added to his/her plateful.

And yet, we in the U.S. need to pay serious attention to Latin America. To begin, Latin America has been over the last twenty years the second most economically dynamic area in the world, second only to Asia but ahead of the U.S., Europe, and *all* other areas. Second, Latin America has vast resources – oil, natural gas, minerals, and agricultural products – that we can use. China has recognized that fact and is pouring investment into the area even if we have not fully done so. Third, Latin America is our closest and most closely connected neighbor among global regions; a glance at a map and a serious consideration of the complementarity of our economies and societies bear out how interdependent we are with the area. Fourth, Latin America is mainly Western and its democracy and human rights situation are much improved over the last thirty years, which makes it much easier for us to have good relations and deal with the area on the basis of mutual interests. And fifth, one can make a strong case that Latin America is *the most important area in the world* for us due to its effect on our everyday lives and society through immigration, the flow of labor, drugs, petroleum supplies, tourism, music, people, etc. We are *inter-dependent* with Latin America in a host of ways unparalleled anywhere else in the world, whether we want to be or not.

But is Latin America a model of or for anything? Of course, Latin America still lags behind the U.S., Western Europe, and Japan in per-capita income. But as compared with the rest of Asia including China, Russia, South and Southeast Asia, the Middle East, and Africa, Latin America is not doing altogether badly. Latin America, where the U.S. has concentrated its development efforts over the last five decades, may thus be a model for other developing areas. Latin America may also be a model for the Third World of how successfully to achieve democracy and human rights. Finally, Latin America, rather like Japan and now India and others, offers us a model of how to absorb Western ways, to democratize and modernize, while also remaining true to its own culture and ways of doing things. If Latin America can democratize and modernize while at the same time keeping its own culture intact, that is both a major accomplishment *and*, perhaps, an example for others to emulate.

History and Political Culture

We will not dwell on Latin America's indigenous background, fascinating though it is, except to make the following points:

1. At the time of the European conquest (1492-1570), Latin America had *ten times* the number of indigenous peoples as did the United States – twenty million versus three million for the U.S. Therefore, Latin America could not deal with its Indian population as did the United States, through subjugation, slaughter, and confinement

on reservations. Rather, because of the sheer numbers, Latin America's indigenous population, while subjugated, remained in place, dominated but yet present, and mixing with their conquerors to a degree unknown in the U.S., producing in many countries a majority *mestizo* population (mixture of Indian and white) outnumbering whites.

2. Through both conquest and culture shock (their gods "defeated" by the gods of their colonial masters), the Indian population retreated or was forced into an inferior, secondary, and subjugated position that persists to this day.

3. Because of this continuing and large indigenous population, Latin America remains closer to the Third World, predominantly Western but with a large non-Western component, than is the United States.

4. Today, this large, "sleeping" indigenous population in Latin America is only beginning to make its presence felt; its role in the future is likely to be far greater.

Consider this: Spain and Portugal, the two main colonial powers in Latin America, arrived in the Americas fully a century and more before the Pilgrims arrived and settled at Plymouth Rock. By 1570, still fifty years before the first English settlement in North America, and two-and-a-half *centuries* before the United States reached the Pacific Ocean, the conquest of *all* of Latin America was already completed.

These dates and time differences are important for the following reason. Latin America, discovered, conquered, and colonized in the sixteenth century, was still, predominantly, a product of feudalism, the Middle Ages, what we refer to as "traditional society." Whereas the U.S. was settled a full century and more later, after feudalism had largely disappeared from Europe, "born free" as it were except the U.S. South, a society founded on and in modernity, not any longer the Middle Ages. These essential, founding differences based on entirely different situations, time periods, and socio-cultural differences, help explain why already-modern North America would forge ahead while semi-feudal Latin America would lag behind.

Think of the following five contrasts: first, the economic system of Latin America was basically feudal in the sixteenth century, while that of the U.S. in the seventeenth century was entrepreneurial, commercial, and nascently capitalistic. Second, Latin American society was essentially two-class and caste – whites on top, indigenous below – while that of North America was middle class, farmers, and small businessmen. Third, Latin America's political tradition and structure, inherited from Spain and Portugal, was top-down, hierarchical, and authoritarian, while that of the U.S. inherited from England was already representative and democratic. Fourth, in the religious sphere, Latin America was monolithically Catholic while the U.S. had a plurality of religious beliefs that eventually gave rise to political pluralism. Fifth and finally, reflecting the religious monopoly of the Catholic Church, Latin America's intellectual tradition was closed, scholastic, absolutist, and based on revealed truth; while that of North America was more inquiring, empirical, and scientific. These fundamental differences between North and South America, helping account for the future development of the North and the retardation or underdevelopment of Latin America, are summarized in Figure 8.1.

An understanding of these contrasting structures and societal orientations goes a long way toward explaining Latin America's underdevelopment, as compared to the U.S. In one word, Latin America was basically feudal while North America was modern or modernizing. What is surprising actually, given the time frame, is not that Latin America was founded on this quasi-feudal basis but that it lasted so long. It lasted through the sixteenth and seventeenth centuries as Spain and Portugal established and consolidated their top-down, closed, pyramidal colonial administration and structure of society. Then under the Bourbon monarchy in Spain in the eighteenth century, the system became even more autocratic, centralized, and authoritarian.

When independence finally came to Latin America in the early nineteenth century following the American (1776) and French (1789) revolutions, it came under conservative auspices, not liberal or democratic ones. The Latin American elites who led these independence movements favored republicanism and independence, but the last thing they wanted was true democracy. They wished to preserve the existing conservative and elitist structures, social hierarchies, and privileged landholding system as against the then liberalizing currents of the Spanish Crown. Independence came as a result of the efforts of these Creole elites, those born in the New World, to preserve their power and place in society, not to overthrow it.

The nineteenth century in Latin America was chaotic and divisive which prevented much internal national development. In the early part of the century Latin America was dominated by authoritarian men-on-horseback (*caudillos*) who sought to impose order on unruly societies.

In the mid-nineteenth century, some liberal governments came to power for the first time, but that was episodic and short-lived. The preconditions for democracy and liberalism to survive and thrive – greater wealth and literacy, a strong middle class, and civil society – had not yet been established. Liberalism was quickly supplanted by a new wave of authoritarian leaders, or else in some countries by a reconsolidation of oligarchic rule. These regimes began establishing what Rostow called the "preconditions for takeoff" – stability, new institutions, foreign investment, population increase, and an export-oriented economy based on minerals and agricultural products.

FIGURE 8.1
CONTRASTING DEVELOPMENTAL FOUNDATIONS THE UNITED STATES AND LATIN AMERICA[47]

Characteristic	Latin America	United States
Economic	Feudalism	Capitalist, modernizing
Social	Two-class	Middle class
Political	Authoritarian, top-down, exclusionary, autocratic	Republican, democratic, pluralistic, inclusionary
Religion	Catholic, monolithic	Protestant, pluralistic
Intellectual	Scholastic, deductive, rote memorization	Empirical, scientific

Source: Wiarda, Howard J., and Harvey F. Kline, eds. *Latin American politics and development*. Westview Press, 2013.

Unfortunately for Latin America, this period of still conservative and oligarchic but nonetheless constructive development did not last. It came crashing down in the world financial collapse (the Great Depression) of 1929-30. We forget sometimes that the Depression was a worldwide phenomenon and not just limited to the U.S. In Latin America the market for the products it had been producing and exporting all but disappeared. As the Latin American economies collapsed, so too did their governments. At the height of the Depression between 1930 and 1935, fifteen of the twenty countries experienced revolutionary overthrows.

The Depression set back Latin America for decades. Clearly the old model of oligarchic or military rule (often the two in combination) was no longer viable. What to do? In the 1930s and 1940s there were many military regimes and dictatorships. Some countries experimented with democratic, progressive, or, alternatively, corporatist regimes. Others reverted again to rule by conservative elites. Some rotated among all of these. Others experienced near-constant instability, upheaval, and the rapid turnover of governments. Meanwhile, in some of the most unstable and noninstitutionalized countries of the Caribbean and Central America, the U.S. Marines had been sent in during the early years of the century to stabilize the situation and advance American interests as the United States emerged as a global power.

In the aftermath of World War II and with the reestablishment of peace and the founding of the UN, a new but again short-lived round of democratic governments came to power. They were soon replaced by renewed authoritarianism in the 1950s followed by still another short-lived opening to democracy, corresponding to the first years of the John F. Kennedy Administration, in the early 1960s.

By the mid-1970s, however, the authoritarians were back in power in seventeen of the twenty countries. Clearly Latin America had not yet found its way, or its developmental formula, after some 150 years of independence.

Although Latin America has been doing very well lately, second among regions only to Asia, its future direction may even now not be entirely clear. Economically, its growth has been powered by this past decade's high prices for Latin America's main commodity exports – minerals, petroleum, and agricultural products – but those prices may not last. Meanwhile, Latin America's industrialization, except in some of the bigger countries – Brazil and Mexico – has been weak and, as state-run industries, is often beset by corruption and wasteful patronage. Politically, we can say that, with the democratic transitions that began in the late 1970s, nineteen of the twenty countries (all except Cuba) are now democracies, but democracy in Latin America is similarly weak, nonconsolidated, and still characterized by incomplete civil society and institutionalization.

So, which way Latin America? It's hard to be certain. Many Latin Americans and their international sponsors, principally the U.S., are proud of their newly established democratic institutions and wish to maintain the Western model. But at the same time, quite a number of the Latin American economies are still buffeted by uncertain international winds, democracy remains not fully consolidated, and civil society is weak. Meanwhile, there remain powerful nondemocratic, and sometimes revolutionary challenges to the status quo: Marxists movements in some countries, indigenous movements in others, and reactionary forces in still others who would like to go back to the earlier model. Given this uncertain situation, what is it that Latin America can offer to the rest of the world?

Socioeconomic Overview

Latin America occupies an intermediary position on almost all indices of wealth and modernization. It is not as wealthy as North America, Western Europe, or East Asia (excluding big but still-poor China). However, on a per-capita basis Latin America is wealthier than Africa, South Asia, Southeast Asia, or the Middle East (except for the oil-rich Persian Gulf states). In terms of growth over the last twenty years, Latin America ranks second only to East Asia, while most of the rest of the world has experienced stagnation or only modest growth. See Table 8.1.

The best performers in Latin America are Chile, Uruguay, and Costa Rica; but they have been outperforming the rest of the hemisphere for over 150 years. More recently Panama (banking and finance) has joined the list of prosperous countries. Not only are these countries thoroughly democratic but they have all recently been promoted to the ranks of what the World Bank calls "Developed Countries."

TABLE 8.1
LATIN AMERICAN COUNTRIES:
POPULATION AND GROSS DOMESTIC
PRODUCT PER CAPITA[48]

Country	Population (in millions)	Gross Domestic Product per Capita
Argentina	43	NA
Bolivia	10.6	6,630
Brazil	206.1	15,893
Chile	17.8	22,071
Colombia	47.8	13,357
Costa Rica	4.8	14,918
Cuba	11.4	20,611
Dominican Republic	10.4	13,262
Ecuador	15.9	11,372
El Salvador	6.1	8,351
Guatemala	16	7,454
Haiti	10.6	1,732
Honduras	8	4,909
Mexico	125.4	17,315
Nicaragua	6	4,918
Panama	3.9	20,895
Paraguay	6.6	8,911
Peru	31	11,989
Uruguay	3.4	20,884
50Venezuela	30.7	18,276

Source: World Development Indicators, The World Bank

Quite a number of other Latin American countries, including the biggest ones – Argentina, Brazil, Colombia,

213

and Mexico – are similarly democratic and right on the verge of making it into "Developed Country" ranks. The Dominican Republic, Peru, Bolivia, Ecuador, and Paraguay have taken off in parallel fashion, but they have not yet reached the level of the others mentioned. Venezuela is rich in oil but the revenues from the oil have been mismanaged and the country has regressed from its earlier democratic opening in the 1950s and 1960s.

That means thirteen, or two-thirds, of the Latin American countries are doing quite well. Only one-third – Cuba, El Salvador, Guatemala, Haiti, Honduras, and Nicaragua – are going badly. Of these, only Haiti is a failed state.

Another way to think about this is to consider the dramatic changes in Latin America since 1960, which is about when the world first began to pay serious attention to the area. In 1960, Latin America was 80 percent illiterate, now it is 80 percent literate. In 1960, Latin America was 80 percent rural and unindustrialized, today it is 80 percent urban and industrial. In 1960 the Church, the Army, and the oligarchy were extremely powerful and constituted a triumvirate of absolutism; today all three of these traditional groups have been marginalized.

In 1960, Latin America was mainly undemocratic, today nineteen of twenty countries are democratic. In 1960, Latin America had few political parties, almost no civil society, and a miniscule middle class; whereas today civil society is much stronger and the middle class – *the* basis of democratic politics – may number 20, 30, 40, or even 50 percent of the population, depending on the country. And let us not forget that Latin America is about ten times richer than it was in 1960 and has greatly diversified and globalized its economy.

Let us think about all those facts set forth in the preceding paragraph for a moment. Separately and, even more impressively, together, they constitute the main building blocks of a modern society. And they represent a repudiation or better, a contradiction and undermining of those traditional features set forth in Figure 8.1. That is, Latin America is no longer authoritarian but mainly democratic; it is no longer feudal but mainly a modern, mixed economy; it is no longer just two-class but mainly middle- or multi-class. In similar fashion, Latin America has largely put its religious orthodoxy to the sidelines while becoming more secular, Protestant, and pluralistic; rather than dominated any more by scholasticism, Latin America's intellectual life is vigorous and inquiring. So, has Latin America definitively left the past and the Middle Ages behind and entered the modern world? Well, mostly but not entirely.

While Latin America's economic growth has been impressive in recent years, we also need to examine the effects of that growth on social change. Specifically, following the early literature on development, we will want to know if recent, impressive economic growth now provides Latin America with the social foundations on which modernization, democracy, and development can stabilize and go forward. In other words, has economic growth now given rise to genuine social and political pluralism which is the only solid foundation for democracy?

Historically, we have seen, Latin America has long been a two-class or semi-feudal society. There was a small elite at the top consisting of Spanish and Portuguese colonizers and their descendants who monopolized land, mines, church, and government institutions. At the bottom was a large mass of mainly indigenous elements and black slaves brought in from Africa – laborers, servants, what we would later come to call "peasants." In between was a tiny middle class, only 2 or 3 percent of the population, consisting of soldiers, government bureaucrats, small-shop owners, and some mixed-race elements. This hierarchical, elitist, top-down system, with most of the population disfranchised and unable to participate in national decision-making, and such an infinitesimally small middle sector, was not conducive to, nor did it provide a foundation for, democratic politics.

By the late eighteenth century, a split had occurred in the elite between those who remained loyal to Spain or Portugal and those favoring independence. Then in the nineteenth century another but different kind of split occurred between the older landed elites and the newer elites of commerce, business, and trade. Despite these splits within the elite, society remained bifurcated: a small but more diverse elite at the top monopolizing all wealth and positions, and a large undifferentiated mass of poor, illiterate persons at the bottom.

In the twentieth century, more rapid social change occurred. The elite groups – Church, Army, and oligarchy – continued to dominate national political life. But no longer exclusively; by this time in most countries the middle class had grown to 15, 20, or even 30 percent of the population. However, the middle class mainly shared the elite's conservative values; when there was a challenge from below and darker-skinned elements to stable, authoritarian rule, the middle class sided with the Church, the Army, and the elites to preserve the traditional hierarchies. Meanwhile, the lower classes, now including industrial workers as well as peasants, were largely kept out of power. Exceptions included Cuba, Bolivia, Nicaragua, and Venezuela where progressive or revolutionary regimes came to power.

The biggest changes have occurred in the twenty-first century. In quite a number of countries – Brazil, Bolivia, Peru, Chile, Ecuador, Uruguay, Costa Rica, Mexico, Argentina, and Venezuela – absolute poverty has been greatly reduced. Second and correspondingly, the size of the middle class has been greatly increased, in some countries now reaching over 50 percent of the population. Third, thanks to regular, democratic elections (nineteen of the twenty countries – all except Cuba – can now be considered mostly democratic), the monopoly of the elites on power or of the elite-middle-class alliance, is being challenged if not broken.

Now, according to Rostow, Lipset,[49] and Almond, once a country reaches a certain level of social and economic modernization in terms of literacy, urbanization, social differentiation and pluralism, and wealth, the odds of its becoming and remaining democratic are much better. Once a country becomes sufficiently socially pluralist that its elites are no longer able to monopolize political power, then political pluralism, or democracy, usually follows. The question now becomes, is Latin America sufficiently socially and politically modern and pluralist that it has reached that point where democracy is assured?

The question is more complicated than it sounds. First, remember that this is a correlation, not causation; while it is generally better to be rich than poor if you want to have democracy, there is nothing *automatic* about the process, nothing that says greater wealth or urbanization leads automatically to democracy. Second, keep in mind that many of these social changes in Latin America are still weak, fragile, and incomplete. Third, while Latin America has modernized a great deal in recent decades, it remains the area of the world where inequality is the greatest. And fourth, Latin America is still often ambivalent about the democracy it has achieved. Rather like Russia, Latin America is still torn between its Western and its non-Western orientations. It wants to be like the West and achieve the West's prosperity, but it also wants to go its own nationalistic and culturally conditioned ways. At times of disorder and chaos Latin America, like Russia, may prefer "strong" or authoritarian government. And that may, or it may not as nowadays, be in accord with the preferences of the Western model.

Let us only briefly say that, while Latin America is at present majority-democratic, it is not liberal democracy that we are seeing in most countries, nor even pluralism. Latin America is "democratic" in the sense that most countries hold regular elections but it also practices "illiberal democracy" in the sense that the liberal freedoms – speech, press, assembly, etc. – are regularly denied or curtailed. In addition, while Latin America is democratic and republican at some levels, it is corporatist (like Russia) at others: official trade unions and peasant groups rather than free associability, limits on civil society and interest group activity, and restrictions on the number of interest groups and their aggregation or lobbying efforts.

Latin America has lived in the shadow of the U.S., and sometimes under the eagle's talons, for so long that it harbors strong anti-American sentiments. Its roots are "Western," we have seen, but it is also anti-Western or at least anti-U.S. It wants to be considered "civilized" and "advanced" in the Western sense but its anti-American sentiments force it to be nationalistic and even xenophobic. Even while following a generally Western path, it must declare its independence, vote against the U.S. in international forums, and go its own nationalistic way.

This attitude explains also why Latin America admires Cuba, Bolivia, Nicaragua, and Venezuela – because they have mostly been able to thumb their noses at the U.S. and get away with it – even while not wanting to imitate these countries non-democratic and anti-Western ideologies. For the same reasons, Latin America harbors admiration for anti-American, left-wing, progressive, radical, Marxist, and even revolutionary politicians – Fidel Castro, Hugo Chávez, Daniel Ortega, or Evo Morales – who similarly defy the U.S. and stake out, like Iran and other Third World Marxist regimes, anti-American positions. And all this while wanting to retain Latin America's close and historic ties to the West.

Government Institutions and the Role of the State

We need to understand Latin America in ways similar to our understanding of Russia or Africa. That is, of a vast, "wild," empty, underpopulated, unruly territory that has never been governed effectively. A territory, historically without roads, without civil society, without institutions, without means of communication and transportation, without *civilization*. And in which the role of the state or government is to fill that empty space, provide the institutions otherwise lacking, and bring civilization to a large area previously bereft of same.

Only strong men or strong regimes can fill this near-empty vacuum. The arguments are the same in Russia or in Africa. In the absence of strong institutions, and given the development needs of a vast unruly territory, only a strong "czar" like Putin or a "strong man" as in Africa can fill the void. The argument put forth by such authoritarian leaders (the term in Spanish is *caudillo* or "man on horseback") is that you can't speak of democracy in countries that have no roads, no schools, no telephones or internet, no literacy, and no civic life. Only a strong leader, the argument runs, can hold the country together, prevent anarchy, and provide for growth and development. Democracy, in the Rostow stages of growth, may come later, once the country has had a chance to build itself up, but not now. Once the country has had thirty or forty years of stability and development, then it may be possible to have democracy, but any attempts to develop democracy before the national infrastructure has been built up would be naïve, premature, and doomed to failure.

The government, therefore, must be strong, centralized, and top-down. And, in the absence of much home-grown or natural civil society at grassroots levels, it is the state's role to step in and create it. Hence, the formation in many developing countries like those of Latin America of official or government-created trade unions, government-created peasant leagues, official or government-created women's associations, student associations, even business groups. Where civil society is weak or nonexistent, the state must step in to create it.

Usually this "statism" in the political realm is accompanied in developing countries by statism in the economic realm. If the private-sector economy is weak, then the state must again step in to create state-led industrialization or what we may call "state capitalism." This model of economic growth, which is also practiced successfully in China, is very attractive to many developing countries, in contrast to the slow-growth model currently of both the U.S. and Western Europe.

In the political sphere, the counterpart of state capitalism is usually called corporatism. Corporatism exists when the state creates its own structure of civil society. Corporatist civil society means the government creates and then also regulates and controls its own trade unions, farmers' groups, business associations, professional associations, and the like. In this way the state helps fill the organizational space previously lacking, just as in the economic sphere it creates a system of state-led capitalism.

However, since the government controls the funds and keeps close watch over all these associations, it means the government also controls the nation's associational life. No strikes by organized labor or lockouts by business can be allowed. In this way, the corporatist model advocates, the thirty to forty years of stability necessary for economic takeoff can be achieved; the government allows but also controls and regulates any potential pluralism and discord.

Corporatism is very popular in Latin America and other developing areas as a transitional regime or half-way house. It is not totalitarian (*total* control) because it allows considerable room for civil society and associational life to organize, even if under government control. On the other hand, it is certainly not democratic, liberal, or pluralist either because the main associations and interest groups are monopolized, dominated, and subservient to the state. At the same time, corporatism is often seen by many of these same Third World leaders as a transitional system that can eventually evolve into a more liberal and pluralist structure.

If we understand these features of Latin America (or Russia or Africa) – the vast empty spaces, the wild unruly territory, the lack of infrastructure or institutions, the weak civil society or associational life, the lack of "civilization," hence the need for the state to step in to correct these faults – we are a long way to understanding Latin American politics, its operating assumptions, and the main model, corporatism, it has used to overcome these faults. The need for strong, centralized leadership, for example, helps explain why Latin American presidents have exercised strong power while the parliaments, court systems, and local government have always been weak. The weaknesses of the economy, of the private sector, and of private entrepreneurship help explain why the state must step in to stimulate the economy and why Latin America must have state-led industrialization and state capitalism. Similarly, the absence or weakness of civil society explains why the government, using corporatism, steps in to create its own form of *official* civil society under state control. Seen this way, a system of state-led economic growth and state-dominated civil society seems like a quite reasonable and rational choice for Latin America even if it does not quite conform to our own Western, liberal, democratic values.

But now, here comes the kicker: the changes that may force Latin America to abandon its own model and opt for something else. First, ever since independence in the early nineteenth century, the goal, judging by its laws and constitutions, that Latin America has set for itself has always been republican, liberal, and democratic. It may not have always lived up to those laws and constitutional precepts, but that at least was and is the aspiration. Second, all the Latin American countries are now under tremendous pressure, from the U.S., the EU, the World Bank and IMF (which loan them money), and the Organization of American States (OAS), to adopt and maintain democratic standards. The result, if these norms are broken, is international ostracism and being cut off from international assistance.

Third, Latin America *wants* to be democratic. It *wants* to be free with the rights of its people respected. It *wants* regular and democratic elections, for the votes to be counted honestly, and for civil society to be free and open. It *wants* to join the civilized world and to be a part of the West. It has often accepted the notion from the past that its lack of institutions and civil society historically may have served as a pretext for authoritarianism and corporatism, but now it is being held, and is holding itself, to a higher standard.

So, is Latin America now ready for full-scale democracy, pluralism, and liberalism, or is it still a victim of the past? More than that, has Latin America now advanced to a level sociologically and economically where it has the ability to support full democracy? Does it now have, after several decades of economic growth, the economic base to support democracy and the sociological infrastructure – a large middle-class independent civil society, no longer state-created – on which a strong and stable democracy can be based? These seem to be the key questions.

And on these issues Latin America is still ambivalent. First, it depends on which country or countries we are talking about. Argentina, Brazil, Chile, Colombia, Costa Rica, the Dominican Republic, Mexico, Panama, and Uruguay are all probably safely in the democratic, Western camp; but Bolivia, Cuba, Ecuador, El Salvador, Guatemala, Haiti, Honduras, Nicaragua, Paraguay, Peru, and Venezuela are not. So the first priority is to distinguish between countries and groups of countries. Some – about half – "get it" and are "making it" into the modern, democratic, globalized world; the other half have not made it yet and may not make it any time in the near future.

Second, among Latin Americans themselves, there is still considerable ambivalence and uncertainty on these matters. Many Latin Americans, including many in the countries listed above as "getting it," still doubt their own capacity for democracy. They don't know if they are advanced enough for democracy. They are often chock full of inferiority complexes about their country's capacity for democracy. They do not trust their leaders or even themselves. Such self-doubt and lack of confidence is among the major factors holding back both development and democracy.

Third, let us recognize that there are powerful vested interests, on both the Left and the Right, who do not want the democratic, Western option to succeed. And who may try to sabotage it at every opportunity. On the Right, probably no more than 20 percent of the population in most countries, and concentrated in the armed forces, the Church, and white elite groups, are persons who don't want democracy to triumph, don't want to sacrifice their own power, and doubt the capacity of the masses (and darker-skinned!) to govern. On the Left, again no more than 20 percent in most countries but higher in Bolivia, Cuba, Ecuador, Nicaragua, and Venezuela, are those who so hate the U.S. and the West, or so love the Russian, Iranian, or Chinese models, that they, too, want the liberal-democratic model to fail.

In most countries of Latin America, neither the Rightist elements nor the Leftists can, in normal circumstances, come to power by themselves. But if there is an economic crash (as at present with depressed commodity prices), or if there is widespread civil unrest, or if (not unheard of) Left and Right come together to oppose the middle way of the moderate democrats, then it's quite possible that the Western democratic model could be abandoned and something far scarier – authoritarianism or totalitarianism – take its place.

The Latin American Model

What can we learn from Latin America? Many Americans and other readers will think that a silly question, doubtful that there is *anything* that *we* can learn from Latin America. I disagree with that position: There is a lot that we, and especially the developing world, can learn from Latin America.

First, let us dispense with the scenarios that are *unlikely* to happen. To begin, it is unlikely that Latin America will again experience the wave of military, repressive coups that it experienced in the 1960s and '70s; the area is now too advanced and developed overall for that to occur, although we could still see coups and military regimes in some individual countries. Likewise, it seems highly unlikely, despite some romantic and ideological wishes to the contrary, that we will

225

see many more Left-wing and revolutionary takeovers in Latin America; despite Ché Guevara's famous call for "fires up and down the Andes," most of Latin America has passed beyond the stage – too developed, too urban, too literate, too middle class – where a leftist revolution is possible.

A third "null hypothesis" is that Latin America will rediscover its indigenous past, abandon its Western trajectory, and reconstruct an indigenous society from before 1492. But, except in such "Indian countries" as Bolivia, Paraguay, Peru, Ecuador, and Guatemala, this is unlikely to happen. And even in these countries, indigenous groups are tending demographically toward becoming a minority and are unlikely to want to go back to that earlier, pre-Western condition. Once modernization begins, you can't go back to a more primitive feudal condition.

What *will* likely happen is that Indian groups in specific countries will demand and receive more rights and privileges, but nowhere are they likely to seize power or reestablish a pre-Columbian Indian civilization. For good or ill or however incompletely, Latin America has embraced the Western world; it cannot at this stage erase all those five centuries of Western (albeit Luso-Hispanic or Southern European) history and go back and join the non-Western world.

That leaves two main options for Latin America: liberal democracy or corporatism. Some see these two as diametrically opposed models, incompatible; but I do not see the need for that. First of all, there is no reason why one cannot conceive of a model where elements from both of these systems are present at the same time. Indeed, that is the situation in most of Latin America at present. On the one hand, it has democracy in the electoral arena, congress, the political party realm, alternation in the presidency, most areas of human and political rights, et cetera. On the other, it has corporatism, or a mixed system of corporatism and liberalism, in the areas of state-society relations, interest-group activity, and public policy (by group) implementation. I see no reason why Latin America cannot go on in this fashion, with competing, overlapping corporatist as well as liberal-pluralist forms, both existing side by side and interacting in all kinds of complex, interesting ways.[50] One could even agree that corporatism or organic-statism is *the indigenous model* for Latin America and, therefore, an extremely powerful influence, while liberal democracy is the weaker, imported system of rule.[51]

But I think there is an evolutionary element operating here as well. Corporatism may be the historic, traditional, and indigenous "model" for Latin America, but it is gradually fading. At the same time, democracy and liberal-pluralism are becoming gradually ascendant. The two may continue for a long time to co-exist and overlap, but such powerful forces as economic development, social change, globalization, and changing political culture are ever-so-slowly pushing the corporatist features and institutions aside as the liberal-pluralist ones become more powerful.

Another and parallel way to conceive of this process is to see corporatism as a transitional regime in Latin America, intermediary between the traditionalism and semi-feudalism of the past and the greater democracy and pluralism of the future. In this view Latin American corporatism is not fixed in place now and forever more but is part of a dynamic and evolutionary process helping guide Latin America away from its historic past and into a more democratic and socially just future. In this view, it is not useful for Latin America to try to jump immediately and prematurely from its historic feudal past into a democratic future; that is too abrupt and too upsetting of traditional forces, produces premature democracy, and is likely to provoke counter-revolutionary reactions as in the 1960s and 1970s. Far better, the argument is, to proceed slowly, to combine the corporatism of the past with the democratic needs of the future, to *ease* into the transition process, and thus avoid all the conflicts, civil wars, violence, fragmentation, and breakdowns that accompanied the earlier efforts at bridging this transition.

And that is what makes the Latin American model of broader interest and gives it considerable appeal in the Third World. For what Latin America has done, after more than a half-century of huffing and puffing and instability, is arrive at a model that combines traditional and modern, liberalism and corporatism, change and stability, indigenous or home-grown, and outside-imported. We know, for example, that the Chinese Communist Party leadership is reading the literature on Latin American corporatism to see how they might manage their own transition away from Leninist totalitarianism, but without going in China's case toward full democracy. Other non-Western and transactional regimes – Indonesia, the Philippines, and Vietnam – are reading that same literature and hoping to control the change process. It may be that corporatism will turn out to be a transitional regime that many non-Western countries will see as useful in bridging the gap between tradition and modernity. In that case, the Latin American experience of semi-corporatist development and democracy will have a lot to offer.

* * *

Latin America has now joined Eastern Europe as a major success story for United States foreign policy. After the great fear of communist insurgencies in the 1960s and then the wave of military authoritarianism in the 1970s, Latin America has settled down into a more-or-less democratic, free-market path. Rather like Eastern Europe after the Soviets withdrew, Latin America in the 1990s came to largely accept the main elements of the "Washington Consensus": democracy and human rights; a modern, mixed (capitalist and social-democratic) economy; and free trade. In addition, although some countries – Cuba, Venezuela, Argentina, and Brazil – often go their own way to pursue an independent foreign policy, for the most part Latin America has accepted the Western system of international relations. In these ways, both on the domestic and the international front, Latin America has accepted the main tenets of the Western model and may well be locked into it.

CHAPTER 9

SUB-SAHARAN AFRICA: IS THERE ANY HOPE?

Sub-Saharan Africa is the poorest, most traditional, most troubled, and least developed of all the regions with which we deal in this book. We all know the adjectives that are used to describe Africa: poor, miserable, diseased, violent, starving, and consumed by conflict and civil war. These are the images that dominate our television coverage: poor, starving children, bones sticking out of emaciated bodies, flies crawling over them, and death from disease or starvation or both. The question is, is this an accurate portrayal or not?

The answer is: yes and no. There *is* great hardship, poverty, violence, and chaos in Africa. Africa is, by the numbers, by far the poorest of all world areas. There is not a single, developed country in all the continent. Africa's annual per capita income, at only $3,206 average for the entire continent, is only one-half that of South Asia, one-third that of East and Southeast Asia, and one-quarter that of Latin America. As compared with developed countries, Africa lags even farther behind: one-*tenth* that of Japan and

Western Europe, one-*seventeenth* that of the United States, and even farther behind such high-flyers as Hong Kong, Kuwait, Singapore, Luxembourg, and the United Arab Emirates (UAE). We need to be honest here: Africa is so poor that it is doubtful if it will *ever* catch up to these others.

On the other hand, of the fifty African countries listed in Table 9.1, six are doing pretty well and another half-dozen are doing okay, accounting for about 20 percent of the continent.

TABLE 9.1
AFRICA: POPULATION AND GROSS DOMESTIC PRODUCT PER CAPITA[52]

Country	Population (in millions)	PPP GDP per capita
Angola	25	6,949
Benin	10.9	2.03
Botswana	2.3	16,099
Burkina Faso	18.1	1,620
Burundi	11.2	770
Cameroon	23.3	2,972
Cape Verde	0.5	6,520
Central African Republic	4.9	594
Chad	14	2,182
Comoros	0.8	1,429
Congo, Dem. Rep.	77.3	746
Congo, Rep.	4.6	6,277
Cote d'Ivoire	22.7	3,258
Djibouti	0.9	3,270
Equatorial Guinea	0.8	34,739

Eritrea	5.2	1,411
Ethiopia	99.4	1,500
Gabon	1.7	19,430
Gambia, The	2	1,631
Ghana	27.4	4,082
Guinea	12.6	1,221
Guinea-Bissau	1.8	1,386
Kenya	46.1	2,954
Lesotho	2.1	2,638
Liberia	4.5	842
Madagascar	24.2	1,439
Malawi	17.2	822
Maldives	0.4	12,530
Mali	17.6	1,599
Mauritania	4.1	3,803
Mauritius	1.3	18,585
Mozambique	27.2	1,129
Namibia	2.5	9,956
Niger	19.9	938
Nigeria	182.2	5,911
Rwanda	11.6	1,660
São Tomé and Principe	0.2	3,176
Senegal	15.1	2,333
Seychelles	0.1	26,422
Sierra Leone	6.5	1,966
Somalia	10.5	NA
South Africa	54.8	13,049
South Sudan	12.3	2,019
Sudan	40.2	4,069
Swaziland	1.3	8,292

Tanzania	53.5	2,538
Togo	7.3	1,429
Uganda	39	1,770
Zambia	16.2	3,904
Zimbabwe	15.6	1,792

Source: World Development Indicators, World Bank

Africa has abundant natural resources: oil and natural gas, diamonds, precious metals, vast hydroelectric power, valuable woods, and an abundance of good agricultural land. Foreign investment has, selectively, been pouring into Africa over the last decade, raising the standard of living and the health conditions by quantum leaps over previous decades. Both populous China and India (less so the United States) have been pouring investment as well as settlers into Africa recently in the hope of not only utilizing Africa's vast resources but of feeding their own, billion-plus populations. Do they know something about Africa that the rest of us don't?

That is, in fact, our main theme regarding Africa in this chapter: lots of despair over poverty, corruption, failed states, and lack of good governance; but at the same time a measure of hope. For that is actually the reality of Africa: some countries doing OK-to-good while others seem to be locked into poverty and lack of progress. We should not have romantic and unrealistic expectations about most of the continent; on the other hand, the situation is not hopeless and we should not give up on Africa either.

In terms of the main themes of this book, we need to ask what Africa has to offer the rest of the world? Domestically, Africa so far has been an *importer* of foreign development models. It is here, as well as in Asia and Latin America, where the main battles over competing development theories – Rostow's developmentalism, dependency theory, Russian Marxism, Chinese Marxism – have been fought out. *None* of these imported models seems to have worked out too well or delivered much in the way of development. At the same time, Africa along with Iran and the Middle East, has been one of the key places – because of the repeated failure of these foreign models – where the argument for an indigenous theory of development has been put forward most vigorously. Countries like Ghana, Tanzania, Senegal, Kenya, Nigeria, and the Ivory Coast have led the way in setting forth a home-grown or "authentic" model of *African* development. Unfortunately, the quest for a unifying indigenous model has been no more successful in achieving development than the ill-fitting imported ones.

Similarly, on the international front: Africa has been mainly an importer of conflicts originating elsewhere. Africa itself is not a major actor in world affairs but especially during the Cold War the great powers – the U.S., the Soviet Union, and belatedly China – often fought out their conflicts by proxy on the African continent. Africa was the subject and often the victim of international great-power machinations and seldom itself a vigorous participant in the conflicts that affected it most closely. Some African countries were all but destroyed and their developmental prospects severely set back by these outside conflicts. In response, Africa was at the center of the non-aligned movement and contributed to global affairs thereby, not only refusing to align itself with either of the great superpowers but seeking to play them off against each other to Africa's advantage. Even today, however, although that may be changing, Africa remains marginal to the world's great conflicts; how often, except for instances of mass starvation, refugees, and civil war, do African issues make it onto our television screens?

At both the domestic and the international levels, therefore, with the exceptions already noted, Sub-Saharan Africa has been a net importer of ideas and models of world affairs, both with regard to strategies of development *and* global power politics, and not an exporter of them to other regions. That is because scholars, public officials, and the general public have generally denigrated Africa, asking what if anything it has to offer. Africa has thus been a victim both of its own inadequacies and of other peoples' and nations' negative, even sneering attitudes toward it. Is that, finally, beginning to change?

History and Political Culture

Archeology tells us that life, including eventually human life, began in Africa, probably close to the equator and near the lakes region of East Africa. Africa is the setting for what has been termed "the long dawn of human history." Humans then migrated north, up the Nile River, around the Fertile Crescent, and on to the Middle East, Europe, and Asia. From Asia, the evidence shows, humans migrated across the Bering Sea and throughout the Americas, North, Central, and South.

Although human life may have begun in central Africa (China sometimes claims this honor for itself), we know relatively little about the earliest African peoples and civilizations. We know a lot about the earliest Egyptian, Cretan, Phoenician, Hebrew, Syrian, Babylonian, Persian,

Indian, and Chinese civilizations of two, four, or even six thousand years ago, but almost nothing about Sub-Saharan African civilizations of the same time periods. The reasons for this are complicated, having to do with the absence of very many archeological explorations in Africa, the lack of funds available, disinterest by governments in the region who have other priorities, and doubtless the disintegrative effects on possible sites of heat, rainfall, and tropical moisture and parasites. But perhaps the greatest cause is that the African tradition is more an oral tradition than a written one, which causes a great loss of historical memory over the centuries. Most areas of Africa, unlike the other civilizations mentioned, lacked an alphabet or a written or carved record to which future generations, to say nothing of future social scientists, could refer.

We should not be entirely surprised if deep-grained prejudice had something to do with the lack of attention to Africa as well. Westerners have long had deep, including blatant racial prejudices toward Africa. Africa was dubbed, with obviously racial connotations, "the Dark Continent" by those early, mainly European explorers and imperialists who traveled there. The terms used to describe Africa – "primitive," "backward," even "underdeveloped" – convey similar bias. The attitude often is seldom expressed in polite company but always there just below the surface, that underdeveloped countries such as those in Africa are populated by "underdeveloped people," a dangerous and race-based concept that we must seek to avoid. Even today, racial prejudice toward Africa remains strong even while no longer quite so blatant as in the past.

Africa's history goes back *millions* of years. Neolithic rock carvings indicate that early hunting and gathering communities existed in Africa long before they arrived in Europe or the Middle East. Organized agriculture in Africa goes back to at least 6000 B.C.; early Africans had also learned to work iron, to cultivate grains and forests, to fashion tools, and to domesticate animals. Some of the early cave paintings found in Africa rival the more famous ones found in France and Spain. Africa pioneered in long-distance trade, in social organization, and in having settled cultures. Some of the world's first large-scale kingdoms and civilizations emerged in Africa, but for most of its history the continent was a patchwork of diverse, usually smaller cultures and organized groups. We have almost no *written records* of these events.

While Africa's ancient history is obscure for the reasons cited above, we do know quite a bit, in fragments, about some sub-areas of the continent. Thus, for example, the Sudan and the headwaters of the Nile River were all part of an ancient and rich civilization centered in Egypt. In the fourth century A.D., when Europe was still mainly pagan, the ancient kingdom of Ethiopia was already a center of Christianity, one of the oldest Christian kingdoms in the world. During the Middle Ages, when justice in much of the world was still determined at the point of a sword, several African kingdoms already had courts of law and an early system of justice.

There are other surprising facts that emerge from a clear-eyed and non-prejudiced examination of African history. Thus, as far back as the eleventh century, the kingdom of Ghana was able to organize and raise an army of 200,000 men; in contrast, the Norman invasion of England in 1066 was carried out by a force of only 15,000. We know that in the late Middle Ages there were already caravans across the Sahara Desert from Mali, Niger, and points south all the way up to North Africa, the Mediterranean, and, hence, to Europe. Similarly, in the fourteenth century at Jenne and Timbuktu, Africa had centers of learning that rivaled most European university centers.

These examples show that Africa is not without history, *its own* history, even ancient history, as well as culture and civilization. The trouble is not only a lack, for the most part, of a written\ history, but also that the history we do have is fragmented. That is, if we are looking for a single, all-encompassing history of "African civilization," we are bound to be disappointed. There is no one, single history of Africa. Rather, what we have are fragments of history, from different time periods, and from different regions of this vast continent. Instead of a single "African history," we would be better off to focus on regional histories (in the plural), local histories, ethnic or tribal histories. When we do that, we often discover a rich but varied cultural and ethnographic background.

This rich culture, tradition, and history of Africa was rudely interrupted by heavy-handed European colonialism and imperialism beginning in the fifteenth century. As early as the 1440s the Portuguese, the first European imperialists, were exploring down the Western coast of Africa, eventually rounding the Cape of Good Hope (South Africa) in 1497 and then exploring East Africa, the Indian Ocean islands (most of which still have Portuguese names), and sailing all the way to India and eventually to Japan. Though mainly interested in gold, ivory, and spices, the Portuguese found the African slave trade to be even more profitable. Soon the other great European powers – Spain, France, Holland, and England – joined in this nefarious but highly profitable trafficking in human slaves. Africa began to be divided up by the European powers, each of whom had a "colony" or *entrepot* for the gathering and shipping of slaves rounded up and provided by greedy African tribal chiefs.

While Europeans dominated the coastal areas of Africa from the sixteenth century on, the vast interior of Africa had yet to be explored. That would occur mainly in the nineteenth century when these countries, now plus Belgium, Italy, and Germany, staked out claims to virtually all of the African continent. It perhaps goes without saying that the colonial powers were not interested in developing Africa but only in exploiting it and its riches. Hence, there was no interest whatsoever in bringing education to Africa, improving health conditions, raising literacy or building infrastructure beyond what was used to exploit its natural resources. These long centuries of colonialism, imperialism, and exploitation meant that Africa, like Latin America, the Middle East, and South and Southeast Asia, missed out on the enlightenment, the industrial revolution, the knowledge revolution in science and technology, and the democratic revolution – all the great modernizing revolutions that led to the modern world. Modernization and development didn't simply pass Africa by; rather, Africa was *deprived* of these possibilities by rapacious colonialism.

Africa was carved up by the colonial powers seemingly without regard for existing clans, tribes, ethnicities, kingdoms, or even geographic realities. Thus Portugal, a tiny European country, seized tracts in Africa – Angola, Mozambique, Cape Verde, Guinea, and Bissau – that were *hundreds* of times bigger than the mother country; Spain took Morocco, the Canary Islands, and other enclaves both on Africa's Mediterranean and Western coasts. The Dutch seized virtually all of Southern Africa (later ceded to Great Britain) while England itself garnered territories in West (Ghana), Central (Nigeria), South (Rhodesia), and East (Kenya) Africa. France took most of Africa just south of the Sahara Desert (Chad, Niger, Mali, Senegal, and Cote d'Ivoire), and Italy moved down the Red Sea to capture Ethiopia and Somalia. Belgium and Germany were both late-comers to the "game" of dividing up Africa; in the late nineteenth century, they took huge territories in Central and East Africa.

Colonialism was not just cruel, exploitive, and based on blatant racism, it postponed Africa's chance to develop in tandem with other global areas for four and even five centuries. Among the colonial powers, it is usually conceded that the Belgians in the (Belgian) Congo were the worst in their treatment of their colonial subjects, followed by the French. There is, however, lots of blame to go around.

The picture we should have of colonialism, nevertheless, is not necessarily all evil. The Europeans brought some, limited schools, hospitals, roads, docks, technologies, improvements in agriculture, health, and mining, as well as Christianity, to Africa. Some were more paternalistic and caring than others in their treatment of the native Africans. And even Marx conceded that colonialism was necessary as a *first step* in stimulating African development. But let us make no mistake about it: the basic role of Europe in Africa was exploitive, the extraction and exploitation of African resources not for the good of Africa but for the benefit of the colonial powers. In its wake, colonialism left Africa all but completely unprepared for independence: no universities, no civil service, no government institutions, no trained police or armies, no civil society, and no training or preparation for democracy or self-government.

A handful of African countries became independent after World War I. But the bulk of them achieved independence only after World War II had exhausted the main colonial powers: France, Great Britain, and Belgium. There was one spurt in the late 1950s to early 1960s when so many African countries became independent that it *doubled* the membership of the United Nations' General Assembly – and then the membership doubled again. Portugal tried stubbornly to hang onto its large colonial possessions in Africa, seeing them as a key to Portugal's own economic development; but in the mid-1970s, after a revolution in Portugal itself, it was forced to relinquish its colonies as well. We now had a *host* of "New Nations" on the world scene, and a considerable literature now sprang up to try to explain, understand, and assist these New Nations.

The first task after independence (what Ghanaian leader Kwame Nkrumah had called "the kingdom of God") would be to write a new constitution for the new country. But where to look for a model? Having mainly been educated at universities in Europe (Oxford, the Sorbonne, and the London School of Economics), the leaders of these new countries fashioned their constitutions on the European or American model, often translating whole sections of the Bill of Rights, for example, into their native language and incorporating these into their own basic laws. But often doing this without adapting these imported constitutions to their own national realities. The assumption was, apparently, that merely adopting the basic laws of the West on paper would make them work in practice in their own countries. But, of course, nothing could be farther from the truth: you can't just adopt the constitution of one country, in this case the U.S. or Europe (highly literate, industrialized, etc.), and expect it to work in the same way in another quite different cultural and geographic context.

National borders presented another difficult problem. The colonial powers had divided Africa among themselves using boundaries that had everything to do with European power politics and nothing to do with the realities of African geography or ethnic, clan, or tribal differences. These borders were carried over into the new states where in some cases specific ethnic groups would find themselves divided and located in two or more countries; in other cases, there would be so many incompatible ethnicities, cultures, and languages within a single territory that it was all but ungovernable. Much of the subsequent instability, violence, and civil wars in Africa stemmed from this basic fact that the new nation-states of Africa had little to do with the basic geographic and sociological realities underneath.

Much the same applies to other hastily organized institutions in the New Nations: the civil service, police, government ministries, armed forces, political parties, and bureaucracies. First, you can't borrow these institutions from some other country and expect them to work the same in your own country. Second, it takes *time* for new institutions to take hold and work effectively. And third, you must adapt these institutions, or the overall general model that you use, to the actualities of our own society. If you do not, the result will certainly be dysfunction and breakdown, precisely what happened to the new states of Africa by the mid-1960s.

Independence in Africa in the 1950s and early 1960s had been accompanied by great hope and optimism. But after the first few years the early optimism had dissipated. Things weren't working very well, governments were ineffective, political parties were poorly organized, the state was not delivering promised social policies: education, housing, health care, and the like. In addition, violence, civil strife, and even national breakdowns were spreading. Into this void created by ineffective governments, ethnic rivalries, societal strife, and – let us not forget – ongoing Cold War clashes between the United States and the Soviet Union, soon stepped the armies created by these new nations. By the mid-1960s and early 1970s, the initial democratic hopes in many nations had given way to the realities of repressive military governments, strong men, and long-term dictatorships.

Military rule in Africa lasted, depending on the country (and there was considerable variation in regime types), for roughly the next twenty to thirty years. These authoritarian governments were often cruel, bloody, and oppressive. In some countries, military rule and dictatorship alternated with usually brief periods of civilian government; in others, it produced civil war; in still others, it led to national breakdowns. In almost all countries the human rights situation deteriorated; in a few, there were mass genocides directed against opposing ethnic groups, peoples, and religions. Perhaps of equal importance in long-range terms, amidst all this tumult over a three-decade-long period, roughly the mid-1960s to the mid-1990s, there was precious little economic development in most of the African nations, *nor*, in Rostow's terms, was there even much infrastructure development for Africa to build upon in the future.

We are cheered by the recent emergence of greater democracy, more elections, a better human rights record, and greater stability in quite a number of African countries over the last twenty years. But what really turned the tide in Africa in this period was the global rise in oil, minerals, and general commodity prices. This leap in the prices for Africa's principal exports led to greater foreign investment, a growth in jobs, more prosperity, and more money in circulation. It led commodity-hungry countries like China, India, the Europeans, and, belatedly, the United States not only to invest in Africa but also, especially in the Chinese case, to send thousands of their own people to buy African land, emigrate there, become farmers, and ship their crops back to China.

Rising commodity prices and more money sloshing around led to a sharp rise in government corruption, bribery, and payoffs to keep opposition groups and tribes from revolting. Vast patronage networks developed in which not just key individuals but often whole tribes or ethnicities or at least their leaders were put on the public payroll as a way of buying their loyalty. You do not revolt against a government that is paying your salary!

But is this real development or democracy? We should be encouraged by the steps, often halting, toward greater democracy and better human rights, and it is advantageous to have more money in circulation which also raises per-capita income. But the levels of corruption, bribery, and patronage remain very high and much too wasteful. And what if, as at present, those high commodity prices that have financed Africa's development over the last decade begin declining? Then will we see not just a decline in the level of development that Africa has recently enjoyed, but also a renewed squeeze and undermining of Africa's still-fragile democracies?

Recall from our earlier analysis that only six countries out of fifty in Africa could be said to be doing well economically and only twelve of fifty (fewer than a quarter) doing either well or moderately well. But that leaves thirty-eight out of fifty not doing so well and six of these among the world's poorest countries. It is not an impressive record; moreover, the continued reliance almost exclusively on instable commodity prices may not bode well for the future.

Socioeconomic Overview

It hardly needs repeating that Africa is a very poor area, the poorest in the world. Take a look again at those figures in Table 9.1: not a single wealthy country, only a handful (out of fifty) doing moderately well, most (80 percent of the countries) mired in extreme poverty. Here in Africa is where most of the problems we read about lie, of mass malnutrition and widespread disease. Here too are most of the countries where people must try to get by on an average of one or two dollars a day, where the vast majority of the population has no income at all. No other continent in the world has so many poor countries (in Latin America only one country out of twenty, Haiti is as poor as the majority of African countries) and so many poor people. One may find it hard

245

to believe that the numbers in Table 9.1 are entirely accurate; they are at best only estimates, often pumped up by the country providing them, and my own belief is that most of the countries are even poorer than the statistics indicate.

Let us start at the top and work our way down the scale. What we will find is that *all* the rich countries are anomalies in different ways. They do not represent the continent as a whole. Nor, as the wealthiest countries, do they represent a path, let alone a model for the other countries to follow?

Only two countries in Africa have annual per-capita incomes above $20,000. But the richest one of these, the Seychelles, is not even an African country. It is a group of islands in the Indian Ocean off the eastern African coast. It is classified as "African" because it lies "close" (600 miles) to the main continent. But culturally, ethically, religiously, sociologically, and racially, the Seychelles is not an African country; it is something else, mixed, partly Asian and Middle Eastern, a trading center, which also helps explain its relatively successful development.

Equatorial Guinea is another anomaly. It lies *on* the African continent but, like the Seychelles, it is not representative of the continent as a whole. That is because Equatorial Guinea almost literally floats on diamonds. In this sense, it is an accident of history or, better, of geology, like Bahrain, Qatar, Kuwait, Saudi Arabia, or the UAE. It has the sheer "dumb luck" of having the world's richest diamond mines. Like the Persian Gulf countries mentioned, Equatorial Guinea's wealth is due not to merit or achievement but to pure serendipity. It is also not representative of the continent as a whole nor could other countries hope to emulate its "model."

Four countries – Botswana, Gabon, South Africa, and Mauritius – have per-capita incomes between $10,000 and $20,000. Two others, the Maldives and Namibia, are so close to the $10,000 threshold that we will include them in that category. But look carefully again at this list. South Africa, with its mix of black and white, is the most European of the African countries; it is no accident that it has the largest gross national product in Africa and is often considered among the BRICS: Brazil, Russia, India, China, and South Africa.

Two of our group, Botswana and Namibia, border on South Africa and benefit from the jobs, prosperity, and economic activities of the larger South African economy. The Maldives is another group of islands far off the African coast and is, like the Seychelles, not an "African" country. Finally, Mauritius is also an island which, like the Seychelles and the Maldives, has long benefitted from ocean-going trade, business, investment, and commerce. Another case of a geographically African but culturally, ethnically, and sociologically a non-African country.

It is striking that *all* the relatively well-off African countries are anomalies in some ways. Their *relative* prosperity, compared to the other countries, seems mainly based on the good fortune of location. Three of the top eight countries are islands off the African coast and thus have a history of beneficial trade and commerce. Two of the countries have the advantage of lying on the border of wealthier South Africa, and two others are swimming in diamonds. The eighth, South Africa, had the advantage of European business, trade, and technology for 450 years.

Our next group of countries has per-capita incomes between $5,000 and $10,000. The list includes four countries: Angola, Cape Verde, Nigeria, and Swaziland. These are countries that are doing moderately well. Angola and Cape Verde are former Portuguese colonies; they have the advantages of vast oil reserves and other mineral resources (Angola) or of being on major trade, commerce, and airline routes (Cape Verde). Nigeria has the advantages of a large, English-speaking population and is one of the largest oil producers in the world. With these advantages, Nigeria should be developing much faster than it is but ineffective government, corruption, disorganization, and terrorism (Boko Haram) hold it back. Swaziland, like Botswana and Namibia, is on the northern border of South Africa and similarly benefits from the jobs and economic dynamism of its large neighbor.

The next classification includes countries between $1,000 and $5,000. This is the largest group in Africa, with thirty countries (60 percent) falling into this category. *All* of these countries are struggling. There are *no* major developmental breakthroughs or successes here, and certainly no "models" of development. There are countries that are crawling, not running, racked by poverty and underdevelopment, with only limited modernization. These countries often have limited developmental success for a brief time; tend often to fall back into chaos, bad government, and public insecurity; then raise themselves up again. In general, in these countries infrastructure is underdeveloped, civil society is weak, and civil strife (class, ethnic, and political) is endemic. A *few* of these countries may succeed over the long term in raising themselves out of poverty and underdevelopment, but as a whole they offer more discouragement than hope.

Our last category is countries with under $1,000 per-capita income. These are the poorest of the poor: Burundi, Central African Republic, Democratic Republic of the Congo, Liberia, Malawi, and Niger. These six countries, in general, have very few resources, almost no infrastructure, and are off the main routes for trade, commerce, and investment. Five of the six are racked by violence, conflict, ethnic strife, and/or civil war. How can you develop under these conditions? Answer: you can't. How can you achieve democracy if you have no infrastructure, weak civil society, and none of the prerequisites (literacy, economic development, and social modernization) for democracy? Answer: you probably can't succeed at that either. So what do you do in cases like these that are almost hopeless? Answer below.

This quick survey of social and economic development in Africa does not leave one optimistic about the future. Of the top eight countries, it is striking that *all* of them are doing well (compared to their neighbors) only because of accidents of history or geography: two receive the rub-off effect of being next-door neighbors of wealthy South Africa, three are islands not only on the major trading routes but also isolated from the continent's internal turmoil, two are awash in diamonds or oil, and one, South Africa, benefitted from being a European outpost (like Australia or New Zealand) for so long. *None* of the top eight made it mainly on the basis of its own skill, endeavor, or hard work (like Taiwan, South Korea, Hong Kong, or Singapore), although those traits may have been involved as well.

Much the same conclusion applies to the second tier of countries. Of the four countries in this group, two virtually float on oil, one has the advantage of lying on all the coastal trade routes, and a fourth, like the other two above, benefits from being in South Africa's economic orbit. One would have to say, therefore, that *all twelve* of Africa's leading countries are sure-fire bets, guaranteed not to miss, because of (1) oil, (2) diamonds, (3) international trade, and (4) location, location, location: proximity to the big South African market.

But where in this accounting are countries that made it on their own, without natural resources, or without the benefits of a prime location? The answer is: there are none. And that is the reason many analysts are pessimistic about Africa, not just the present but the future, too, especially for the three-quarters of Africa, unlike these others, not so blessed or richly endowed. Where is the formula, the pathway, the model for growth other than the pure good luck that these leading countries enjoy?

Or should we not be quite so pessimistic? Read on!

Government Institutions and the Role of the State

In Sub-Saharan Africa, as in other developing areas that we've dealt with, the precise form of government, a parliamentary or a presidential regime, probably doesn't matter very much. One can make an argument for either of these two forms. On balance, given the disintegrative, centrifugal forces in African society and politics, a presidential system is probably better since a strong president can better hold a divided country with weak infrastructure and weak civil society together than can a parliamentary regime with only a weak prime minister.

The reason the experts say the form of government doesn't matter very much is that other, what we can call existential, issues are so much more important than that one. The list includes establishing security, avoiding rebellion and civil war, keeping the various ethnic groups satisfied, providing at least a minimum of public services, maintaining law and order, keeping out foreign invaders, and sheer state survival. These are all first-order, existential requirements without which the state or the nation might not survive. *Of course,* you also want to get your laws, constitution, and form of government correct, but these issues pale into insignificance compared to the higher-order priorities listed above. If you cannot provide the basic requirements of a state, then the precise form of government doesn't matter very much.

What Africa requires, under whatever form of government it chooses, is good, honest, effective government that delivers real goods and services to its people. That can be done under different types of regimes: parliamentary, presidential, or various hybrids. Experience as well as Africa's preferences have led in most cases to a presidential system with especially strong presidents and weak congresses and judiciaries. The risk in such a system is presidents that are so strong that they become autocrats, only weak checks and balances, and, in the absence of well-institutionalized court systems, the absence or weakness of the rule of law.

If the precise institutional form that the government takes is of lesser importance, what is, or has been, the big governance issue? In addition to those existential issues of state maintenance and survival listed above, the big issue has been civilian versus military regimes, including under both of these widespread human rights abuses and lack of either political rights or civil liberties. Most African states started off in the 1960s as civilian, constitutional governments; by the 1970s the armed forces were in control or operating just below the surface of civilian government in most countries. Often these military regimes gave rise to long-term dictatorships – Robert Mugabe in Zimbabwe, Joseph Mobutu in the Congo – that stayed in power for twenty years or more and were often gross abusers of human rights. In the 1990s the pendulum began to swing back, though incompletely, to civilian rule, although some of these governments were just as destructive of human rights as were the military regimes.

The issue is not just human rights abuses or violations of civil liberties but, more broadly, widespread citizen insecurity. Here we often have weak governments, with limited reach, weak court and judicial systems, corrupt police and military forces, and irregular militias, terrorists (Boko Haram) revolutionary groups, and outright criminal gangs operating in both cities and countryside. In this context, neither citizens, farms, schools, mines, factories, or even homes can feel secure. How can you have either democracy or development in a situation of such widespread violence, chaos, breakdown, absence of law and order, and citizen insecurity? Answer: only marginally, sporadically, and with great difficulty.

Terrorism is important to consider when discussing the widespread instability in Sub-Saharan Africa. Regions within sub-Saharan Africa that are host to regional extremist groups include Sahel, the Lake Chad Basin, and the Horn of Africa. The terrorist groups in these areas include al-Qaeda in the Islamic Maghreb, al-Mourabitun, and Ansar al-Dine, Boko Haram, and al-Shabaab respectively[53]. Harakat al-Shabaab al-Mujahidin, more commonly known as Al-Shabaab, an Al-Qaeda affiliate controlled many parts of Southern Somalia between 2006 and 2007. While having lost some ground, they continue to plan and execute terrorist attacks in Somalia, and have claimed responsibility for some attacks in Kenya and Uganda[54]. Boko Haram, based in Nigeria, promotes a version of Islam in which Muslims are forbidden from taking part in any political or social activity with Western society. Since its founding in 2002, the group has carried out many attacks including bombings, and multiple kidnappings that shook Nigeria, neighboring states, and the world[55]. The lack of governments or governments' ability to effectively monitor and control radicalizing elements have allowed the groups to dominate territories and trade. Widespread poverty and unemployment in the region also makes radicalization and recruitment for these groups relatively easy. Affiliations with international groups such as Al-Qaeda and ISIS provide increased resources for these groups.

Under whatever system of government Africa opts for, the state usually plays a large role, in aspiration if not always in actual practice. The state is strong because the private sector is weak, often almost non-existent. In addition to honest, decent government, what Africa needs is a dynamic, entrepreneurial, private sector to provide jobs and raise living standards. Some countries – South Africa, Nigeria, and a few others – have such a dynamic capitalistic class, but not very many. When the private sector is so weak, the state must step in to provide the economic leadership that would otherwise be lacking.

The trouble with this model, of a strong state, often patterned on the examples of China or Singapore, is that it concentrates a large amount of power and money in a very few hands. And with that, the opportunities and possibilities for corruption, even corruption on a massive scale, become huge. The temptation to accept bribes, to dole out patronage and sinecure jobs, or to skim a little (or a lot!) off the top of government contracts and business deals becomes too great. Some economists have argued that the best way to reduce this kind of corruption is to reduce the size of the African state and thus reduce the amount of money available. But if both the state and the entrepreneurial class are weak, where will the thrust and the dynamism for development come from?

If presidentialism-parliamentarianism has not been a big issue for Africa, the issue of Federalism-Unitarianism merits greater attention. Most African states are unitary because local and regional governments are weak or nonexistent and because almost all African regimes have opted for centralized state power. But given Africa's tribal or ethnic makeup, perhaps a more decentralized federalism deserves a second look. That, after all, is Africa's reality; why not recognize that in law and constitution by devolving greater decision-making power on local government organizations that reflect the country's ethnic makeup?

Already, many of Africa's social services – schools, hospitals, welfare, and police protection – are being administered *de facto* at the local tribal level; why not formalize that reality constitutionally? The answer is that

African central governments fear that such a devolution and decentralization of power may produce a particular group or region going its own way, as recently in the South Sudan, leading to the division or breakup of the state itself. But could federalism be much worse than the many corrupt as well as ineffective governments that we have now?

The state in Africa aspires to be strong, and it is sometimes brutal, but the reality is that state power seldom reaches much beyond the capital city. That is *overwhelmingly* where power, money, and coercion (police and army) are concentrated. Hence, while the elites and politicians in the capital city debate such lofty issues as capitalism, socialism, or corporatism, that discussion or the policies that may flow from it seldom reach out into the countryside. In this sense, the argument over which *model* to use to achieve development, in such under-institutionalized countries as many of these, is simply not relevant to the lives of the great mass of the people. They must cope and manage on their own regardless of the decisions reached by the central government. Here, then, is perhaps another argument for experimenting with a federal form of government. Certainly, federalism in some African states could not be worse – more honest, effective, and closer to the people – than the unitary forms they have at present.

This debate also relates to the realities of civil society in Africa. Most of what Westerners think of as belonging to the realm of civil society – labor unions, professional associations, business groups, and political parties – are either exceedingly weak or entirely missing from the African political scene. What *does* exist, and what forms the African version of civil society, is largely organized at the local, clan, tribal, or ethnic level. Here exists a quite rich civil society even if it does not always conform to the West's notion of civil society. Here there are schools, health clinics, churches, local organizations, social services, etc. that form a vast web of *African* civil society. Ways must be found to tap into and build upon this form of African civil society rather than calling for the development of *Western* forms (political parties and the like) that hardly exist in the African context, or denigrating these institutions as "tribal" and "traditional," and, therefore, to be abolished or not paid serious attention. In fact, one could envision an entirely new network of *African* civil society and infrastructure grounded on these ancient, indigenous, societal organizations.

Some African regimes have attempted to build upon this notion of an indigenous, home-grown, *African*, model of society and development. In Tanzania, this effort was called "Authenticity," as articulated by the country's charismatic but soon disillusioned independence leader Julius Nyerere. In Guinea the notion of an indigenous, nationalist, and revolutionary ideology was set forth by its independence leader Sékou Touré who favored a single-party state over a multiparty one. Other African regimes, like Putin in Russia, have advanced schemes for authoritarian or illiberal government, arguing that top-down rule was closer to the African tradition than was imported liberalism. Corporatism has similarly made inroads into Africa, but with a system of internal representation based on tribalism or ethnicity rather than, as in Europe, on occupational categories. But this approach runs into the African taboo of seeing anything worthwhile in tribalism, an institution many African leaders would like to consign to the dustbins of history.

While we may applaud some of these efforts to develop an authentic, local, Africa-centered model of development, the sad reality is that such indigenous models of development and national organization have delivered no more, and often less, in the way of goods and services than have the imported Western ones. And while the intellectual elites and political leaders in the capital city are busily debating these hot issues of grand theory, public opinion surveys tell us that what most Africans want is not an indigenous model of some kind but rather Western imports like Coca Cola, blue jeans, cars, washing machines, and maybe even democracy and human rights.

Is There an African Model?

The short answer to this question is: maybe. After what has gone before in this chapter, with its emphasis on violence, chaos, and breakdown, this at least half-way-positive answer requires some explanation.

In the first decades after independence, 1950s-1970s, Sub-Saharan Africa was a net importer of models from the outside. These included the favored U.S. developmentalist model à la Rostow, a European social-democratic model, a Soviet or Russian communist model, and a competing Chinese Maoist model. Because African independence leaders had mainly been educated in Europe (Paris and London), they tended to favor European social democracy led by a strong state over the U.S. limited-government model, but the U.S. had the money in those days and so the U.S.-favored solution also gained currency. The Cold War now seems so far away that we often forget that not only were the U.S. (capitalism) and the Soviets (Marxism) competing in Africa, but so were the even farther-left Chinese, Maoist, guerilla communists. These Cold War rivalries and machinations and the chaos they left behind provide one more reason (still another?) for Africa's difficult development path.

It is striking that *all* these model – the Western one in both its U.S. and European variants and the Eastern or communist one in its Russian and Chinese variations – were all *imported* from the outside. *None* of them had anything, or at least not much, to do with African culture, history, traditions, or realities. *All* of them were based on the rather narrow and quite unique experiences of North America, Europe, the Soviet Union, and China. A few years later these 1960s models imported from outside were joined by some others also imported from Western intellectual discourse: dependency theory which posits that the non-West is dependent and exploited by the West, bureaucratic-authoritarianism which was used to explain the 1960s-1970s rise of military regimes, and corporatism, a theory in the West designed to explain the relations of an interest group to the state but now applied to Africa through an analysis of ethnic pluralism.[56]

It took a decade or two, until the 1970s, for African intellectuals and political leaders to come to the conclusion that *none* of these models was right for them. Neither the Western model nor the socialist one, in any of their variations, fitted Africa very well; nor did they deliver in the way of goods, services, or development. With this growing realization on the part of the continent's elites, there ensued a renewed questioning, a prolonged period of self-examination. The questions asked were similar to those asked in other Third World areas at about the same time: who are we as a culture and a people, how are we unique, is there a model of development that fits *Africa* better than the imported ones that we have been using so far, can we do it our way?

Astute readers will recognize that at about the same time these same questions were being asked in the Middle East, East Asia, India, and other non-Western areas. The main overarching questions were: (1) are the Western ways of development the only ways of doing things, and (2) are there elements in our own culture and tradition on which we could build *our own, indigenous* model of development? Obviously, this quest would play upon local pride, cultural identity, and nationalism.[57]

African intellectuals like Sékou Touré, Julius Nyerere, Kwame Nkrumah, and Ali Mazrui began this quest to find a home-grown *African* model to replace the often ill-fitting foreign and imported ones.[58] The result was such movements as the Tanzanian quest for "authenticity," the effort in Kenya and elsewhere to construct a political system based on corporate-ethnic pluralism, various attempts to develop a single-party-inclusive state, and even some efforts to justify authoritarianism by invoking unity and nationalism. All of these efforts so far have foundered on the same shoals that destroyed Africa's earlier efforts at democracy: corruption, poverty, and lack of organization and infrastructure.

The jury is still out on some of these experiments, just as it is still out on the Iranian Revolution (1979) of this same time period. On the one hand, it led to a lot of African self-examination and soul-searching, which was probably beneficial. On the other, not a lot concretely came out of this process; the indigenous models set forth, unfortunately, were no more successful in solving Africa's manifold problems and achieving development than had been the earlier imported ones. Meanwhile, third, the African people, as always skeptical of grand plans coming from the elites in the capital cities, "voted with their feet" by opting for Western movies, Western cellphones and iPads, and a Western consumer society over some vague notions like "authenticity" or a "home-grown" model.

The quest, therefore, for an effective, workable, "African model" still goes on.

CHAPTER 10

CONCLUSION: ONE AND MANY PATHS TO DEVELOPMENT

The world has changed enormously in the last twenty-five years. Three themes dominate the discussion. The first is the relative decline of the United States, both in terms of the dominance of its, or "the West's," political-economic model *and* in terms of its strategic ability to dominate events abroad. The era when the U.S. model of governance and economic policy – the "unipolar moment," the "Washington Consensus," or the "only game in town," – seemed like the wave of the future, indeed the only wave, is over. Or, so it seems, *mostly* over. The time when, as Charles Krauthammer put it, in his "unipolar moment" essay, the U.S. could *impose* its system on other countries is similarly over. That *is* gone. And these trends call for a fundamental rethinking of U.S. foreign and development policy.

The second theme, closely related to the first, is the rise or resurgence of other challenging powers, which have undermined the U.S. position of a quarter-century ago of unparalleled superpower dominance. Here we are speaking of a resurgent Russia under Vladimir Putin and the reassertion by him of an aggressive, nationalistic, autocratic model; the rise of China since the 1990s as the world's biggest economy and China's assertion of a similarly aggressive and expansionist foreign policy; and the rise of Iran, ISIS, and the broader Middle East as a main challenge and preoccupation of U.S. foreign policy.

In addition, we have the success stories of East Asia – first, Japan, then South Korea, Taiwan, Hong Kong, and now especially Singapore – which serve as alternative models for other Third World countries. To the surprise of many, in addition, India has now surpassed China in economic growth and will soon surpass it in population too, to become the world's biggest country/democracy. "The Rest" are also rising – Argentina, Brazil, Indonesia, Mexico, Nigeria, South Africa, Turkey, and Venezuela – and offering, sometimes brazenly, "their own" models for others to emulate. *All* of these countries are going their own way regardless of U.S. wishes and blandishments.

And that gets us to a third theme of this Conclusion: the inability or unwillingness of the U.S. or the Western Alliance to exercise the power to force or *impose* its will and its model on the rest of the world. This point has several causes and dimensions: unhappy and disappointing experiences in Iraq and Afghanistan, a declining inclination in the U.S. and Europe to get so deeply involved in other people's problems or to serve any longer as the policeman of the world's conflicts, and a certain decline ("declinism") in the U.S. itself – educationally, financially, politically, and perhaps in other ways.

In addition, to add to this list of problems, the U.S. and Europe have drifted apart over the years so that what was once referred to positively and strongly as "the West" or "the Atlantic Alliance" is now only an "alliance of the willing" – i.e., those willing, but not obliged, to join our efforts abroad. We need also to say that Europe itself, is no longer so united as it once was and lacks that unity of purpose that was present during the Cold War; this is highlighted by the 2016 Brexit referendum, with Great Britain leaving the EU.

All this makes it very difficult for the West to recommend, let alone impose, its model on the rest of the world. Not only is the West (if there still is such a thing) considerably weakened, by comparison, but many other nations and regions have become stronger. Hence, we begin our conclusion by reviewing and assessing these other nations' and regions' models and development plans, seen from a comparative politics perspective. Later in the Conclusion, we offer some more general comments growing out of the discussion on the current seismic shifts in global politics, viewed from an international relations and foreign policy point-of-view.

The Western Model

We began this book by discussing the Western model of development, as set forth a half-century ago by W. W. Rostow, S. M. Lipset, Gabriel A. Almond, and an entire school of academics and policy experts. The Western Model was set forth, recall, at the height of the Cold War as an alternative to the Communist Model. Indeed, Rostow had entitled his path-breaking book on economic development "a noncommunist manifesto." The Model was aimed especially at "new" or "developing" countries precisely at the time that the Cold War was shifting focus from Western Europe to the emerging nations.

The Western Model was based almost entirely on the experience of "the West": the United States and Western Europe. And Rostow was an economic historian, after all. His research showed that all societies went through five stages of growth: from purely traditional and semi-feudal, to a stage where the preconditions for growth were laid, to what he called the "takeoff" stage, then the drive to maturity, finally the age when development problems are overcome and the country enters a stage (which the U.S. and Western Europe were already in) of democracy, social justice, and high mass consumption.

Lipset and other 1960s-era sociologists echoed the Rostow thesis by showing the correlations between economic development, social modernization (education, urbanization, literacy, and the like) and democratization. Political scientist Almond and his colleagues in the then-influential Committee on Comparative Politics of the Social Science Research Council (CCP/SSRC) picked up on this theme by positing a set of seven functions that *all countries* had to perform (political socialization, interest articulation. interest aggregation, political rule making, rule enforcement, and rule adjudication), all of which bore a striking resemblance to the U.S. political system of democratic participation, interest group pluralism, and the three-part division of powers.

In the Rostow-Lipset-Almond framework, which fitted U.S. policy goals perfectly, *all countries* went through all of these stages and ended up, conveniently, looking exactly like we do – democratic, participatory, wealthy, socially just, etc.

The process was both inevitable and universal. No country could deviate from this model. There was only one path to development and we were it. In a twist on Marx, we would show all countries the mirror of the true, non-Marxian path to development. It was all very antiseptic: no coups, no thieving elites or dictators, no revolutions or civil wars; just one long, but inevitable, and eventually glorious highway to democracy and development.

What's wrong with this rosy picture? So many things; let us count the ways:

- The model was based entirely on the Western experience – and was not even an accurate portrayal of that. So far as we know, at the time (1960) neither Rostow nor Lipset nor Almond had ever visited a developing country.
- The model completely left out international influences on development: the World Bank, the International Monetary Fund, the Vatican, market trends, the U.S. and other meddlesome embassies, etc. The assumption seemed to be that only domestic forces are important in development.
- The model was overly peaceful and linear. There were no setbacks on the path to development: no revolutions, no coups, no civil wars, no violence, no class struggles, no counter-revolutions, no reversals of any kind. It was all peaceful and one-way, leading inexorably to a happy outcome.
- Culture, geography, resources, and history were all completely ignored. *All countries*, supposedly, went through the same stages and processes. But

some countries are richer in resources than others, some countries are closer to other rich countries and benefit from their proximity, countries have different histories which shape their current prospects, and surely, we know by now that cultural differences (for example, in the Islamic Middle East, Russia, East Asia, Africa, and Latin America) impact development in all kinds of important ways. In short, far too much was left out of the Rostow model.

- The developmentalist interpretation, as it came to be called, ignored the Cold War origins of the model and its purpose. The model was designed by Rostow et al. to be a non- (read, "anti- "} communist manifesto and to keep developing countries out of the clutches of the Soviet Union. This fundamental bias would continue to dog the Rostow model throughout its existence, and particularly after the fundamental Cold War purposes of the model ceased to exist in 1991.

- The model posited only a single path to development, one that looked exactly like we do. But that was wrong even at the time that Rostow and these others were writing. There were, in the 1950s and 1960s, already a *variety* of democratic regimes, a variety of authoritarian or military regimes, kingships and sultanates, multi- as well as single-party regimes, several (not just Russian but also Chinese, North Korean, and Eastern European) kinds of Marxist regimes, etc. Already in the 1960s other scholars were suggesting we be open to the idea of *multiple* routes to development, a lattice image or a trellis on which all the multiple flowers could climb, instead of only a single stem leading to development.

- Most scholars at the time ignored or failed to pay sufficient attention to the financial sponsors and Cold War origins of this model. In fact, most of the money for those new centers at Massachusetts Institute of Technology and Harvard (hence, the designation of the Rostow approach as "the Charles River School") to study and advance this particular model of development came from the CIA, the U.S. government, and foundations closely linked to the government. This bias ought to have been pointed out from the beginning but, in fact it was not, either because of ignorance of the true facts or, more darkly, because the scholars involved or hoping to be involved wished to protect their own possibilities for access to these funds. To be fair, we should also say that, at the time, almost no one associated with the Charles River approach saw any contradiction between their academic approach to development and the fact of U.S. government or CIA sponsorship.

The Rostow Model of development, which was, or became, "the Western Model," was thus flawed from the beginning – maybe fatally flawed. It was based on some very large assumptions that already, by the mid-to-late-1960s, were known to be flawed,[59] even false. But the Model was a product of the Camelot-like, romantic, John F. Kennedy, pre-Vietnam, pre-Watergate era; it was a time of great hope, optimism, and good will – what one writer called "the Peace Corps Mood" of the time. Which meant that *we* would lead while also sending our "best and brightest" out to the Third World to teach them how to do it. And that was to emulate *our* ways, our democracy, our economic system. At the time, almost no one saw the potential contradictions between our *wishes* for the Third World, our foreign policy goals, and the *realities* of development in difficult new and emerging nations.

Countries and Regions

The "Western Model," we have said, began as a conceptualization and an amalgam of the combined U.S. and Western European experience with development. The model began in the West, was conceptualized in the West, and was entirely a Western product. And so long as the Cold War was on and the U.S. and Western Europe were basically unified in their purposes, this model, which in its later incarnations was called "the Washington Consensus," would enjoy considerable official approval and support, even while academics and others had begun to attack it and, on the ground, the model was not working very well or delivering very much.

In our analysis of America, Europe, and the Atlantic Alliance and its model, three things happened. The first is that the Cold War ended, Russia was defeated and, therefore, the need for unity and common purpose between the U.S. and Western Europe disappeared, almost literally, overnight. Without a common enemy, there was no longer common purpose or a need to stick together. Such Cold War and Alliance institutions as NATO *struggled* to find a new role. The commonalities and mutual interests between the U.S. and Europe had always been overstated anyhow, but now, without the Cold War struggle to hold them together, the two partners increasingly went their separate ways.

The second thing that happened to the U.S.-European alliance and common model is that, over this twenty-five-year period, the U.S. changed. The U.S. is now much more divided, more fragmented, more isolationist, more polarized, and less inclined to get involved in other countries' affairs than previously. We are less confident as a nation, less sure of the universality of the American model and way of doing things, more chastised, and less-oriented toward foreign interventions or to putting out global brushfires. Without getting into deeper discussion or arguments over America's decline or the issue of "declinism", it seems incontrovertible that, in terms of the economy, governance, education and schools, and politics as well as intellectual life, America is relatively less of a global leader now than it was two-and-a-half decades ago. This decline in our main institutions undoubtedly has a negative effect on our willingness to continue serving as a global leader.

The third major change involving the Western Alliance is in Europe itself. Europe is more internally divided, the European economic model is even less productive than is the American one, and Europe is affected with a continent-wide malaise. In addition, on a host of issues – religion, capital punishment, the UN, the use of military force, drugs, and euthanasia – the U.S. and Europe are growing very far apart culturally and socially, making it hard for us to work together any more. Expecting to be "whole and free" after the Cold War, and with no more enemies, Europe has unilaterally disarmed, but now has a difficult time facing a resurgent and aggressive Russia. Additionally, Eastern Europe, bordering on and more fearful of Russia, is presently closer to the U.S. as an ally than are our erstwhile former Cold War partners in Western Europe. The Western Alliance and, therefore, what used to pass as a common Western model, looks to have frayed around the edges and may not be capable of being put back together again.

The West's greatest successes, from a policy point of view and in terms of exporting its particular model of development, appear to have been some twenty-five years ago and in two specific regional areas: Eastern Europe and Latin America. With regard, first, to Eastern Europe: in 1991 the Soviet Union disintegrated, it had already begun pulling its troops out of the Eastern European countries, and over the next few years all of Eastern Europe became independent of Soviet control for the first time in nearly half-a-century. Almost all of Eastern Europe *rushed* to democratize, to convert to a modern/mixed (free-market/social-democratic) economy, and to join the two great European/Western "clubs": the EU and NATO. Eastern Europe wished to join the EU because they associated it with freedom, prosperity, and progress; they embraced NATO because it offered military protection from any future aggression by the Great Russian bear.

Both the EU and NATO required significant reforms as a condition of membership: democracy, human rights, elections, government reform, financial reform, freedom for civil society groups, anti-corruption measures, and literally *thousands* of others.[60] There was considerable fudging of the criteria to allow some marginally qualified countries – Bulgaria, Romania, Slovakia; now Croatia, Serbia, and others – to come in. But by-and-large we can say that the West's Eastern European policy has been a great success. Although there has been some slippage recently in Hungary, whose president Victor Orban expressed admiration for Russia's Vladimir Putin and the Russian autocratic or "illiberal" model[61], over the last twenty years Eastern Europe has been steadfast in its continuing commitment to democracy, human rights, economic development via the Western model, integration into the EU, and defense modernization in support of NATO. At this point some two-and-a-half decades later, it would be inconceivable for Eastern Europe to abandon democracy, free markets, or the West's security blanket. The recent resurgence and, therefore, threat to Eastern Europe of Russia has reinforced all these earlier trends.

Latin America's model for change may be considered in much the same light as Eastern Europe's: democratization, adherence to orthodox and mainstream economics, and at roughly the same time period. Except that Latin America's transition to democracy began somewhat earlier, in the late 1970s, and carried right through the 1990s. Meanwhile, its economic reform program came at precisely the same time as the decline of the Soviet Union and the discrediting of the alternative Marxist or Import Substitution Industrialization (ISI-statist) models. Hence, its adherence, for the most part, to a free-market model.

Latin America provided, moreover, the main setting for the working out of the "Washington Consensus." With the emphasis on democracy, open markets, and free trade, the "Consensus:" was essentially a continuation and extension of the earlier Rostow/Western model. Indeed, Latin America went *beyond* the Washington Consensus by attaching to the Organization of American States (OAS) charter the "Charter of the Americas" which insisted not just on democracy for all the countries of the hemisphere but also provided for penalties against any country that violated democratic precepts – for example, Honduras in 2009.[62]

Latin America thus strapped itself into a straightjacket of a certain time and place, an orthodoxy from which there could be no deviation. While one may be in favor of open markets, and free trade, countries ought to be free to choose. In fact, at the time the Washington Consensus was still being debated, a strong critique of it argued that democracy had not been secured in the area (and is currently in decline – down to 50 percent in public support), that statism was alive and well, and that free trade depended more on the *U.S.* lowering trade barriers (which we have not done) than Latin America.[63] In addition, a transitional solution, various half-way houses of conditional, limited, or controlled democracy in Latin America, a greater role for the state in the economy in the absence of a vibrant private sector, and an updated form of liberalism combined with corporatism in the social sphere would have been more favorable. These recommendations are, of course, controversial but they would provide Latin America a measure of flexibility in keeping with its transitional development status.

Russia is a completely different story – or is it? After the Soviet Union collapsed in 1991, Russia was, for a time, completely open to the Western model: democracy, capitalism, and integration into Europe. In Russia at the time, the early 1990s; some efforts were directed at creating new political science and international affairs departments and helping reform Russian universities overall.[64] But the elected democratic president at the time, Boris Yeltsin, proved to be a drunken disaster, the economic reforms disintegrated into complete failure and chaos, and a greatly reduced (in size, population, and strength) Russia lost its superpower status.

By the mid-to-late 1990s, there was widespread discontent in Russia with the existing state of things: poverty, high unemployment, lowered life expectancy, corruption, internal chaos, and loss of international power. Moreover, there was rising impatience and resentment at the ineffectiveness of the democratic reforms the U.S. had helped usher in, the failures of the free-market model, and Russia's reduced international status[65]. Vladimir Putin would, a few years later, ride these rising discontents to power, eventually to autocratic power. In the course of things Putin began asserting the authoritarian, illiberal (with respect to basic rights), nationalistic, chauvinistic, aggressive (with regard to foreign policy) model that we described in Chapter 3. For the purposes of this book and its main themes, therefore, and in sharp contrast to both Eastern Europe and Latin America, Russia is important for two things: (1) an outright rejection of the U.S.-Western-EU model of politics, economics, and world order, and (2) the assertion of *its own* autocratic, statist, and newly assertive model. For a time, the Putin model was also popular in Belarus, Egypt, Hungary, Kazakhstan, Moldova, Serbia, the Ukraine, Cuba, and Venezuela; but Russia's downward economic slide will diminish that model's attractiveness.

With respect to East Asia, we are talking about the Asian Model of development. But it was not always this way. Right after World War II, a defeated Japan was not only obliged to accept a U.S.-imposed constitution but also the Western model of democracy and free markets. South Korea, after its civil war with the North in 1950-52, and Taiwan, under a U.S. protectorate following the 1949 expulsion of the Kuomintang from Mainland (and Communist) China, were similar: countries under the U.S. wing that, at least initially, were obliged to follow the main tenets of the U.S. economic and political model. In short, the East Asian economic model at least at the beginning was similar to the Eastern European and Latin American experiences in adapting the Western model, but at a time a couple of decades earlier and when the Cold War – and the Soviet menace – was still on.

But then something funny happened. East Asia went its own way. It was the first global region outside the West to develop its own home-grown, indigenous, non-Western model of development. It accomplished this spectacular feat in two main ways. First, the countries of East Asia were *selective* in adopting Western ways. They never accepted the Western model in toto. Rather, they selectively borrowed from Western technology, industrial production, and ways of doing things, and adapted these to Asian (Confucian) culture.

Second and within that framework, they devised their own particularly East Asian model. That model, as distinct from Western free market capitalism, involved close collaboration between the state, the private sector, and especially the trade ministry. It was a particularly effective form of state capitalism under which East Asia achieved its miracle growth rates. By this point, Hong Kong, Singapore, and possibly others have joined the original three (Japan, South Korea, and Taiwan) in achieving miracle growth. Meanwhile, the U.S. Pacific Fleet and American foreign policy provided the international security blanket necessary for East Asia to thrive domestically.

At this stage there is no one, single "Asian Model"; instead, there are two or two-and-a-half models. The first is the democratic but statist model of Japan, South Korea, and Taiwan. The second, really only a half because it is so small and probably non-repeatable elsewhere, is the tight, autocratic model of Lee Kuan Yew in Singapore, now evolving toward the more open and democratic model of the other three. And the third is big, dynamic China which is using a state-capitalist/state socialist model coupled with an evolving (toward somewhat greater openness) Leninist system of political controls. Elsewhere in Southeast Asia the newly emerging economies of Indonesia, the Philippines, Malaysia, Thailand, and others are mainly following a not-very-efficient (not Confucian) statist model, coupled with electoral democracy in the political realm, but with considerable admiration for China's accomplishments. And its potential *threat* to them; hence, their, in general, seeking of protection (no NATO in Asia) through U.S. security.

India is clearly the most important country and the dominant power in South Asia, with aspirations to surpass China not just in economic development but in population, to become the world's biggest country, itself a measure of national power. The Indian case is distinct because its trajectory is just the opposite of that posited by Rostow et al.: democracy *first*, *then* economic development and social change. For India was, in a sense, "born free" and democratic like the United States, with democracy inherited immediately upon independence from its British colonizers.

Thereafter, India followed an irregular and tumultuous path: first, the disastrous "cottage industries" plan advocated by Gandhi (a great moral leader but not a great economist), then large-scale industrialization and state socialism under Nehru and the Congress Party, a continuation of statism on into the twenty-first century, followed by in the last decade a freeing up and liberalizing of the economy which produced the dramatic results noted above: surpassing China in economic growth. India's strategic position paralleled its economic model: a long-time alliance with the Soviet Union, followed by a more pragmatic foreign policy as India emerged as a major power, and culminating in India's recent strategic alignment with the United States. Overall, rather like Eastern Europe, Latin America, and East Asia, we can consider India's democratic/free market development, unorthodox though it is in terms of sequences, to be a major success for Western foreign policy and the Western model.

We seldom pay much attention to the rest of South Asia – Sri Lanka, Bangladesh, and Pakistan – except perhaps as they relate to the war in Afghanistan. But Pakistan was/ is a major U.S. ally (in contrast to India) during the Cold War, Bangladesh is one of the five largest countries in the *world* in terms of population, and Sri Lanka was long torn by a brutal civil war between the majority Hindus and the ethnic/religious minority Tamils. None of these three countries could be said to be a close ally of the United States; none of them has consistently followed the Western model of development although Bangladesh and Sri Lanka are moving in that direction away from statism and socialism, and none of them provides us with a distinct *model* meriting special or separate treatment.

When we turn to the Middle East, the issues become both more confusing and more complex. First, there is no one, single, dominant country in the Middle East comparable to Russia in Eurasia, China on the Asian mainland, or India in South Asia, although several countries – Egypt, Iran, Turkey, and Saudi Arabia – have aspirations to fill that role. Second, Iran and ISIS are both vying to be the leader of a more virulent, aggressive, and expansionist form of Islam; Iran, and perhaps ISIS now too, lays claim to having formulated a home-grown or Islamic model of the state and society, however anathema that model is to most Westerners. And third, we have in the Persian Gulf states (Kuwait, Bahrain, Qatar, Saudi Arabia, and the United Arab Emirates) a model of economic development that is possibly two-thirds of the way to the Western model: rapid economic development, accompanied now by vast social change, but with political systems still under monarchy or sultanship rather than democracy. And again, protected by the U.S. fleet and security forces.

So, which way the Middle East? It is the global area today that is most in conflict internally and with the West, most at odds with the Western political model though not necessarily its economic one, and where the Huntingtonian "clash of civilizations" is most manifest. One may wish that the Middle East was evolving in the direction of the Rostow-Lipset-Almond model (economic development to social change to democracy), but at this point we cannot say that. Nor can we rule out continued conflict and struggle for dominance among the Middle Eastern countries themselves, or with the United States. Of all the critical global areas covered in this book, the Middle East is clearly the most uncertain and the most dangerous.

Seen in contrast to the Middle East, Sub-Saharan Africa, even with all its manifold problems, looks positively benign. In part, that is because Sub-Saharan Africa is still at a lower level of development. It is, for the most part, just beginning the development process, at Rostow's first stages. Some countries, those with valuable oil or minerals, on the trade routes, or with locations close to wealthy South Africa, are doing well, while most, three-quarters of the countries, still have a very long way to go. In these early stages, infrastructure development *begins*, economic development begins, social change is just starting. And the political outcomes are still uncertain although the prospects for greater democracy seem hopeful. Sub-Saharan Africa is thus a work-in-progress, a *candidate* for the Western model and maybe even a hopeful one. Meanwhile, other outside powers – BRICS, BEMS, and "The Rest" – such as Brazil, India, China, and Russia – are all making inroads into Africa and challenging Europe (the former colonial powers) and the United States for dominance in the area.

Overall, if one views the macro picture, the Western model, for all its faults and problems, is not doing badly on the world stage. That conclusion comes as a bit of a surprise since the initial hypothesis of this book going in was that the Western model and the West itself were fraying, decaying, and unraveling. But look at the world: the Western Model is still healthy and doing well in *all* the places where it began or took strong root: North America, Europe, Australia, and New Zealand. Post-World War II, the Western Model also triumphed in much of East Asia: Japan, South Korea, Taiwan, Hong Kong, Singapore, and now in other Asian countries, too.

Additionally, with the collapse of the Soviet Union and the end of the Cold War, the Western model similarly triumphed in Eastern Europe and Latin America, virtually *all* of which have accepted the Washington Consensus. Similarly, now in South and Southeast Asia: in all these areas democracy, a modern, mixed economy, and free trade have become the only game in town. Sub-Saharan Africa is at this stage an open book, a *tabula rasa*, but in its better moments it seems to be tending in that direction.

That leaves three main, what we will call "holdout areas." Russia under Putin as well as some other (Belarus and Kazakhstan) nearby autocratic regimes; China and its influence in some neighboring states; and Iran, ISIS, and the turbulent Middle East. But Russia is already partly Western and Putin cannot last forever; China has liberalized its economy, if not yet very much its political system; and even in the Middle East the Gulf States are modernizing economically and socially, even though there is not yet much democracy present. Overall, then, it is a quite impressive record for the West and the Western model, and certainly not (although that is good for headlines and best-selling books) deserving of the "declinism" or "decayism" literature that is out there and seeping into the popular mindset.

The World of the Future

The world of the future, obviously with some nuances and adjustments, will likely not look all that different from the world of today. It may be audacious, and even dangerous, to speculate on what the world of years hence will look like; on the other hand, some of the main macro trends are quite clear. We begin with a discussion of the United States, the West, and the Western model, and then proceed along the same region-by-region lines as we did before, but this time with more of an international relations/foreign policy focus.

The United States is in decline according to some markers but not others, and overall the U.S. is likely to retain its elevated position in the world on into the future. It is discouraging that U.S. education scores are in decline, that the U.S. has slipped out of the top ten on several school tests, and that a significant percentage of Americans lack the skills and education to function effectively in the modern world. *Relative* to some others, in addition, the American economy is not quite as robust as it once was, the American political system is deeply divided and ineffective, and at several levels America seems to have lost both its direction and its moral compass. These are worrisome but certainly not fatal trends, and certainly not signs of predetermined declinism.

On the other side of the ledger, America has *by far* the world's most powerful armed forces, it leads the globe in technological innovation, and it is the world's only superpower.[66] The American economy is recovering faster from recession than either Europe's or Japan's and, while China has recently tied the U.S. in gross national product,

U.S. income on a per-capita basis is *three times* that of China. Foreign graduate students, including Chinese, Korean, Japanese, and Taiwanese, *flock* to U.S. graduate schools because they are *by far* the best in the world; and if you want to rise up quickly in the world, the U.S. is one of the only places where, with brains, dedication, and hard work, you can do it in one generation. Clearly, it is way premature to write off the U.S. or the American model; ever more, the U.S. is seen or indeed *is* a place that facilitates upward mobility. The main difference between today and thirty years ago is not so much the decline of America (although some trends in the U.S. are obviously worrisome) but what Zakaria has called "The Rise of the Rest."[67] That is, the rise of other countries to achieve parity with the U.S. in terms of living standards, or even to surpass America. Among the countries or regions that have reached economic equality with America in per-capita income terms are Western Europe (Southern Europe lags behind the U.S., the Nordic countries are ahead); Japan, Hong Kong, and Singapore in East Asia; and Qatar, Bahrain, Kuwait, Saudi Arabia, and the United Arab Emirates along the Persian Gulf. Other countries like South Korea are fast closing in on the United States in terms of the rankings, and some offshore banking centers like Bermuda or the Cayman Islands have also reached this advanced level. But by "The Rest" Zakaria has in mind a core group of developing countries that still lag behind the developed countries but nevertheless have really "taken off," à la Rostow, over the last thirty years: Argentina, Brazil, Chile, China, Colombia, India, Indonesia, Malaysia, Mexico, Nigeria, South Africa, Thailand, and Turkey. As these countries develop, it is, of course, only natural that the

U.S.'s share of global gross world product would be reduced somewhat.

Western Europe is one of the world's great success stories of the last seventy years and, along with North America, the historic center of the Western model. It is quite remarkable how successful this model was all through the forty-five years of the Cold War and the twenty-five years since the Soviet Union unraveled. While Western Europe has by now achieved economic parity with the United States and its advanced welfare state is the pride of most Europeans (even to the extent of being incorporated into the European definition of "democracy"),[68] in recent decades and with the Cold War over, Western Europe has increasingly gone its own way, independently of the U.S.

Culturally, socially, politically, and in terms of economic policy, Europe stands considerably to the left of the U.S.; more worrisome is the fact that since the Cold War ended Europe has so unilaterally disarmed as to be only a limited military force in international political and military affairs. And now that Russia is resurgent, Europe finds itself with only limited resources to counter Russian aggressiveness and can chiefly muster only moral condemnation, economic sanctions, diplomatic pressure, and votes in international assemblies – but precious little military might. Nevertheless, although it is not so easy anymore, when it comes to international terrorism, Russia's invasion of the Ukraine, or its threats to the Baltic countries and others, "the West" can still muster sufficient unity to act quite forcefully and the "Western model" still carries enormous weight and attractiveness in the world.

Two places where the Western model has triumphed most decisively are Eastern Europe and Latin America. Eastern Europe is one of the Western model's great success stories: the adoption of democracy virtually across the entire region; of modern, mixed, free-market economies; and of integration into the two great "clubs" of the Western world, the EU and NATO. Today it would be unthinkable for Eastern Europe to repudiate any of these features, and there would be immediate and hard-hitting sanctions if any of the countries of the area attempted to reverse course. Problem areas remain, certainly, in the Balkans, Hungary, and Southeastern Europe; but to most observers it looks like Eastern Europe has made a lasting and definitive commitment to the West and the Western model. That assumes, of course, that a resurgent Russia does not lay claim to or even invade its former Eastern European territories. Meanwhile, since it seems that Eastern Europe's fate is now a settled matter, the main centers of contention in this part of the world have moved several hundred miles to the east (and closer to, as Putin puts it, the "gates of Moscow"): Belarus, Moldova, the Ukraine, Georgia, and the Caucuses.

Latin America may, or may not, be a different story. On the one hand, Eastern Europe's per-capita income and levels of socioeconomic development are considerably higher, which helps its success story a lot, than those of Latin America. At the same time, Eastern Europe had the great advantage of prosperous Western Europe right next door and its willingness to spend *billions* in investment, aid, and subsidies to bring the East up to EU standards. But in the 1980s and 1990s, in roughly the same time period as Eastern Europe, Latin America embraced democracy, free markets, and all the essential ingredients of the Washington Consensus

One wonders, however, how deep this commitment to the Western model runs. First, Latin America is far poorer, less developed, and its democracy less institutionalized than Eastern Europe's. Second, in the United States, Latin America has a far less attentive and generous benefactor than is the EU in Eastern Europe; the policy is widely known as "benign neglect." Third, Latin America is not all that wedded to either democracy (just over 50 percent in the most recent public opinion surveys) or free markets (under 50 percent); polls indicate continuing strong support for either "strong government" (authoritarianism) or for a leftist-populist regime like that of Cuba, Ecuador, Venezuela, Nicaragua, Bolivia, Peru, or El Salvador (fully one-third of the twenty countries). Meanwhile, fourth, a number of the bigger countries that Zakaria would call "The Rest" – Argentina, Brazil, perhaps Mexico – are chafing to go their own independent way regardless (and sometimes in spite of) U.S. direction and guidance. Despite the OAS's "Democratic Charter" which seeks to lock in and guarantee Latin America's democratic and Western orientation, these large, macro issues are far less settled in Latin America than they are in Eastern Europe.

In Russia these issues are not settled at all. In the early 1990s after the fall of the Soviet Union, it appeared Russia might be on the democratic-free market path. But that proved not to be the case, as massive corruption, mismanagement, and national disintegration set in under Boris Yeltsin. We forget that totalitarian regimes as the Soviet Union tend to produce in their wakes *total vacuums* of politics, society, economy, and institutions.[69] An astute observer could note that in the early 1990s, the U.S. Embassy's hopes for democracy and a free-market economy were not working out. However, committed strongly to its democracy agenda, the overly optimistic writings of Francis Fukuyama, and policies of National Endowment for Democracy (NED), the U.S. government was not then inclined to listen to dissenting views.

Out of this period of confusion, breakdown, and national embarrassment emerged Vladimir Putin. Putin has championed Russian nationalism, the Army, the Church, the Secret Police, aggression (in the Ukraine), and the restoration of Russian great-power statues. He has also violated and cracked down on Russian democracy, human rights, and civil society. In the process he has created a new and particularly Russian model of authoritarianism, corporatism, and "illiberal democracy" that is attractive and gaining adherents in Belarus, Hungary, Moldova, Myanmar, Kazakhstan, Egypt, Kyrgyzstan, Thailand, and possibly Turkey as well as half of the Ukraine.

But while Putin blusters and, though with oil prices high he has restored a degree of prosperity and renewed Russia's military might, there are many reasons why the Russian model will not prove all that attractive, long-lasting, or popular on the global level or even within Russia itself. Already, with oil prices falling, corruption widespread, and the human rights situation deteriorating, some of the gas has gone out of the Putin model, although it, or variations of it, will continue to find favor among the 40 percent or so of countries on the world stage that are not democratic.

East Asia, on the other hand, looks much more hopeful now. Japan, South Korea, and Taiwan, all of which embraced the Western model early on, are solidly democratic, prosperous, and doing well – except that Taiwan is traumatized by the overwhelming presence of gigantic and aggressive China which may pull the plucky island under its control. Hong Kong, though a part of China, continues to resist absorption under the mainland's hegemony; while tiny Singapore provides a model to the world of how to achieve miracle economic growth under a statist (but democratizing) regime. Democracy and the requirements of a free market have also spread to Southeast Asia including Indonesia, Malaysia, the Philippines, Thailand, and others.

That leaves a handful of authoritarian regimes plus big China outside of the democratic consensus. China is, of course, a rising, nationalistic, and expansionist power, probably destined to be a twenty-first-century superpower. And, while China has liberalized economically and to a certain extent culturally, socially, and politically, its model remains that of a top-down, statist, authoritarian, and Leninist regime. We know, for example, that the leadership of the Chinese Communist Party has been reading the literature on Latin American corporatism as a way of allowing for some limited social change but without that producing a demand for pluralism and democracy.[70]

China clearly represents, like Putin's Russia, an alternative to the Western model and one that is attractive to some Third World leaders. But China is also changing rapidly, it may succumb to some upheaval as it undergoes unprecedented urbanization, and we should not forget that China is hemmed in by a not-so-subtle balance-of-power strategy on the part of the United States that includes treaty agreements with nearly all of China's neighbors: Japan, South Korea, the Philippines, and India. The goal is to so envelop China in international linkages, obligations, and domestic preoccupations that its international ambitions are ameliorated and tamed over time.

India is our main case study in South Asia. In this country, the world's largest democracy, recently the engines of economic growth have revved up under a less-statist and more-entrepreneurial regime. India also has ambitions to surpass China both in population, growth, and, surprising to some, economic growth. All these factors – democracy, market-led growth, a check on China – make India a fitting partner for the U.S. and a recent success story for the Western model. U.S.-Indian relations are at an all-time high, and the trade and mutual security treaty the U.S. recently signed with India makes India a quite willing collaborator in the effort both to encircle China with defense alliances (with Japan, South Korea, the Philippines, and now India) and to "civilize" China and bring it in peacefully and responsibly into the family of nations. India, now alongside Eastern Europe, Latin America, and East and Southeast Asia, as a great success for both the Western model and for U.S. foreign policy.

The Middle East is the most troubled and dangerous of all our global areas. However, we should not let dramatic, day-to-day headlines overwhelm a bigger picture of the area. Obviously, countries like Afghanistan, Iraq, Libya, Syria, and Yemen are extremely troubled: terrorism, violence, civil war, and failed states – or at least the potential for failed-state status. But other countries – Oman, Turkey, Jordan,

Egypt, Tunisia, Algeria, and Morocco – are doing quite or moderately well, while others – Bahrain, Kuwait, Qatar, Saudi Arabia, and the United Arab Emirates – are, thanks to oil, doing extremely well. While the first group of five troubled countries commands about all of our television coverage, the last two groups, including twelve countries, merit far greater attention.

We need to define what we mean when we say the five "oil sheikdoms" mentioned above are doing "extremely well." Because of their vast petroleum resources, these have become wealthy countries – among the wealthiest in the world. Social change is now following from four or five *decades* of sustained and accelerated economic growth: urbanization, rising literacy, a new middle class, almost no poverty anymore. In addition, the Persian Gulf states have embraced globalization, as centers for international banking, tourism, finance, education, investment, and a travel hub between Europe and Asia, in ways that start to make them rivals to Hong Kong and Singapore.

The great problem here, what political scientists call the "laggard variable," is political. None of these countries is a democracy and, though they have opened up and liberalized (like China or Singapore?) in recent years, their human rights records are often spotty. Most troubling from the point-of-view of the Rostow-Lipset-Western model is that the result – democracy – that was supposed to follow from economic development and social change has not, in fact, followed. Although one can argue that oil wealth and now diversification into other economic sectors will enable these Persian Gulf sheikdoms to continue indefinitely into the future, my own field research there leads me to conclude that these countries will over time move toward greater democracy – maybe not Western democracy but perhaps a form of democracy resembling Lebanon, Turkey, Jordan, or Malaysia. Thus, while it is clear that Western policy in the Middle East cannot be chalked up as a success in the Persian Gulf states and some parts of North Africa we can see partial successes and even a partial, but not yet completed in its final stages, triumph of the Rostow-Western model.

Sub-Saharan Africa is the other great unsettled and unresolved area of the world. Its problems include poverty, tropical heat and disease, poor soils, limited resources, colonialism, racism, national borders that often make little sense, underdevelopment, lack of transparency, corruption, absence of the rule of law, weak or absent institutions (government, police, armed forces, public administration, and civil society), and other problems seemingly too numerous to mention. The problems are so immense that many, including scholars who started off fifty years ago as "Africanists," foreign aid workers, NGOs, and government officials, have given up on the area.

But that is not a useful, constructive, or even rational position to take. First, between a quarter and a third of Africa's fifty nations are doing fairly well and have achieved considerable development. Another quarter, and perhaps even another third, are beginning and have established the groundwork and infrastructure for the development process. Second, many of the earlier quandaries regarding borders, nationhood, sovereignty, and the basic law or constitution have by now been resolved. Third, after a long hiatus, democracy has been restored or established in a growing number of countries. Fourth, recognizing Africa's vast resources and potential, foreign capital is *pouring* into the area, raising the standard-of-living in ways that no amount of foreign aid can do.

A fifth factor is that African governments, ministries, private business, and public administration have become more rationalized, efficient, and transparent as they recognize that the earlier levels of corruption and inefficiency scare away that critically needed investment. Sixth, the United States and other Western nations, to say nothing of emerging powers China and India, have become increasingly interested in Africa, now on security as well as economic grounds. These and other factors suggest that Africa is not "hopeless," that growth and development are occurring, and that democracy is gaining ground. And while China is making inroads into the continent, we should not, therefore, assume that Africa is "lost" to the West. Indeed, it may well be argued that Africa is currently reaching the socioeconomic and developmental level where the Western model is *most relevant*. Clearly, for Africa, a longer time-span beyond the immediate past and present is required.

* * *

Although America's clout and position in the world, *relative* to what it used to be thirty years ago, have been somewhat diminished – politically, economically, diplomatically, and perhaps even morally – America still wields immense power. The United States has the most powerful military forces in the world, its economy is as big as China's with only one-fourth the population, America is the only *global* superpower, and young foreign talent flock to

American universities and start-up enterprises. America may not *dominate* world affairs as it once did but U.S. leadership is *indispensable* in all areas of the globe. While a certain degree of pessimism pervades our political discourse, over 80 percent of Americans think of the U.S. as the best place in the *world* to live. It is mainly our *domestic situation*, not our international power, that is the chief threat to American preeminence; Joseph Nye published a new book in which he argues that the United States will be *the* central player in international affairs at least through the 2040s.[71]

Not only is America still powerful individually but the *Western Model* that it has erected along with its Western allies remains overwhelmingly dominant on a global scale. To reiterate, the Western Model has been firmly institutionalized, not only in North America, Western Europe, and Australia/New Zealand, it has also, overwhelmingly so, become dominant in Eastern Europe, Latin America, East Asia (Japan, South Korea, Taiwan, and Singapore), much of Southeast Asia, India, and parts of Sub-Saharan Africa. Many of the countries in these areas practice a *form* of democracy and a *type* of economy (mainly, more statist and corporatist) that is different from our own, but that is to be expected and does not diminish the really quite astounding triumph of the Western Model on a worldwide basis.

The main "holdouts" are Russia, China, and the Islamic Middle East. Vladimir Putin in Russia has now put forth a revived, rejuvenated, autocratic, authoritarian state-corporatist (like Franco or Salazar) model that has found some camp-followers in the near-abroad (Belarus, Kazakhstan, and a handful of others); but Russia's failing economy and Putin's restrictions on freedom have made that model far less attractive as an alternative to the Western one. China's dynamic (now slowing) economy and one-party, Leninist political system are attractive to some political leaders in Southeast Asia and Africa seeking to emulate China's miracle growth; China seems poised to become a twenty-first-century superpower. But China's rapid, unprecedented, social modernization and urbanization may tear the country apart, its economy is slowing, and China's regimented work force and crowded conditions, to say nothing of the thick pollution, are not attractive.

The Islamic Middle East is troubled and problematic; it is also the world's most disappointing area from either a democratic or a developmental perspective. Although Iran and possibly others may develop some nuclear capacity, no country or movement (ISIS, the Muslim Brotherhood) in the region is or will be in a position to challenge Western dominance anytime soon. The Iranian-Islamic revolution has been a great disappointment to those who once saw in it hopes for a genuinely indigenous, home-grown Islamic model, and surely ISIS is outside the pale of civilization. By process of elimination, that leaves more moderate (and Western-oriented) Turkey, the Gulf states, and Egypt as the best hopes in the Middle East and North Africa.

What about "The Rest," including India, South Africa, Brazil, Mexico, and possibly others? Well, India has embraced the main facets of the Western Model in both economics and politics and could be considered the "world's greatest [certainly the largest] democracy." South Africa has resisted some of its African neighbors' call for an indigenous (but perhaps unworkable and ineffective) model and has, like India, embraced democracy and a modern, mixed economy. Similarly, in Brazil and Mexico: both of these are big, important, nationalistic countries; but Mexico now appears to be locked into the North American (Canada, Mexico, and U.S.) system of trade, business, and democracy; and for Brazil, while it is fiercely independent, it would be inconceivable that Brazil would depart from its Western, democratic orientation.

These results, overall, are somewhat surprising. When this book began, one would have expected that there would be far more and greater challenges to the Western Model than has, in fact, turned out to be the case, that new, nationalistic, and indigenous models would be offering alternatives to the Western one. In some cases – Russia, China, and Iran – that is true, of course. But the real surprise and message of the book is how viable and widespread the Western Model still is, whether in politics, economics, or international affairs and in almost every area of the world. Allowing for some setbacks, reversals, and mixed systems, we see this dominance of the West and of the Western Model lasting well into the twenty-first century.

SUGGESTED READINGS

Chapter 2:

Almond, Gabriel Abraham, and Sidney Verba. *The civic culture: Political attitudes and democracy in five nations.* Princeton University Press, 2015.

Deutsch, Karl W. "Social mobilization and political development." *American Political Science Review* 55, no. 03 (1961): 493-514.

Inglehart, Ronald. *Modernization and postmodernization: Cultural, economic, and political change in 43 societies.* Vol. 19. Princeton, NJ: Princeton University Press, 1997.

Lipset, Seymour Martin. "Some social requisites of democracy: Economic development and political legitimacy." *American Political Science Review* 53, no. 01 (1959): 69-105.

Rostow, Walt Whitman. *The stages of economic growth: A non-communist manifesto.* Cambridge University Press, 1990.

Thelen, Kathleen. *How institutions evolve: The political economy of skills in Germany, Britain, the United States, and Japan*. Cambridge University Press, 2004.

Chapter 3

Gel'man, Vladimir. *Subnational institutions in contemporary Russia*. Palgrave Macmillan UK, 2000.

Goldman, Marshall I. *Petrostate: Putin, power, and the new Russia*. Oxford University Press, 2009.

Lynch, Allen C. *How Russia is not ruled: reflections on Russian political development*. Cambridge University Press, 2005.

McFaul, Michael. *Russia's unfinished revolution: Political change from Gorbachev to Putin*. Cornell University Press, 2015.

Sakwa, Richard. *Putin: Russia's choice*. Routledge, 2007.

Sakwa, Richard. *Russian politics and society*. Routledge, 2008.

Schrad, Mark Lawrence. *Vodka politics: Alcohol, autocracy, and the secret history of the Russian state*. Oxford University Press, 2014.

Thornton, Judith, and Charles E. Ziegler, eds. *Russia's Far East: A region at risk*. National Bureau of Asian Research, 2002.

Chapter 4

Dryzek, John S., and Leslie Holmes. *Post-communist democratization: political discourses across thirteen countries.* Cambridge University Press, 2002.

Kostelecký, Tomáš. *Political parties after communism: developments in East-Central Europe.* Edited by Tomáš Kostelecký. Washington, DC: Woodrow Wilson Center Press, 2002.

Lewis, Paul, and Zdenka Mansfeldová, eds. *The European Union and Party Politics in Central and Eastern Europe.* Springer, 2016.

Triska, Jan Francis, and Paul M. Cocks, eds. *Political Development in Eastern Europe.* Vol. 54. New York: Praeger, 1977.

Perica, Vjekoslav. *Balkan idols: Religion and nationalism in Yugoslav states.* Oxford University Press on Demand, 2004.

Przeworski, Adam. *Democracy and the market: Political and economic reforms in Eastern Europe and Latin America.* Cambridge University Press, 1991.

Schimmelfennig, Frank, and Ulrich Sedelmeier. *The Europeanization of Central and Eastern Europe.* Cornell University Press, 2005.

Chapter 5

Beeson, Mark. *Regionalism and globalization in East Asia: politics, security and economic development*. Palgrave Macmillan, 2014.

Gereffi, Gary, and Donald L. Wyman, eds. *Manufacturing miracles: paths of industrialization in Latin America and East Asia*. Princeton University Press, 2014.

Hayes, Louis D. *Political Systems of East Asia: China, Korea, and Japan*. ME Sharpe, 2012.

Jeffries, Ian. *China: A guide to economic and political developments*. Routledge, 2007.

Madsen, Richard. *Democracy's dharma: Religious renaissance and political development in Taiwan*. University of California Press, 2007.

Ortmann, Stephan. *Politics and change in Singapore and Hong Kong: Containing contention*. Routledge, 2009.

Perkins, Dwight H. *East Asian Development*. Harvard University Press, 2013.

Ward, Robert E., ed. *Political Development in Modern Japan: Studies in the Modernization of Japan*. Princeton University Press, 2015.

Chapter 6

Bayley, David H. *Police and political development in India.* Princeton University Press, 2015.

Bruton, Henry J. *The political economy of poverty, equity, and growth: Sri Lanka and Malaysia.* Oxford University Press, 1992.

Jalal, Ayesha. *Democracy and authoritarianism in South Asia: A comparative and historical perspective.* Vol. 1. Cambridge University Press, 1995.

Kingsbury, Damien. *South-East Asia: a political profile.* Oxford University Press, 2001.

Ollapally, Deepa Mary. *The politics of extremism in South Asia.* Cambridge: Cambridge University Press, 2008.

Rudolph, Lloyd I., and Susanne Hoeber Rudolph. *The modernity of tradition: Political development in India.* University of Chicago Press, 1984.

Von Vorys, Karl. *Political development in Pakistan.* Princeton University Press, 2015.

Wiener, Myron. *State politics in India.* Princeton University Press, 2015.

Chapter 7

Bayat, Asef. *Life as politics: How ordinary people change the Middle East.* Stanford University Press, 2013.

Beinin, Joel, and Frédéric Vairel, eds. *Social movements, mobilization, and contestation in the Middle East and North Africa.* Stanford University Press, 2013.

Brand, Laurie A. *Women, the state, and political liberalization: Middle Eastern and North African experiences.* Columbia University Press, 1998.

Entelis, John Pierre. *Islam, democracy, and the state in North Africa.* Indiana University Press, 1997.

Halpern, Manfred. *Politics of Social Change: In the Middle East and North Africa.* Princeton University Press, 2015.

Henry, Clement Moore, and Robert Springborg. *Globalization and the Politics of Development in the Middle East.* Vol. 1. Cambridge University Press, 2010.

King, Stephen Juan. *The new authoritarianism in the Middle East and North Africa.* Indiana University Press, 2009.

Chapter 8

Franko, Patrice M. *The puzzle of Latin American economic development.* Rowman & Littlefield, 2007.

Frieden, Jeffry A. *Debt, development, and democracy: modern political economy and Latin America, 1965-1985*. Princeton University Press, 1991.

Gough, Ian, and Geof Wood. *Insecurity and welfare regimes in Asia, Africa and Latin America: Social policy in development contexts*. Cambridge University Press, 2004.

Haggard, Stephan, and Robert R. Kaufman. *Development, Democracy, and Welfare States: Latin America, East Asia, and Eastern Europe*. Princeton University Press, 2008.

Przeworski, Adam. *Democracy and the market: Political and economic reforms in Eastern Europe and Latin America*. Cambridge University Press, 1991.

Wiarda, Howard J. *The soul of Latin America: The cultural and political tradition*. Yale university press, 2003.

Wiarda, Howard J., and Harvey F. Kline, eds. *Latin American politics and development*. Westview Press, 2013.

Chapter 9

Ali, Taisier Mohamed Ahmed, and Robert O. Matthews, eds. *Civil wars in Africa: Roots and resolution*. Montreal: McGill-Queen's University Press, 1999.

Hydén, Göran. *African politics in comparative perspective*. Cambridge: Cambridge University Press, 2006.

Mikell, Gwendolyn. *African feminism: The politics of survival in Sub-Saharan Africa.* University of Pennsylvania Press, 1997.

Mohamoud, Abdullah A. *State collapse and post-conflict development in Africa: the case of Somalia (1960-2001).* Purdue University Press, 2006.

Sisk, Timothy D. *Democratization in South Africa: The elusive social contract.* Princeton, NJ: Princeton University Press, 1995.

Wilson, Richard. *The politics of truth and reconciliation in South Africa: Legitimizing the post-apartheid state.* Cambridge University Press, 2001.

Young, Crawford. *Politics in Congo: Decolonization and Independence.* Princeton University Press, 2015.

ENDNOTES

1   Howard J. Wiarda, *Dictatorship and Development* (Gainesville: University of Florida Press, 1968); Wiarda, *Corporatism and Development* (Amherst: University of Massachusetts Press, 1977); Wiarda, *Politics and Social Change in Latin America* (Boulder, CO: Westview Press, 1992); Wiarda, *Democracy and Its Discontents* (Washington, DC: Rowman and Littlefield, 1955); Wiarda, *Non-Western Theories of Development* (Fort Worth, TX: Harcourt Brace, 1998).

2   A wonderful book on this subject by my former mentor and boss, ninety-one-year-old Henry Kissinger, is *World Order* – by which he really means the absence thereof – (New York, NY: Penguin, 2014).

3   (New York, NY: Random House, 1955).

4   (Princeton, NJ: Princeton University Press, 1960).

5   Donald Blackmer, *The MIT Center for International* Studies (Cambridge, MA: MIT, 2002).

6   *Foreign Affairs*, Vol. 70, No. 1 (1990-91), 23-33.

7   (Stillwater, OK: University of Oklahoma Press, 1992).

8   *The End of History and the Last Man* (New York, NY: Simon and Schuster, 1992).

9   Wiarda, *Cracks in the* Consensus (Westport, CT: Praeger Publishers,1997).

10 Wiarda, *Globalization* (Lebanon, NH: University Press of New England, 2007).

11 *World Order* (New York, NY: Penguin, 2014).

12 "The Rise of Illiberal Democracy," *Foreign Affairs* (November-December, 1997).

13 Howard J. Wiarda, *Ethnocentrism and Foreign Policy: Can We Understand the Third World?* (Washington, D.C.: American Enterprise Institute, 1985).

14 *The Post-American World and the Rise of the Rest* (New York, NY: Penguin, 2009).

15 Dennis Bark, *Dancing in the Dark* (Stanford, CA: Hoover Institution Press, 2007).

16 Louis Hartz, *The Founding of New Societies* (New York, NY: Harcourt Brace, 1964).

17 W. W. Rostow, *The Stages of Economic Growth* (Cambridge, MA: Cambridge University Press, 1960); Seymour Martin Lipset, "Some Social Requisites of Democracy," *American Political Science Review* (March, 1959), 69-105; Gabriel A. Almond and James S. Coleman, *The Politics of the Developing Areas* (Princeton, NJ: Princeton University Press, 1960).

18 GDP per capita based on purchasing power parity (PPP). This table shows the GDP per capita converted to international dollars using purchasing parity rates (World Bank)

19 Tony Judt, *Postwar: A History of Europe since World War II* (New York, NY: Penguin, 2005).

20 Francis Fukuyama, *The End of History and the Last Man* (New York, NY: The Free Press, 1992).

21 Howard J. Wiarda, *Corporatism and Comparative Politics: The Other Great "Ism"* (New York, NY: M. E. Sharpe, 1996).

22 In the early-to-mid-1980s the author was one of the founding architects of both Project Democracy and the National Endowment for Democracy. He was, however, skeptical of the more ambitious and universalist goals of those programs then, and remain so today – see Howard J. Wiarda, "Can We export Democracy?" Occasional Paper #157, Woodrow Wilson International Center for Scholars (1984) and republished in numerous edited volumes. In the political battles of those times, his more skeptical, relativistic arguments lost out to the

democracy true-believers; but by now his arguments have been mainly vindicated.

23 Henry Kissinger, *World Order* (New York, NY: Penguin Press, 2014).

24 Zbigniew Brzezinski is very much in this tradition; see his *Second Chance* (New York, NY: Basic Books, 2007).

25 GDP per capita based on purchasing power parity (PPP). This table shows the GDP per capita converted to international dollars using purchasing parity rates (World Bank)

26 Samuel P. Huntington, *The Clash of Civilizations* (New York, NY: Simon and Schuster, 1996).

27 David Landes, *The Wealth and Poverty of Nations: Why Some Are So Rich and Some So Poor (New York, NY: Norton, 1998).*

28 Max Weber, *The Protestant Ethic and the Spirit of Capitalism (1905).*

29 Peter Moody, *Tradition and Modernization in China and Japan* (Belmont, CA: Wadsworth, 1995).

30 Some good books on Indian and South Asian history are: Ganguly, Sumit. *South Asia.* n.p.: New York: New York University Press, c2006., 2006; Keay, John. *India: A History: from the Earliest Civilisations to the Boom of the Twenty-first Century.* Grove Press, 2010.; Guha, Ramachandra. *India after Gandhi: The history of the world's largest democracy.* Pan, 2007.; Phuntsho, Karma. *The history of Bhutan.* Random House India, 2013.; Tharoor, Shashi. *India: From midnight to the millennium and beyond.* Arcade Publishing, 2006.; Spencer, Jonathan, ed. *Sri Lanka: History and the roots of conflict.* Routledge, 2002.; Whelpton, John. *A history of Nepal.* Cambridge University Press, 2005.

31 The states of India are Andhra Pradesh, Arunachal Pradesh, Assam, Bihar, Chhattisgarh, Goa, Gujarat, Haryana, Himachal Pradesh, Jammu and Kashmir, Jharkand, Karnataka, Kerala, Madhya Pradesh, Maharashtra, Manipur, Meghalaya, Mizoram, Nagaland, Odisha, Punjab, Rajasthan, Sikkim, Tamil Nadu, Telangana, Tripura, Uttar Pradesh, Uttarakhand, and West Bengal.

32 The seven union territories of India are ruled directly from the central government of India. The union territories (federal territories) of India are Andaman and Nicobar Islands, Chandigarh, Dadra and Nagar Haveli, Daman and Diu, Delhi, Lakshadweep, and Puducherry (previously known as Pondicherry).

33 The *Rajya Sabha* consists of about 550 members. The exact number varies.

34 The *Lok Sabha* consists of no more than 250 members at any given time.

35 The various sources of India law include the Constitution, statutes based on national, state or union territory legislation, customary law, and case law.

36 Tandon, Rajesh. *Voluntary Action, Civil Society, and the State.* Mosaic Books, 2002.

37 Tandon, Rajesh, and Satgur Saran Srivastava. *Invisible, yet widespread: the non-profit sector in India.* PRIA, 2003.

38 Franke, Richard W., and Barbara H. Chasin. "Is the Kerala Model Sustainable?" in *Rethinking development: Kerala's development experience* ed. M.A Oommeen (New Delhi, Institute of Social Sciences, 1999).

39 Somjee, A.K., "India: A Challenge to Western Theories of Development" in *Non-Western Theories of Development: Regional Norms versus Global Trends* ed. Howard J. Wiarda (Fort Worth, Harcourt Brace and Company, 1999).

40 Rostow, Walt Whitman. *The Stages of Economic Growth: A Non-Communist Manifesto.* Cambridge University Press, 1990.

41 Tharoor, Shashi. *The Elephant, the Tiger and the Cellphone.* Penguin UK, 2007.

42 Robin Wright, *Rock the Casbah: Rage and Rebellion Across the Islamic World* (New York, NY: Simon and Schuster, 2011).

43 GDP per capita based on purchasing power parity (PPP). This table shows the GDP per capita converted to international dollars using purchasing parity rates (World Bank)

44 CIA World Factbook 2015 estimate

45   Howard J. Wiarda, *Ethnocentrism and American Foreign Policy: Can We Understand the Third World?* (Washington, DC: American Enterprise Institute for Public Policy Research, 1985).

46   Selma Botman, *From Independence to Revolution: Egypt, 1922-1952* (Syracuse, NY: University Press, 1991).

47   Howard J. Wiarda and Harvey Kline, "The Pattern of Historical Development," in *Latin American Politics and Development* (Boulder, CO: Westview Press, 2014)

48   GDP per capita based on purchasing power parity (PPP). This table shows the GDP per capita converted to current international dollars using purchasing parity rates (World Bank)

49   W. W. Rostow, *The Stages of Economic Growth* (Cambridge, UK: Cambridge University Press, 1960); S. M. Lipset, "Some Social Requisites of Democracy," *American Political Science Review* (March, 1959), 69-105.

50   Howard J. Wiarda (ed.), *Authoritarianism and Corporatism in Latin America – Revisited* (Gainesville, FL: University of Florida Press, 2004).

51   Howard J. Wiarda, *The Soul of Latin America* (New Haven, CT: Yale University Press, 2001.

52   GDP per capita based on purchasing power parity (PPP). This table shows the GDP per capita converted to current international dollars using purchasing parity rates (World Bank)

53   Thomas M. Sanderson, "Terrorism in Sub-Saharan Africa" in *Global Forecast 2016* (Washington D.C.: Center for Strategic and International Studies)

54   "Al Shabaab", *Counter Terrorism Guide,* National Counterterrorism Center

55   Farouk Chothia, "Who are Nigeria's Boko Haram Islamists?", *BBC Africa* 4 May 2015 http://www.bbc.com/news/world-africa-13809501 last accessed on June 15, 2016

56   Crawford Young, *The Politics of Ethnic Pluralism* (Madison: University of Wisconsin Press, 1976).

57   Howard J. Wiarda, *Ethnocentrism and Foreign Policy: Can We Understand the Third World?* (Washington, DC: AEI, 1985);

A. H. Somjee, *Development Theory: Critiques and Explorations* (London, UK: Macmillan, 1991).

58 Ali Mazrui, *The Africans: A Triple Heritage* (London, UK: BBC Publications, 1986).

59 I wrote critically of the model as early as 1965. In my doctoral dissertation research and later writings, I found that almost none of what Rostow, Almond, et al. had posited about the Third World could, in fact, be found there.

60 Howard J. Wiarda, *The Politics of EU and NATO Enlargement* (Vienna: Austrian Institute for International Affairs, 2002); also published in *World Affairs* (Spring, 2002).

61 Fareed Zakaria wrote the first piece on illiberal democracy (*Foreign Affairs* [November-December 1997]), one of many scholarly works on what we may call "democracy with adjectives" – "limited," "controlled," "top-down," or "corporatist." Zakaria used the term as one of opprobrium, but Orban picked up the phrase to describe a regime that he viewed positively.

62 For the dilemmas involved, see Howard J. Wiarda and Hilary Collins, "Constitutional Coups," Occasional Papers, Center for Strategic and International Studies, July 2011.

63 Howard J. Wiarda, *Cracks in the Consensus* (Washington, DC: CSIS/Praeger Publishers, 1997).

64 Howard J. Wiarda, *Adventures in Research*, Vol. III (Lincoln, NE: iUniverse, 2006), Chapter 19.

65 As early as the spring of 1992, the author had reported to the State Department and U.S. Ambassador Robert Strauss that democracy was not working in Russia, the free-market reforms were producing economic calamity, and Russians were growing increasingly resentful of the U.S. But the U.S. government was so committed to its democracy agenda that it did not wish to hear this message.

66 Joseph Nye, *Is the American Century Over?* (New York, NY: Polity Press, 2015).

67 Zakaria, *The Post-American World and the Rise of the Rest* (New York, NY: Penguin, 2009).

68 Eric Einhorn, "Liberalism and Social Democracy in Western Europe," in Howard J. Wiarda (ed.), *Comparative Democracy and Democratization* (Fort Worth, TX: Harcourt Publishers, 2002, 18-36.

69 Howard J. Wiarda, *Dictatorship and Development* (Gainesville: University of Florida Press, 1968).

70 David Shambaugh, *China's Communist Party* (Berkeley: University of California Press, 2008).

71 Nye, *Is the American Century Over?*

INDEX

W

Z

Y

Printed in the United States
By Bookmasters